Selling the City

Gender, Class, and the California Growth Machine, 1880–1940

LEE M. A. SIMPSON

Selling the City

Gender, Class, and the California Growth Machine, 1880–1940

STANFORD UNIVERSITY PRESS 2004

Stanford, California

Stanford University Press
Stanford, California

Library of Congress Cataloging-in-Publication Data

Simpson, Lee M. A.
Selling the city : gender, class, and the California growth machine, 1880–1940 / Lee M. A. Simpson.
p. cm.
Based on author's thesis (Ph.D.)—University of California, Riverside.
Includes bibliographical references and index.
ISBN 0-8047-4875-6 (cloth : alk. paper)
1. Women—California—History. 2. Property—California—History. 3. Women in business—California—History. 4. Women in politics—California—History. 5. Women in community development—California—History. 6. Urban women—California—History. I. Title.

HQ1438.C2S55 2004
305.4'09794 dc22 2003027045

Printed in the United States of America
Original Printing 2004
Last figure below indicates year of this printing:
13 12 11 10 09 08 07 06 05 04

Typeset at Stanford University Press in 10/13 Palatino

FOR BILL

Acknowledgments

In the ten years it has taken me to see this project through, from graduate research paper, to dissertation, to completed manuscript, I have relied on the insight and inspiration of a number of people. My journey began in 1990 when I entered the graduate program in public history at the University of California, Riverside. I was quickly taken under the wing of Ron Tobey and, by extension, Charles Wetherell. I was a slightly bewildered graduate student with no clear plan for my future. A master's degree in archival management seemed a good goal, but I had not considered an academic career beyond that. I soon found myself propelled into Ph.D.-level work and faced with the need to complete a graduate research seminar. Much to my displeasure, I found that the only course offered at the time I needed it was a research seminar in urban history offered by Drs. Tobey and Wetherell. Much to my surprise, I came to be deeply interested in this field and have pursued a research agenda in urban history ever since. I am grateful for the rigorous training these two scholars demanded of me and for their insistence that I never settle for second-rate work. Their emphasis on excellence and scholarly integrity will be an enduring legacy in my professional career.

This research might have languished after completion of my dissertation if it were not for the tremendous support of Don Hofsommer. As department chair during my tenure at St. Cloud State University he provided me with a model of professional integrity and with unending support in pursuing a scholarly agenda while teaching a four-course load. Don introduced me to a number of publishers and scholars and helped me balance the demands of teaching, research, and family. In addition, he offered valuable comments in reading several sections of this manuscript.

Without the assistance of a variety of librarians and archivists, this project would not have been possible. First, I would like to thank Ron Baker, city historian and librarian for the City of Riverside, who introduced me to this story through the records of the Riverside Women's Club. Christie Hammond, Don McCew, Nathan Gonzales, and Larry Burgess at the A. K. Smiley Public Library in Redlands provided invaluable assistance with sources in that community. Dolores Ritchie, Special Collections Librarian for the University of California, Santa Barbara, allowed me access to the only partially processed Community Development and Conservation Collection. Michael Redmon of the Santa Barbara Historical Society and Lee Goodwin of the Santa Barbara Trust for Historic Preservation also helped with photographs in that city. Finally, Janice Braun opened the Aurelia Henry Reinhardt papers to me at Mills College in Oakland.

The project has sailed through the review and acceptance process with the able and supportive guidance of Norris Pope and John Feneron at Stanford University Press. Norris's continued interest in the project as it proceeded through external review gave me the confidence needed to see it through to completion. The two reviewers provided me with excellent suggestions which have greatly improved the analysis and presentation of the material. I am particularly grateful for the insight of Carl Abbott, whose comments helped me solidify my own growth machine thesis.

I owe a huge debt to my friends and family, who provided the all-important moral support to see me through the days when I thought I would not be able to complete this project. Gabriele Carey offered me first her friendship and then a job, and became my critic, assistant, and friend. My family deserves a special acknowledgment. Not only have my parents been my ardent supporters over the years; they provided me with free room, board, and computer while researching the Oakland section of this work. Along with my grandmother and my sister they have provided needed emotional support. The credit for the inspiration behind this work must go to my grandfather, Dr. Albert R. Parker. He showed me in his own special way the wonderful world of history and encouraged me to undertake a study of women while I was still an undergraduate. Although he died before this work was completed, I believe he would have been pleased with the results. My children, Joseph and Ben, were both born while this project was in process. They have helped pull me back to reality when I might have become too entrenched in my work.

Most importantly I owe my husband and best friend, Bill, an unbounded debt for always having a delicious meal and a sympathetic ear at the end of the day. Although his field is physics, he patiently listened to me expound on women's issues and provided many useful criticisms that kept this project, and me, on track. Without him, this work would not have been finished.

Contents

Illustrations

Selling the City

Gender, Class, and the California Growth Machine, 1880–1940

Introduction

Looking back on her life in 1968, eighty-year-old Pearl Chase of Santa Barbara could identify a defining moment when she consciously chose to become involved in the civic life of her community. She recalled at nineteen, after returning from a semester at the University of California, Berkeley, "how ashamed I was of the dust and dirt and ugly buildings here and I resolved to do what I could to improve Santa Barbara."[1] After graduating from Berkeley in 1909, Chase returned to Santa Barbara and became a civic leader of unprecedented power and influence. Choosing to remain outside traditional politics, Chase created a broad-based network of citizens in the city that drew upon her connections in female social service reform, the arts, and the real estate and building industries. She became the nexus of the Santa Barbara growth machine, shaping the plan and development of the city until her death in 1979. Her life provides strong evidence of the unique position women played in the growth and development of urban California in the early twentieth century.

Pearl Chase was born at a time when the United States was beginning to experience a subtle yet pervasive transformation in regional dominance from the East Coast to the West that was completed with the coming of the Second World War. The rapid growth that accompanied the war vastly expanded the economic, political, and cultural influence of western states, with California providing the main leadership. In order to understand the growth of the West after 1940, it is important to understand the foundation for growth laid in the prewar period. Western cities were able to handle the massive wartime buildup because they had gained important experience with the process of urban growth and development prior to the war. Most western cities, following the lead of California, had experimented with the methods and tools now considered fundamental to modern city planning and successful city growth. Although many cities struggled with an overwhelming influx of immigrants seeking to fill wartime manufacturing positions, the existence of city plans and city planning commissions provided at least a minimal guide as to how to handle the situation.

City growth is a complex process that has been assessed by a variety of scholars from fields as diverse as sociology, history, economics, and political science. Since 1976, urban sociologists seeking to explain contemporary urban crises have been profoundly influenced by Harvey Molotch's city-as-growth-machine thesis. Molotch defined a growth machine as a coalition of land-based urban elites who manipulate local government to pursue policies that protect and enhance the wealth of growth machine members. Because land is the basic unit of wealth, property laws and property taxes become the primary concern of the growth coalition, and hence of city government. In much the same vein as the social control thesis, Molotch's argument asserts that this elite also manipulates the rest of the community to embrace the vision of the elite and thus ensure that the preconditions for growth are met. The outcome, he suggests, is a situation in which only a small proportion of a city's population benefits. Most citizens are negatively affected by higher taxes and never reap the benefits of promised new jobs.[2]

The evidence presented in the following chapters supports much of the growth machine theory, although I conclude that the outcome is far from as negative as the sociologists would have us believe. Indeed, California cities did pursue aggressive growth policies between 1880 and 1940 that benefited property owners. Measured in terms of increased population, western cities grew at a tremendous rate during the latter half of the nineteenth and early part of the twentieth centuries, and property values correspondingly rose. But instead of harming the majority of the population, city growth based on increased population made possible a wide range of economic policies designed to enhance quality of life as well as overall wealth. Indeed, the continued growth of West Coast cities throughout the twentieth century suggests that growth *does* benefit the majority of people.

Eric Monkkonen's work supports this conclusion.[3] In a broadly synthetic work on U.S. cities from 1780 to 1980, Monkkonen argues that population growth in cities led to perpetually rising property values that made it possible for city government to follow policies of conservative taxation while maintaining high levels of bonded indebtedness. City debt in turn, financed the services that attracted more immigrants and perpetuated the cycle. Knowing that increased land values would continue to underwrite the city debt, this sense of unbounded economic opportunity further encouraged more conservative property owners to invest in the city. Thus, Molotch's expectation of higher taxes did not materialize in this period.

What did materialize in California cities was the creation of a "group consciousness" among both the middle class and the elite and the spread of a "we feeling" among all citizens that fostered a sense of community solidarity. Successful city growth required the development of a clear community identity for competing cities, particularly among second-tier cities like the citrus cities of Southern California and the tourist cities of the central coast that would never be able to compete for state and regional dominance like San Francisco and Los Angeles. In many cases this sense of community was based on a shared class identity, not always dependent upon economic or employment status. Instead it represented a worldview or value system centered in the capitalist "will to possess." It was a community identity grounded in home ownership and such subjective criteria as "quality of life."

American society as a whole has evolved as an inherently bourgeois society in which the formation of a capitalist class identity, particularly between 1890 and 1913, shaped political, social, and religious movements as well as economic affairs. Capitalists supported American urban cultural attractions and made them open to all, in part as a means to protect capitalism from threats from labor and entrepreneurial capitalists.[4] By enlarging the area of "high culture" to include "the masses," the elite initiated the lower classes into its corporate capitalist vision and created legitimacy for its existence and goals. After 1890, corporate capitalists expanded their realm by endowing and establishing libraries, museums, orchestras, and expositions and by claiming that they alone were heirs to the civilizing culture of Western Europe. By appropriating American culture, capitalists created the rationale to justify a reorientation of republican ideology away from small-scale entrepreneurial capitalism toward corporate-industrial capitalism. Cultural solidarity also helped mediate the natural competitiveness (both interclass and intraclass) that could destroy capitalism. At the local level, it helped ensure the legitimacy of the growth mentality.

In the larger capitalist marketplace, sustainable growth relied on class cohesion. Without broad political and market authority and the consent of the masses for that authority, prolonged growth would be impossible. A "middle-class" identity had to be created that would appeal to all Americans and would legitimate the dominance of corporate capitalism as both a business system and a social system. The creation and solidification of this identity took place not just in corporate boardrooms and committee meetings in Washington, New York, and Chicago, but in the creation of chambers of commerce and "social service" clubs such as Rotary, Kiwanis, and women's clubs. Thus, civic improvements in the form of parks, public concerts, and museums reflected the extension of the capitalist class vision to the masses. The city became the arena in which capitalists defined and implemented a shared vision of class cooperation.[5]

By building a middle-class identity in social clubs, and a consensus around shared goals for growth, growth coalitions helped to preserve the corporate vision of capitalism in the face of threats from labor and entrepreneurial capitalists. In the process, they found that developing a community identity for their cities contributed to success in California's urban competition, particularly for California's second- and third-tier cities like Redlands and Santa Barbara. Once a community had defined itself in terms of a specific class identity, it fought to preserve and exploit that identity as an asset. In part, this reflected a growing awareness by real property owners that property values could easily be sustained or increased by maintaining an outward appearance of affluence. Only with the assurance of continually rising property values could cities follow those policies of conservative taxation that would continue to appeal to prospective urban investors.

The members of California's urban growth coalitions, both men and women, thus implemented visions of city growth grounded not in speculation, but in investment in both traditional forms of capital and in what Douglass North terms "social overhead."[6] These capitalists shared the corporate vision of capitalism, not the speculative interests of entrepreneurial capitalists. Thus, they created the cultural amenities that would serve to define a middle-class identity for their cities. As investors in education, social organizations, and infrastructure, as well as capital goods, they also demonstrated an understanding of the complex and diverse factors that influenced individual and family decisions to make a home in a particular community. Oakland, for example, could not beat rival San Francisco for regional dominance without supplying its citizens with good schools; churches; social organizations; clean, well-planned streets and neighborhoods; *and* employment and investment opportunities.

In addition, many smaller cities like Redlands, Riverside, and Santa Barbara did not have the industrial base of Los Angeles or San Francisco that would lead to major metropolitan status. Instead, Redlands' immediate competitors were smaller cities like Riverside, San Bernardino, and Pasadena, all of which competed for residential and small-business growth. By the turn of the twentieth century, these cities had developed basic city services to such an extent that perceived levels of investment in social overhead and levels of affluence (or morality) became the deciding factor for individuals considering a move to a certain California city. The Redlands and Santa Barbara growth coalitions recognized this and tried to sell their cities as superior service cities with a long list of cultural amenities. Redlands' promotional literature touted the city as "one of the wealthiest communities per capita in the United States," populated by a "cultivated, refined, moral people."[7] Affluence thus became an important strategy employed by the Redlands growth machine.

California cities, like cities across the country, engaged in a variety of formal actions designed to preserve affluence that became a part of the city planning arsenal in the twentieth century. First, real estate developers used legally enforceable codes, covenants, and restrictions on deeds to protect property from a variety of perceived threats. Deed restrictions could be used to limit property use, to define acceptable landscape and architectural styles, and to place restrictions on the sale and use of property in perpetuity. While many deed restrictions remain in effect to the present, those aimed at restricting access to housing were deemed unenforceable by the U.S. Supreme Court in its 1948 *Shelley v. Kramer* decision. When deed restrictions became unenforceable, real estate developers instead turned to formal city plans, zoning laws, and subdivision regulations to preserve affluence.[8]

Redlining, created by the federal government through the Federal Housing Administration (FHA) in the 1930s, functioned as another tool in the capitalist arsenal against property depreciation. Like deed restrictions, redlining was designed to prevent real estate from being sold to "undesirables." As a more subtle form of discrimination, however, redlining took place not at the level of the deed, but in banks and insurance companies. Capitalists engaged in redlining to prevent members of the lower class, and people of color in particular, from being able to afford to buy homes in certain areas. As with deed restrictions, the Supreme Court declared redlining unconstitutional. Local commercial and civic leaders thus turned to other forms of protecting their neighborhoods, particularly the use of environmental language and zoning to keep business and industry out of certain neighborhoods.[9]

In addition to formal barriers, the California urban elite used another, more subtle form of discrimination that was particularly effective between 1900 and 1940. California's chambers of commerce played a significant role in the growth of the state's cities. Not only did chambers advertise the city, the region, and the state; they responded to personal inquiries from potential emigrants interested in making their home in a specific city. From the evidence found in the Redlands Chamber of Commerce files, chamber responses most often reflected the booster spirit of promotional literature, with encouraging statements about unlimited opportunity. The degree to which a chamber would encourage an individual to emigrate, however, reflected that individual's perceived ability to contribute to sustainable growth. Those who could invest in the city were openly welcomed; those who were only looking for a job were discouraged.

Perhaps one of the most valuable contributions of the growth machine thesis is the insight that growth is the driving force of the North American city and that growth can be achieved only at the expense of one's competitors.[10] Between 1880 and 1940 (and some would say on to the present), California cities generally adopted the belief expressed by W. A. Purrington of Riverside in 1915, that "the chief ambition of almost all cities . . . is to achieve bigness. This would bring added value to real estate, bringing greater returns to property owners."[11] California cities thus engaged in a heated interstate and intrastate competition to attract more businesses, industries, and residents in order to achieve "bigness" and become *the* regionally dominant city of the West; they engaged in what can be termed a "city growth game."[12]

Most urban histories of the West depict this growth game as a gendered game in which both the credit of vision and the benefits of economic growth accrue primarily to men, the owners of wealth and power.[13] Yet because women constituted 50 percent of the population and did enjoy legal protections to property ownership in California, they could not be ignored in creating a growth coalition to win the game. A successful growth strategy required careful planning and marketing by real estate developers and urban entrepreneurs, both men and women. Because most cities by the turn of the twentieth century were providing the basic services of police, sidewalks, and schools, reaching the top of the urban hierarchy required vision and forethought. It was not enough for a city to sell itself solely as a modern service city. Urban boosters had to develop a variety of social and moral services (churches, clubs, and parks) and to demonstrate the growth potential of the city.

Although still constrained by the social imperatives of the Victorian era, California property law and a strong growth mentality allowed and encouraged middle- and upper-class women to assert their rightful claim to a voice in the process of urban growth and development as early as the 1880s. With the founding of the first women's clubs and improvement societies in the 1890s, upper- and middle-class women developed one social vehicle through which they could more openly participate in the growth machine and influence local growth and development. In the early years, this participation tended to be in the provision of social and cultural services that helped solidify the corporate capitalist worldview, but their interests quickly expanded. The records of California's women's clubs demonstrate that club activities extended far beyond maternal or domestic interests in municipal housekeeping and philanthropy. Through club resolutions presented to city councils and chambers of commerce, fund-raisers, and committee work, clubwomen helped define their communities politically, culturally, economically, and intellectually. Often cloaking their behavior in the vocabulary of Victorian womanhood, they used their expertise and social standing as the guardians of public morality, culture, and cleanliness to plan and sell their communities. In the process, along with their male counterparts, women contributed to California's economic success. They shared in the promise of wealth and sense of destiny that fueled the state's growth and development.

A study of women growth machine members, who were excluded from direct political participation before 1911, provides insight into the attitudes and motivations behind the activities of the growth coalition. At the same time that upper- and middle-class women were organizing women's clubs and improvement societies in the 1880s and 1890s, they increasingly entered what I term "apprenticeships" in property ownership and management, in political activism, and in city planning. In these apprenticeships, they confronted the language of capitalism and learned about the connection between city improvements and property values. They became familiar with the economic value of parks and beautification projects, yet they remained bounded in their public discourse by the social mores and language of Victorian womanhood that placed their public activities in the context of domestic and maternal concerns. By entering into these apprenticeships, women developed a capitalist consciousness and a capitalist vocabulary that served them as contributors to city growth. As Sarah Deutsch has said, they "learned to talk more like a man."[14]

The fact that upper- and middle-class women were economically motivated in completing their apprenticeships is evident in the rapid evolution of their vocabulary. In the 1880s, women usually discussed their improvement work in terms of how it would enhance the moral character of the city. By 1891, however, women could argue publicly that "good roads are an investment and not a tax. By the increase in property values, they are paid for many times over."[15] By 1907, women property owners could employ the vocabulary of capitalism to protest city improvements that "would mean a great depreciation in property values."[16] By 1924 the letterhead of one female-headed civic organization could read, "We urge the confinement of all display advertising to commercial locations where it will not injure scenery, civic beauty or residential values."[17] Although to the present day women employ the language of home and family in their political crusades when it is expedient, they learned in their apprenticeships to employ the language of capitalism as well.

This is the story, then, of the emergence of women's influence in the process of urban growth. It explores the evolution of women's economic involvement as California cities developed from small agricultural outposts into thriving metropolitan and residential centers. Returning to Harvey Molotch's contention that a growth machine consists of a coalition of property owners, it seeks to establish women in that position. It thus begins with an examination of evidence of women as property owners and managers. As women gained experience in the real estate market through apprenticeships in property, they gained confidence in their ability to speak the language of capitalism and to function within the urban growth machine. Through these apprenticeships women developed a capitalist consciousness and a community "we feeling" in which preservation of community identity became a paramount consideration such that they came to identify more with men of their same class than with women of other classes.

After establishing women as stakeholders in the city corporation, it is important to explore the vehicle through which they had the most success in influencing city growth. For most women, continuing to feel the bonds of Victorian social mores, women's clubs provided that vehicle. Chapter 2 thus looks at the work of California women's clubs and concludes that women's clubs were more than social organizations or arenas in which women could develop a feminist consciousness. They were also a vital part of the growth machine and an avenue through which many women completed apprenticeships in public and political activism.

Next, I turn to a more conventional assessment of growth machine activities by exploring the work of women with various chambers of commerce throughout the state. This is a heretofore unexplored area of women's work in the city. Chamber of commerce activities do not fit with the standard interpretations of women's work with the emphasis on gender-specific clubs and power relations. The inclusion of women in chambers of commerce suggests that women were indeed members of the growth machine and interested in far more than moral uplift, self-improvement, or sisterhood in their public work. They were also deeply motivated by the same capitalistic and economic concerns of men of their same class and status. Since chambers of commerce exist solely to sell cities, evidence of women's work with chambers of commerce provides the most compelling evidence of the capitalist interests of urban California women and of their inclusion in the growth machine. In addition, this evidence also suggests that chambers of commerce were not the exclusive purview of greedy male capitalists. At least in the cities included in this study, members of chambers of commerce were local citizens interested in pursuing economic success, but also in developing morally upright cities with a high quality of life.

Chapter 4 turns to the function of city government and politics and explores the role of women as political actors. Once again, the growth machine thesis offers insight into women as political actors. As property owners, women had a concrete reason to become involved in the business of the city. Property ownership provided women with the status of stockholders in the city corporation. It propelled women into the political arena long before they had the power of the vote in 1911. The imperatives of the growth machine seem to have constrained sexism in local politics.

Chapters 5 and 6 conclude this study by exploring the role of women in the adoption of city planning ordinances and comprehensive city plans prior to 1940. Throughout California women influenced the development of city plans, and in the 1920s and 1930s, one woman came to dominate the field. Through her work with the Better Homes in America campaign and the Plans and Planting Branch of the Community Arts Association, Pearl Chase personally guided the development of both a city and a county plan for Santa Barbara. Building upon the City Beautiful tradition, Chase worked to make Santa Barbara the most aesthetically pleasing city on the West Coast. She recognized that the Santa Barbara tourist economy relied on developing the region's natural and historical assets rather than on industrial development. In addition, she found that by working within the context of female moral authority and domesticity, she could achieve far greater influence over city growth than through more overt political activism. She masterfully blended the language of capitalism with the language of domesticity to realize her vision for the city over a fifty-year period. Over time, her influence on city planning was felt as far away as New York and Washington, D.C.

In California's second- and third-tier cities, middle- and upper-class women realized that protecting and enhancing the natural beauty, the cultural assets, and the services of their cities through comprehensive planning protected and enhanced property values. As they worked with male booster organizations, there developed a division of labor, not entirely drawn along gender lines, in which women supported programs designed to build up the residential areas and men the commercial areas. Together, these programs sold California cities as ideal places where families could find unlimited economic, social, educational, recreational, and spiritual opportunities.

By exploring the means through which California women became property owners and managers, and eventually reached the highest ranks of city planning professionals, I offer new insight into the effects of gender and class on the process of western urbanization and the workings of the growth machine. The evidence suggests that the unfettered capitalism of western development introduced women to the language of economic growth and broke down Victorian social mores regarding women's public activities. Once property-owning women realized that their economic security depended on continued urban growth, they joined the growth coalition and shaped it by their own concerns and interests. While city life may have altered gender roles and perceptions, the larger issue is how women joined with men of their social class to shape the process of urbanization and contribute to the growth and development of the western United States.

By examining the story of California cities prior to 1940, we gain new insight into the emergence of the West as a pacesetter for the nation. In order to gain a broader understanding of this period, we need to explore the contributions of both men and women and address the differences between residential and commercial development. We need to understand the ways in which the job of selling the economy and the home were shared by both men and women and by a variety of civic organizations all with the ultimate goal of achieving economic security. By examining city growth in terms of potential long-term investment prospects, as well as through male and female contributions, a new picture of the urban West emerges that counters interpretations of a history of greed and speculation.[18]

Women and Property Ownership

Staking a Claim to the City

In late 1886, Will Eddy, a Presbyterian minister in New York, received the devastating news that he had been diagnosed with tuberculosis. Following his doctor's advise, he packed up his wife, Elizabeth, their baby daughter, Ruth, and all of their belongings and moved to the drier climate of Southern California. Leaving behind the support network of family and friends in New York, Elizabeth Eddy faced an uncertain future. While her husband's health could improve and he might be able to provide for the family, the more likely scenario was an early widowhood for Elizabeth in which she would become the sole support for her daughter. Under these circumstances, the couple entered into a true economic partnership. Together they scoured the Riverside and Redlands citrus region for available citrus investment property and eventually purchased a lot on Fern Avenue in Redlands. Upon Will's death in 1888, Elizabeth became an independent private property owner and thus a stockholder in the City of Redlands' corporate ambitions for growth.

Private property ownership is a defining feature of Western civilization and is often considered a sacred right of Americans. John Locke argued that protection of private property is one of the central reasons for the creation of government. From national to state to local government, protection of private property and the mediation of property disputes have been at the center of a vast majority of legislation and legislative debate. At the local level, property determines both "place" and "process." It is the impetus for creating community. One's interest in the activities of others increases as concern grows for the value of individual property holdings. An individual's first concern lies with his or her personal piece of property and the ability to attain profit from it. Property owners expand the orbit of their interest to neighboring properties if concern arises that use of those properties might impair the value of their own. Over time, property owners come to see that their personal future begins to be bound to the development of an ever-expanding area. Thus, a "we feeling" is created that can also be defined as "community." Cities can thus be seen as geographical settings defined by legal, political, and topographical features in which competing land interests must give up some of their rights in order to achieve security through strategic coalition and action. Property ownership thus provides the impetus for joining the urban growth coalition.[1]

In the historical context, with personal wealth based in real property, property owners regardless of gender found their personal fortunes dependent on successful city growth. Consequently, private property owners had to participate in civic affairs in order to protect or enhance that personal wealth. For property owners, the public and private spheres became inextricably intertwined. By viewing the growth machine as an intersection of public and private concerns, an alternative interpretation of women's entrance into public activities emerges. As middle-class women increased their property holdings, they could not afford to distinguish between a public and private arena. Women property owners thus became part of the public sphere because private property ownership was a domestic concern. Rather than extending the domestic sphere to the public through moral reform efforts, middle-class women instead reacted to the encroachment of the public sphere into the domestic.[2] The same decision-making process that took place on the private level influenced decision making at the public level. The city growth game and the private wealth accumulation game were one and the same. In confronting capitalism through property ownership, women also took the first step in developing a twentieth-century "capitalist consciousness" and a capitalist vocabulary that slowly replaced the nineteenth-century language of separate spheres.

Because of legal arrangements that protected their right to own property, California women could participate in the real estate market and thus stake a claim to stockholder status in the city corporation with few legal impediments (social and political impediments would remain in place well into the twentieth century). Growing out of a Spanish tradition of community property rights, California law has always protected the rights of women to own property both before and after marriage. California's constitution of 1849 protected women's rights not only to property acquired prior to marriage but to property acquired independently after marriage. Inherited from the Mexicans, this law set the standard by which all future community property law would be evaluated.[3]

Prior to 1870, as community property law evolved, women slowly gained the right to control finances separate from their husbands. In 1852, the California state legislature enacted a law permitting married women to engage in business as "sole traders." Sole trader status guaranteed that the business and profits a married woman acquired independent of her husband belonged exclusively to her; a lien could not be placed on them to pay off the debts of her husband. Once registered as a sole trader, a married woman's assets attained after marriage were no longer at the disposal of her spouse. In 1870, the legislature repealed the registration requirement and gave women the protection they needed to pursue their independence as capitalists. The legislature further amended the law to permit a husband and wife to determine for themselves the status of their property as joint tenants, tenants in common, or community property. Although the husband continued to have the sole right to manage community property, recognition of separate property status for women opened the world of business and real estate to California women.[4] Between 1872 and 1917, only small changes were made in the wording of community property law. In the twentieth century, as the social status, political importance, and economic position of women developed, community property law evolved to give the wife ownership rights commensurate with her contributions to the marriage, family income, and industrial society.

While separate property ownership gave women legal economic equality with men in California, socially and politically they continued to lag far behind. Between 1880 and 1940, however, middle- and upper-class women increasingly fought against the social and political barriers to property ownership and management for all women. They asserted their rights by demanding that cities respond to their claims and protect and enhance one of the few economic assets they had. Individually and through their women's clubs, women confronted city councils on issues as diverse as street grading and widening, tree planting, eminent domain, beautification ordinances, curfews, and zoning. Women's clubs in particular took it as their special mission to inform women of their property rights and to act as women's advocates by petitioning local, state, and federal governments to protect those rights. In the process, they found themselves drawn into the nexus of their local city growth machines.

Although women may have had the legal right to own property, breaking down the social and political barriers to economic independence proved a daunting task and one that only a few overtly political women took on. For most women, taking advantage of their legal right to own property required what I call an "apprenticeship" in property owning and managing. The evidence suggests that between 1880 and 1910 women evolved into active members of the growth machine by completing an apprenticeship that introduced them to the workings of the land market and the language of capitalism. Through this apprenticeship they mastered the knowledge necessary to manage their own financial affairs and to be vocal and successful members of the growth coalition.

It appears that middle-class women's emergence into ownership and management of their property in California generally followed a two-step process. First, women could enter an apprenticeship with either their fathers or their husbands overseeing the initial purchase of property. In this first phase, women were being prepared for economic independence by gaining experience in the overall process of home buying and building. Second, women attained direct ownership and management of property through either inheritance or personal investment. As independent property owners prior to 1911, these women achieved a semblance of economic emancipation before they gained political enfranchisement.

A good example of this process can be found in the experience of Elizabeth Eddy, who entered into her apprenticeship in 1886 under the guidance of her husband, Will, and her friend John P. Fisk, who was a real estate broker. By learning the rules of the real estate market, and its intimate relationship with the mechanisms of city government, Elizabeth's apprenticeship introduced her to the language of capitalism and the strategies employed by the growth machine. It prepared her for a life outside the home, ensured her interest in the process of city growth and development, and equipped her with the skills necessary to remain financially independent following Will Eddy's death in 1888 (she married John P. Fisk in 1890). Far from existing within a restricted sphere, Elizabeth's apprenticeship in property integrated her into the Redlands growth coalition and hence made her a participant in the urban com-

The Fisk family—John, Ruth, Helen, and Elizabeth—ca. 1900. From the Archives of the A. K. Smiley Public Library.

petition for regional dominance that characterized western urban growth.[5]

By the time Elizabeth's daughters were ready to enter their apprenticeships in property acquisition and management in the 1910s and 1920s, they no longer required the economic assistance or business expertise of male relatives. In part this reflected the breakdown of Victorian separate spheres that accompanied the emergence of women as capitalists. Because the first generation of middle-class women had established their capabilities as competent property owners and managers, their daughters, entering the marketplace between 1910 and 1940 could purchase and improve property independently. The rules were also changed by a nationwide shift away from an apprentice system of training to academic training, credential programs, and a growing movement for professionalization in business.[6] While fathers, brothers, and uncles continued to provide one avenue of entry into an apprenticeship, the proliferation of women's colleges and professional and business schools after 1900 offered alternative approaches.

Elizabeth's daughter Helen Fisk, for example, entered an early apprenticeship with her father by helping him in his real estate business as a teenager. She then attended Mount Holyoke in the 1910s, where she majored in English and economics and made contacts with other business and professional women. After graduation she returned to Redlands, where she took business courses through the local business school in order to expand her skills. Her experiences as a working woman in the 1920s and 1930s prepared her to assume full ownership and management of the family's citrus groves and land holdings as an unmarried, independent businesswoman.[7]

Getting a handle on who California women property owners were is difficult in light of the fragmentary record they left behind. Only a limited number of diaries and letters that address the issue of property ownership and management are available. The rest of the story must be pieced together through newspaper articles, tax assessor records, and probate records. Keeping in mind the powerful influence of Victorian social mores, the story is even harder to flesh out. One woman who left us a detailed account of her activities as a property owner was Elizabeth Eddy Fisk of Redlands. Through her detailed family records, including her complete diaries, we can see how one woman became a property owner and a member of the growth machine.

Elizabeth Eddy's apprenticeship in property ownership and management began in 1887 when she and her husband, Will, joined the flood of easterners emigrating to the booming citrus region of Southern California. A minister, not a businessman, Will had accumulated enough wealth to afford the move with relative comfort and to be able to purchase citrus investment property upon arrival. Will and Elizabeth, however, did not purchase property rashly. Instead, searching for real estate that would provide both income and an ideal homesite, they chose to rent a house for several months and to explore the region. Together, they traveled throughout the Riverside and Redlands orange-growing areas looking at property and discussing the merits of the various communities.

Far from being relegated to a secondary domestic role, Elizabeth shared equally in this property search. She and Will "talked as usual all manner of plans for living here, building, renting etc."[8] Elizabeth learned about the operation of the land market and participated in the entire process of purchasing property and building a home. In her diaries, she carefully recorded the prices of property, the date and amount of purchases, and any other significant financial information. On November 18, 1887, Elizabeth recorded that the couple purchased a five-acre lot on Fern Avenue in Redlands, next to a ten-acre orange grove.

The home Elizabeth and John Fisk eventually built on the Fern Avenue property, purchased by Will and Elizabeth Eddy, ca. 1900. From the Archives of the A. K. Smiley Public Library.

Three months later, Elizabeth noted in her diary that they had sold off investment property in Riverside that had nearly doubled in value in less than a year.[9]

In the process of purchasing a home in Redlands, Elizabeth spent a year in the first stage of her apprenticeship. In this period, she gathered knowledge about the operation of the Southern California citrus real estate market. In addition to recording land prices and acreage in her diaries, Elizabeth noted her conversations with real estate developers and other investors on the advisability of purchasing property in either Riverside or Redlands. As she and Will spent more time in Redlands and discussed the situation with friends, they concluded that even high-priced land would be a worthwhile investment. In considering a 13½-acre lot priced at $300 per acre, Elizabeth and Will conferred with their friends Jane Hale and Austin and Marion Park on the matter. The Hales and the Parks were members of the Redlands citrus elite, and they agreed with the Eddys that although the price was high, the quality of the land would make it an investment worth considering.[10] Elizabeth gained further knowledge about the local real estate market by discussing it with local surveyor and engineer Isaac Ford. He recommended that the couple purchase at the minimum a half interest in ten acres in Redlands (ten acres was the average size orange grove at the time). This would provide a modest income until they could purchase land on which to build their home and plant their own orange grove.[11] The couple recognized the wisdom of this advice, but because they still planned to make their home in Riverside at this time, they chose to purchase there first.

The care with which the Eddys considered their purchase provides insight into the growth machine as a coalition of real people with genuine concern for their lives as well as their economic success. Far from being a collection of coldhearted, greedy capitalists intent upon manipulating others for personal gain, members of the Redlands growth machine were also genuinely caring people.[12] In the case of Will and Elizabeth Eddy, they were Christians with a deep sense of community and responsibility to others. They may have been interested in purchasing property and increasing wealth through it, but they also wanted to live in a community where they could raise children with a high quality of life. Eventually Redlands proved to be that place.

At the time the Eddys arrived in Redlands in 1887, the town had enjoyed nearly a decade of growth on the heels of the Southern California citrus boom of the 1880s.[13] Located sixty-five miles east of Los Angeles in the San Bernardino Valley, Redlands' growth relied on the creation of a real estate market, a primary agricultural product (citrus), and a thriving tourist business. From the town's founding in the 1870s, Redlands property owners, like most citrus growers throughout Southern California, demonstrated their interest in long-term investment opportunities by making their homes where they owned land. *Redlands Citrograph* editor Scipio Craig noted that investors bought property in Redlands and settled to stay. He predicted that this stability would bring long-term prosperity to the community:

> Each family comes in, settles down, goes to work quietly developing the marvelous richness of the soil and that is all there is to it. No feverish excitement; no 'making a pile and going home' about it. *This* is home from the time they get here. To wait for the collapse of such a movement is equivalent to waiting for the stars to fall, so as to gather up the fragments of jewelry.[14]

Although tinged with a heavy dose of booster rhetoric, this observation was grounded in fact. A "get-rich-quick" mentality was not possible in citrus because it took from five to seven years for citrus trees to bear fruit and return dividends.

Citrus also provided Redlands with the closest thing to a guaranteed return on investment. Speculation was not an issue because of the substantial profits available from even a small grove.[15] One California newspaper editor compared growing oranges to mining gold, noting that in 1904 alone the orange harvest was valued at nearly 50 percent more than the yield of gold for that year.

> Last year California produced gold worth $16,835,500. It was 18 per cent of the gold mined in the United States, Alaska included. Only three countries in the world, outside of America, beat that one American state. The California gold yield was equal to about $10 for every man, woman and child in the state. This year California shipped eastward oranges valued at $24,375,000. The golden fruit of the groves was worth nearly 40 per cent more than the metallic gold of its mines, probably fully that proportion above the gold yield, taking account of the oranges consumed in the state.[16]

As a result, owning a citrus grove provided both men and women with their greatest economic opportunity in Southern California.

Women did make substantial profits in the citrus real estate market, and one in particular came to dominate the industry through the 1890s. Planting Redlands' first orange seed bed in 1888, Sarah J. Morey established the most successful citrus nursery in San Bernardino County. Obtaining seed from the nearby Barton ranch, she originally sold trees to the town's founders and leading real estate developers, E. G. Judson and F. E. Brown, for ten acres of land with water rights. Reinvesting her profits in more seedlings, she eventually planted and successfully raised twenty-five thousand young trees, which she sold to Mathew Gage of Riverside for twenty thousand dollars.[17] Until her death in 1897, Mrs. Morey was considered *the* source for nursery stock as well as a leading expert on all aspects of the citrus industry.

Sarah Morey completed her apprenticeship in property and had gained the status of an independent property owner and businesswoman by the 1880s. Unlike Elizabeth Eddy, who inherited her independence from her husband, Sarah pursued her own business interests while her husband was living. As a successful property owner and businesswoman, Sarah became a role model for other women in Redlands such as Elizabeth Eddy. Elizabeth enjoyed both a social and a business relationship with Sarah, who provided Elizabeth with most of her nursery stock and also with advice on all aspects of raising citrus.[18] Perhaps this relationship inspired Elizabeth to maintain separate finan-

The Morey mansion and a portion of the citrus groves planted and tended by Sarah Morey, ca. 1890. From the Archives of the A. K. Smiley Public Library.

cial accounts from her husband after she married John P. Fisk in 1890.

Sarah Morey was not alone in investing in Redlands real estate or in completing an apprenticeship in property ownership and financial management by the early 1880s. Indeed, many women played a key role in Redlands' early history as individual entrepreneurs and investors. The *Redlands Citrograph* reported in 1891 that eight women were among the top fifty property tax payers in the city.[19] In addition, the *Citrograph* regularly printed new building permit filings and construction statistics, in which the names of women frequently appeared. In the early 1880s, Dr. Ellen B. Seymour (Redlands' only physician from 1881 to 1887) established the Prospect House, the first hotel in the Redlands Valley. Functioning primarily as a sanitarium, this hotel helped establish Redlands' reputation as a health resort that drew eastern immigrants in search of a healthful climate.[20] In addition, women were responsible for the establishment of the Redlands Bowl (an outdoor amphitheater), they pushed for the development of city parks and a public library, and they worked with men's organizations in the ongoing effort to make Redlands an attractive and clean city. Growth and develop-

The Prospect House was the first hotel in Redlands. It was run by Dr. Ellen B. Seymour, at the left of the two women shown here in front of the building, ca. 1885. From the Archives of the A. K. Smiley Public Library.

ment relied not merely on an investment of dollars in real estate, but also on an investment in those cultural and social organizations and attributes that would attract permanent residents as well as businesses.

As Redlands tried to assert itself as a regionally dominant city in the 1880s, the elite sought to develop its vision of a residential city. The *Citrograph*'s editor suggested that the only thing preventing Redlands from attaining her destiny as San Bernardino County's leading city was a lack of available housing for eastern immigrants. Scipio Craig believed that there was an overwhelming demand for residences, and if more were built, more people would follow:

> If there is anything that this section needs more than any other, it is tenement houses. Not a dwelling can be rented anywhere, and not a room to be rented for sleeping purposes. Workmen coming here have great difficulty in getting sleeping accommodations, and if they have families, cannot bring them here at all, unless they have capital enough to buy property and build a house. There would be a large interest in building a number of cottages to rent. Our local capitalists ought to divert a portion of their wealth into this channel. It is not a wild prediction to say that fifty cottages would be rented to families

> in a short time if they were to be had, and fifty families would be quite an addition to our population. Think over the matter, you who have money, and see if you cannot make money by investing in neat, cheap cottages for workingmen.[21]

A month later, Craig continued with his exhortation for more houses, noting that as winter approached, so did tourist season. Second only to citrus, tourism provided Redlands with its economic base. Again calling for building more rental property, Craig stated that small houses could be built for a cost of between five hundred and eight hundred dollars and would rent for from eight to fifteen dollars a month. "Including the price of the lots an average of $10 a month would afford a good investment, to say nothing of the enhancement in value to the property by the increase of population."[22] Both men and women answered Craig's calls for more building and investment in citrus property; by the end of 1887, assessments in Redlands had nearly doubled.

Couples like Elizabeth and Will Eddy responded readily to the investment opportunities available in Redlands. A booming citrus land market provided an ideal setting in which a woman like Elizabeth, facing an early widowhood, could complete her apprenticeship. As her husband grew weaker from tuberculosis in the spring and summer of 1888, Elizabeth entered the second phase of her apprenticeship, in which she assumed management of the family property. Seeking advice and support from her friends Mary and Christopher Sanborn and John P. Fisk, leading land investors in Redlands, she found that she could make her property pay for itself. In June 1888, Elizabeth sold 130 pounds of potatoes, procuring the first cash the property had generated.[23] She had learned not only how to buy property but how to exploit its resources to produce income. In further preparation for widowhood, Elizabeth began to manage Will's business arrangements during his lengthy trips to Pasadena or Los Angeles for medical care.[24] She also demonstrated her knowledge of family finances by handling the sale of the family's used horse and buggy and the purchase of a new rig. Although her training as a New York society woman had not entirely prepared her for such undertakings, she demonstrated an aptitude for business that is evident in her diary entries.

As part of her apprenticeship in property management, Elizabeth also gained an intimate knowledge of the citrus business and developed the skills necessary to oversee the management of her own groves. Her education had actually begun soon after her arrival in Southern California. While staying with friends who owned a grove in

Riverside, Elizabeth observed the pickers and packers who came to harvest the crop. She was outraged that "they took 195 boxes and had estimated and paid for only 155."[25] Following Will's death in 1888 and her subsequent marriage to John P. Fisk in 1890, Elizabeth continued to administer the family groves. She supervised the installation of irrigation pipes, kept herself informed of the latest techniques for treating infestations of scale from Sarah Morey, and carefully monitored the harvest to ensure that pickers and packers did not cheat the family of profits.[26] In addition, Elizabeth became a member of the Redlands Orange Growers Association, with accounts separate from those of her husband. Through this process she began to share in the economic vision of the citrus elite and to define a role for herself as an independent stockholder in the city corporation.

Elizabeth's diaries also shed light on the coalition-building strategy among property owners of the growth machine. In her apprenticeship, Elizabeth met the very people who became the power brokers in Redlands. They included real estate brokers and developers like John P. Fisk and Isaac Ford, but they also included the women of Redlands. Elizabeth noted in her diaries that when she and Will went property shopping they usually went with other couples. In addition to Christopher and Mary Sanborn, Jane Hale, and Austin and Marion Park, Elizabeth consulted with Tilla and Frank Hamilton, who owned a large tract of land in Terracina, and Agnes Sloan, who co-owned the Sloan House Hotel with her husband, Henry. All of these men became prominent in the Chamber of Commerce, and their wives were founding members of the Redlands Contemporary Club.

For these women, property ownership drew them into the civic life of the community, and many of them found a voice for their public concerns in the Contemporary Club. As a member and later president of this women's club, Elizabeth gained valuable experience as a public speaker and leader. Membership in the Contemporary Club thus supplemented her apprenticeship in property by providing her with an apprenticeship in public affairs.

Elizabeth's involvement with the Contemporary Club increased as the club's programs turned to civic issues in the 1900s. While she regularly noted club day in her diary, she usually did not record the program offered unless it pertained to civic matters. For example, in 1900, she wrote, "Club was interesting. Studies as a *civic factor* in Redlands."[27] Other noted programs included a 1904 program on women's law by Mrs. Willoughby Rodman of Los Angeles and a discussion on finance in 1908 by Helen Kimberly and Emma Greenleaf (two of Redlands' leading business and property owners) and by Mr. and Mrs. Robert Burdette (of Los Angeles).

Elizabeth's increased interest in the civic work of the club reflected her growing awareness of business prospects in the city as her apprenticeship drew to a close. Between 1898 and 1910, when she became president of the Contemporary Club, Elizabeth's business activities expanded greatly. In 1898, her concern lay primarily with the price and quality of her oranges.[28] By 1900 she had regained her active participation in the local real estate market by consulting with her husband on investment property and by investigating slum conditions in the city.[29] Four years later, she demonstrated her independence in business matters by purchasing, against the wishes of her husband, an inventory of furniture. At this time, John Fisk's real estate business acquired a furnished home as part of the settlement of an estate. The house furnishings were auctioned separately from the real estate. Elizabeth noted in her diary on June 20, 1904, that John had received two bids for the furniture: $500 from the family purchasing the home, and $400 from the "second hand man." On June 21, Elizabeth decided to offer $550 for the furniture. "John does not favor the move for me but I want to make it. I guess I shall." The next day her offer was accepted, and by June 29 Elizabeth had sold the entire inventory, surprising even herself. "Beats all how fast that furniture has sold."[30] At the same time, Elizabeth became more aware of city elections and the work of the Chamber of Commerce, in which she participated along with her husband.

Throughout this period, Elizabeth expanded her property holdings by purchasing a lot next to the Contemporary Club's clubhouse. This property, which included a small cottage, she intended to sell to the club in the future. In the meantime, the property provided Elizabeth with a modest income from rentals. She sold the property to the club in 1917 for thirty-five hundred dollars. It is interesting to note that she decided to sell the property the same day that she heard a club talk on California development.[31]

While the story of Elizabeth Fisk helps put a human face on the growth machine, her experience alone is not enough to argue that women were a significant part of the California growth machine. Although no hard statistical data exist for the percentages of women owning property in California, additional anecdotal evidence suggests property ownership clearly influenced the evolution of women's capitalist consciousness and capitalist vocabularies. The tax assessment records for San Bernardino County record a significant number of women owning taxable property on which they regularly made improvements. For many, the property provided income through rentals.[32]

Beyond Southern California, women property owners can be found in the booming and competitive cities of the San Francisco Bay Area. One of the more vocal advocates of full equality for women in politics and a California property owner was Clara Foltz of San Francisco. Unlike Elizabeth Fisk, who was content to emerge slowly as a player in public affairs, Clara Foltz came out swinging. Widowed with five children to support, she fought hard to become a lawyer. When she first applied, she found that the law did not permit her admission to law school. Undeterred, she appealed to state legislators to change the law, which they did by a narrow margin. She also had to sue to be admitted to Hastings College of Law, which was closed to her only by the dean. In 1877 she was admitted to the California bar and established her own legal firm. In addition to working as a lawyer, she worked for a brief year and a half as editor and publisher of the *San Diego Daily Bee*.[33]

As both a home owner (she owned her own home on Van Ness Avenue in San Francisco) and a lawyer, Clara Foltz became committed to increasing the rights of women to own property and to gain economic independence. In addition to speaking before the state legislature on bills affecting women, she also became a regular speaker on the women's club circuit. Her appearances at statewide meetings, where she frequently spoke on women's property rights, provide evidence of her commitment to economic empowerment for women. Once again, she had completed an apprenticeship in property and in law long before the law recognized her as the political equal of men.[34]

Clara Foltz was joined by another Redlands citizen, Mary Lynde (Hoffman) Craig, as both a San Francisco property owner and an activist for women's property rights. Mary Lynde Hoffman was a San Francisco widow and treasurer of the Pacific Coast Women's Press Association. Through her Press Association contacts, she met Scipio Craig, editor of the *Redlands Citrograph*. The two eventually married, and Mary made Redlands her primary residence. Nonetheless, she continued to own property in San Francisco. She also attended law school after her marriage and was admitted to the California bar in 1893. She, along with Clara Foltz and Laura de Norce Gordon, were three of only four women practicing law in California in 1893. Again, like Foltz,

Mary Craig used her position as an activist in the cause of women's property ownership, and she, too, became a regular speaker at statewide women's club meetings. Perhaps this explains her husband's strong support for women's property ownership and women's involvement in civic affairs.[35]

Across the bay in the emerging commercial center of Oakland, middle-class women also found opportunities to buy both business and residential property and to stake a claim to "stock" in the city corporation. Property ownership and taxpayer status legitimated women's involvement in civic affairs and supplied the *Oakland Enquirer* with the evidence it needed to endorse women's suffrage throughout the period from 1900 to 1911, when state suffrage was finally granted. As in Redlands, property ownership also helped break down Victorian concepts of acceptable behavior for women and an antiquated vocabulary that confined women's public concerns to domestic and maternal issues.

As Oakland boomed at the turn of the twentieth century, women entered the public arena of property ownership in increasing numbers. Women like Bessie J. Wood added to the commercial development of the city by owning commercial property and running a successful business. Established in 1897, Wood's undertaking business grew rapidly and became a rallying point for the city's boosters, who pointed to it as evidence of the commercial opportunities available to both men and women in Oakland.[36] As her business continued to succeed throughout the 1910s and 1920s, Wood assumed leadership of Oakland businesswomen and became an advocate of using the vocabulary of capitalism to express women's views regarding city growth. In 1909 she joined the Chamber of Commerce and in 1915 assumed leadership of the Woman's Bureau of the Chamber of Commerce. From the membership of the Woman's Bureau, Wood garnered enough support to organize the Business and Professional Woman's Club of Oakland in 1917, which became a major Oakland booster organization in the 1920s.[37] Wood represented a new breed of single, independent career women in the early twentieth century who had successfully adopted the language and techniques of capitalism to ensure their personal financial well-being. When asked in 1910 if she would not rather have pursued a more traditional woman's role, Wood responded, "From the observance of the lives of married friends of mine, and the experience of my own independence, I think I would never hesitate to choose my own way of life to the other [marriage], were I doing it all over again."[38] She would, however, eventually marry.

Bessie Wood was joined as a property owner by many other Oakland women, some of whom owned extensive investment property throughout the Bay Area and others who owned only modest homes. Theresa Fair Oelrichs, for example, heiress to a Nevada silver fortune, represented the large, absentee investor. Although best known as the owner and builder of Rosecliff, an estate in Newport, Rhode Island, Oelrichs was also a majority stockholder in the Pacific Land Investment Company and a heavy investor in Oakland and East Bay property. Prior to a massive sell-off in 1906, "Tessie," as she was known to friends, controlled the Park Hotel property in Alameda, the Neptune Gardens resort in the South Bay, and the property occupied by the F. L. Coghill Lumber Company in Oakland. This property, originally valued at $250,000, was sold in March 1906 for $500,000.[39] Oelrichs also owned property in San Francisco, most of which was destroyed in the April 1906 earthquake. The *Oakland Enquirer* reported, "When the news arrived of the complete loss of the Rialto and Crossley buildings, which [Oelrichs] had lately come into possession of, she made little of it, but felt keenly for the destruction of the Fairmont Hotel, which she built but recently sold. . . . Mrs. Oelrichs intends rebuilding her destroyed properties as soon as affairs shape themselves properly."[40] Stories like that about Oelrichs that appeared in the *Oakland Enquirer* sanctioned women's economic lives and provide evidence of more than just domestic concerns. Although Mrs. Oelrichs was not directly involved in Oakland's civic affairs as an absentee landlord, she represented the type of investor Oakland boosters and the Oakland growth machine sought to cultivate, regardless of gender.

Following the April 1906 earthquake, real estate sales in Oakland boomed and women joined in the general frenzy of land purchases. Mrs. M. E. Effey, who lost her San Francisco home in the earthquake, was one of many San Francisco home owners to relocate across the bay. She purchased a two-acre lot in the Piedmont hills for ten thousand dollars. Other, more modest home purchases by women as reported in the *Oakland Enquirer* included a house and lot in the Humphrey tract by Mrs. J. B. Anderson for thirty-five hundred dollars and three lots in the Santa Fe tract to a Miss McMeekin. Miss McMeekin intended to build rental cottages on her property, thus taking advantage of the large number of displaced residents from San Francisco.[41] After a dip in the real estate market in the fall of 1906, sales increased in the spring of 1907. Among the buyers at this time were Eva M. Shamp, who bought a bungalow for $3,750, and Mrs. P. H. Lamoureux, who bought a business building to be placed on the corner of Nineteenth and Market streets.[42]

The importance contemporary Oaklanders placed on women's property ownership needs to be addressed. Gender distinctions in economic opportunity were not important to Alameda County historian Joseph E. Baker. Writing a booster article for *Sunset* magazine in 1907, Baker used anecdotal evidence of women's property ownership to illustrate Oakland's ascendance as a metropolitan city of distinction. To illustrate the growth of the business district, Baker recounted the story of Mrs. Mary Canning, a woman who rose from a domestic servant to a major owner of business property. In 1867, Baker reported, Mary Canning was an unmarried domestic employee of Horace Carpentier, one of Oakland's leading developers. Pooling her meager savings with that of a woman friend, Canning asked Carpentier to invest this eight hundred dollars in property at the corner of Broadway and Thirteenth streets. Subsequently, Canning bought her friend out for fifteen hundred dollars and became the sole owner of one hundred feet on Broadway. Canning turned this property into rental property and watched it increase in value from eight hundred dollars in 1867 to five hundred thousand dollars in 1907.[43] The rags-to-riches story of Mary Canning provides evidence not only of the opportunities open to women in Oakland but also of the opportunities open to members of all classes who partook of the capitalist value system.

Middle-class women also staked their claim to the city through the creation of women's clubs and clubhouses. For women who did not own property independently, ownership in a clubhouse represented an alternative form of "stock-holding" in the city. In building their clubhouses, women entered another type of apprenticeship in property. Owning a clubhouse represented a major investment of time and money, and managing the building required business knowledge and acumen. Like women across the nation, California women understood the importance of location in building clubhouses that would produce revenue and took time to investigate property before purchasing. For several months in 1909, as members voiced their concerns about location, the Oakland Club debated building a new clubhouse. "Sites in various parts of the city have been discussed for comparative advantages. A faction of the club has stood for a less costly site further out, while others of the club have stood as staunchly for a site more immediately down town where they maintain a clubhouse would be a source of greater revenue."[44]

Founded in 1876, the Ebell Club built this clubhouse on Harrison Street in Oakland in 1907. The building was destroyed by fire in 1959. Courtesy of the Oakland Public Library, Oakland History Room.

Nationally, middle-class women shared in the clubhouse movement that grew in force between 1900 and 1930. Through *The Club Woman,* the official magazine of the General Federation of Women's Clubs, clubwomen shared information about the entire process of clubhouse building, from purchasing the right lot, to hiring an architect and contractor, to providing maintenance and upkeep. Regular articles on clubhouses kept women apprised of building efforts nationwide and of the practice of raising funds by forming a stock company in which members could buy shares.[45] Forming a stock company and buying stock are clearly economic activities and demonstrate that women had knowledge of and employed the language of capitalism in their club work. One can argue that if women applied capitalistic language to their group home buying and building, that they probably did the same in their private affairs. In Oakland, the Oakland Club, the Ebell Club, and the Woman's Civic Club all paid for their clubhouses through stock options, as did the Contemporary Club in Redlands and the Riverside Woman's Club.

In the early 1920s, the Business and Professional Women's Club joined Oakland's other women's clubs in the movement to build and own its own clubhouse. By this time, however, women could openly discuss the economics of clubhouse building and claim their rightful place as an asset to the city. They could employ the language of city growth and discuss the vision of Oakland's growth, to which they sought to contribute. The women endeavored to "build income property" with their clubhouse, and the club leadership was concerned that the funds be raised within the club so that the women would not lose control of the property and the income derived therefrom.[46] The women demonstrated their understanding of the investment potential of property, indicating their full maturation as capitalists:

> We must raise this amount *within the club as only in that way will the club control the property* and receive the benefits which will accrue from the investment—*and it will be an investment!* If each one of us could realize what a desirable way this is to use our savings to bring us a reasonable profit and still be entirely safe, we would each buy all the stock we could and our problem would be solved. When you realize that we paid $550 per front foot for our lot and that one just a few doors south of us sold for about $1,000 cash, that the property all about us is being held at that price while the lot at the corner of 13th and Webster is held at $1300 and will be raised to $1500—just as soon as 15th Street is open for traffic—you can readily see that our lot is bound to increase in value continuously. Surely we are all women of vision with an all-abiding faith in Oakland which is growing by leaps and bounds before our eyes and will loan our money for this purpose with the assurance that we will help the club to secure a HOME OF ITS OWN and make a profitable investment for ourselves at the same time. The stock will begin to bear interest when the building is completed and rented.[47]

The clubwomen were clearly invoking the vocabulary of investment capitalism. There is no doubt that they grasped the concepts behind rising property values—street improvements and expanded city services—and that they would benefit personally by investing in a "public" building. If they understood this as club members, it is unreasonable to assume that they followed a different path in their personal finances.

Property ownership was the great equalizer between men and women and between classes. At the same time that women were increasing their real estate holdings in Oakland, the *Oakland Enquirer* kept its readers updated on what women were doing in business and real estate across the nation. It reported on U.S. Census Bureau findings that over 14 million women were reported as breadwinners in the 1900 census; it reported on the business success of a Pennsylvania woman who managed two clothing factories and admonished businessmen to follow her rules for doing business; it reported on women's success as bankers, noting that there were about twenty-five women officials or directors of California banks in 1908; and it reported on the presence of a prominent real estate woman at the annual meeting of real estate men in Oakland.[48] All of these examples were used by the editor of the *Enquirer* as evidence that women were the equals of men in the business world and should, therefore, be accorded suffrage, particularly at the municipal level. The editor felt suffrage was particularly important for women property tax payers, who, he said, should be allowed to vote on bond issues.[49]

The *Enquirer's* editorials sanctioned the economic behavior of women and provided them with the vocabulary and the facts to justify their public presence. Relying on the U.S. Census returns, the *Enquirer* could prove that in 1906 women were moving beyond the private sphere and thus deserved political recognition of their economic lives:

> No matter by what authority we may try to account for it or whether or not it is best for society, women have become economic factors in the United States, and one which is constantly assuming larger proportions. That women have a right to support and to make a career for themselves are no longer debatable questions. That they have the capability to do so, is proven by the census returns.[50]

The *Enquirer* once again used these data to support women's suffrage.

As it encouraged women to embrace the public sphere, the newspaper reprinted an article by Cynthia Gray for the *Seattle Star.* Gray argued that all women should have business training, "not merely that they may be companions to their fathers, husbands and brothers, able to talk intelligently about business affairs, but for their own protection. . . . A knowledge of business rules and forms is a weapon, and a very valuable one, too, when a woman is left to fight the world single handed."[51]

In 1910 the *Enquirer* stepped up its campaign for women's suffrage, and it turned to local professional women themselves for evidence that career women could find happiness and success outside the home. The newspaper interviewed eight women who it deemed had proved women's right to a place in business and in the professions. These included Denice Hughes, Dr. Luella Stone Sauger, Grace Wishaar, Ella S. Mitchell, Bessie J. Wood, and Jessie V. Berry. Although the women generally agreed that home life should provide most women with satisfaction, they were unwilling to recommend a particular course of action for all women. Miss A. E. Walton perhaps summed up their views best: "Business women and professional women, like home women, are born and not made. One cannot advise for the average woman, for there isn't any average woman. . . . There is no rule to be set down for women to follow."[52] Real estate dealer and manager of a mercantile, Ella S. Mitchell, however, unreservedly recommended a business life for a woman, "unless she can have a professional career":

> Housework gives a woman no chance for the development of her mind and capabilities. . . . Yes, I think a woman unquestionably has a place in the business world, though I do not believe in either business or the professions to the exclusion of the home. Every woman, naturally, wants a home. . . . But I certainly don't believe in a woman marrying just to get that home. And I believe that a business training not only does not unfit a woman for marriage, but rather it tends to make her a better homemaker and manager. The success that women are attaining in every branch of business and professional life, proves their right there.[53]

Helen Kelley and Denice Hughes, also real estate dealers, seconded Mitchell's viewpoint, noting that marriage for marriage's sake made no sense if a woman became entrapped in an unhappy home life.

Women from across the country and across the socioeconomic spectrum were attracted to the economic opportunities available in California in the early twentieth century. Many women investors looked for opportunities in both business ventures and real estate. Miss E. B. Wilmarth of New Rochelle, New York, for example, made contact with the Redlands Chamber of Commerce regarding the feasibility of a small investment in a ceramics business, with a sideline investment in citrus property. Miss Wilmarth's request for information proved to be beyond the scope of the chamber secretary's expertise. While he was more than willing to encourage a potential investor in citrus, he was unprepared to answer a question about the potential demand for art and ceramics classes. Recognizing Miss Wilmarth's potential, however, and unwilling to lose a potential citrus investor, he forwarded her letter to "one of our leading ladies," who highly encouraged the venture. The secretary sent the following endorsement to Miss Wilmarth:

> It is the opinion of the lady to whom I mailed your letter, and who called to talk with me about it, that there is a field here for an artist in such work, providing, however, she is prepared to wait for the business to grow, and providing also, that she is a lady of culture and intelligence. We have now a

> population somewhat above ten thousand, and one of the wealthiest communities per capita in the United States, also a cultivated, refined, moral people. You would be pleased with Redlands in every respect, if your business prospered.[54]

The Redlands Chamber of Commerce strongly supported inquiries from women who sought both business and real estate investment opportunities. These women would contribute equally to the city's commercial success and to the city's drive to increase property values and property sales. Often these women were older, seeking to relocate to Southern California for their health. They were looking for the class of community the chamber sought to promote: a saloon-free, morally upright (Christian) community in which a home and business could be purchased and run for a manageable price. To one such woman, the chamber wrote, "It is conceded that Redlands is the most attractive suburb of Los Angeles for a country home. The climate, scenery, parks, homes, churches, schools and character of the people make it so. We have no saloons and never shall have."[55]

The chamber's strongest endorsements went to women who could contribute to either the citrus economy or Redlands' second-leading industry, tourism. When Emma Blair Gray asked if the city could support a rooming house, the chamber suggested she relocate immediately. Mrs. Gray had been running a successful rooming house in Vancouver and desired to relocate to Redlands to avoid the damp climate of the North. She had about one thousand dollars to invest in a five-room cottage, but she could supplement her income by raising chickens. The chamber wrote to her:

> With the experience that you have had and the success you have made in keeping a rooming house I believe you would also make a success in Redlands, but let me advise you to come before the exodus of tourists from the east commences in the fall and take a month or two to look around and familiarize yourself with conditions, location etc. During last winter, every rooming house, boarding house and hotel in the city did the banner business and there were no vacant houses, the demand beginning earlier than ever before.[56]

Like Miss Wilmarth, Gray represented the class of people the chamber sought to attract. She was a successful entrepreneur with enough savings to afford a reasonably sized house in Redlands. She would invest not only in property but in the tourist business and thus contribute to both the city growth game and the city's economic foundation.

In addition to information regarding business opportunities from women, the chamber received a myriad of requests for more general information about the real estate market. Women from Washington, Massachusetts, Missouri, Pennsylvania, Nebraska, and Florida, among other states, wrote for information about buying and building homes in Redlands. When these women indicated they were seeking to buy a home in a family-oriented town such as Redlands, they received strong support.[57] General responses to letters such as these suggested that "if you are looking for a home city Redlands certainly should be considered. Our schools, churches, homes, parks, streets, and improvements, make it the most attractive little city in the Southland."[58] These letters demonstrate the depth of penetration of Redlands booster literature. In addition, they are suggestive of the degree to which women were aware of and interested in the entire process of home buying and building in a city that could offer both services and amenities. Far from relying on male family members to provide economic security, women from across the country entered the real estate market and successfully owned and managed their personal property.

In 1907, for example, Mary M. Robinson of Homer, Michigan, took responsibility for her family's economic security by initiating a move to Redlands. In considering Redlands as a potential destination, Mrs. Robinson considered not only the price of real estate but also the employment prospects for her son. She would consider purchasing acreage outside the city limits or a vacant lot within the city limits suitable for home building. More important, however, was the potential for her son to find employment. He had five years of experience as a head clerk in a grocery and china store and could supply good references. Mrs. Robinson had initially intended to move to Los Angeles, but booster literature and the advice of friends had turned her attention to Redlands.[59]

The chamber responded favorably to Mrs. Robinson's letter. The chamber secretary assured Mrs. Robinson that "a strong, willing young man will have no difficulty in securing work, and frequently a good position in one of the many grocery stores and mercantile houses."[60] Evidence of the Robinsons' knowledge of luxury goods and their ability to purchase investment property placed them within the cultural value system espoused by the Redlands elite. This family was, apparently, hardworking and thrifty, and as potential residential investors they would contribute to the city growth game.

While Mrs. Robinson was concerned with employment opportunities for her son, Jodie Ansley of Dathan, Alabama, looked for employment opportunities for her husband. Mr. and Mrs. Ansley made the decision to move to California together. Mrs. Ansley, however, took the initiative in writing to the Redlands Chamber of Commerce for information about both the city and Southern California in general, of which they knew little. The couple were not wealthy, but they earned a comfortable income farming and through Mr. Ansley's carpentry business. The demand for skilled carpenters was so great in the growing city that the secretary strongly encouraged the couple to emigrate: "If your husband were here today, he could get all the carpenter work he could do and in a few months the finish will be going into one of the finest residences on the Pacific Coast. It is to cost, with the grounds, $450,000, and a great college has just been located here, but work will not commence on it for a year and a half, or just about when the Green mansion is completed."[61] Noting the variety of crops grown locally that would provide a family with a modest income, the secretary further encouraged the couple to invest in a small farm.

The experience of the Ansleys suggests that wealth alone was not the determining factor in ascertaining whether a potential emigrant would fit the community ideal for Redlands. Rather, the chamber was more concerned with a work ethic, the potential for independent support, and a family's ability to follow an asset strategy of economic security. In other words, if a family could purchase a home or property of some sort, it would be considered part of the class vision of the Redlands elite and thus deemed a desirable immigrant. The *potential* to contribute to the Redlands growth game was, therefore, more important to the Redlands elite than mere ability to contribute upon arrival.

Family decisions to move were not made by husbands and wives alone. Indeed, a fair number of letters to the Redlands Chamber of Commerce came from adult children. In 1909, Emma Bellinger of Fresno wrote to the chamber for information on the availability of carpentry work, the price of rental property, and the price and availability of five- or ten-acre tracts suitable for raising poultry or growing vegetables. The Bellinger family was relocating from Fresno because Mrs. Bellinger suffered from bronchitis that was aggravated by the foggy damp winters in the San Joaquin Valley. It is interesting that Emma Bellinger, an apparently single daughter, took the initiative to write for information. In her letter she does not refer to a male relative who would be the carpenter or farm laborer. This indicates that she and her mother ran their farm in Fresno and had control of the family finances. The chamber of commerce strongly encouraged families like the Bellingers to come to Redlands. Not only did they bring a needed skill (carpentry) to the city, they would, most likely, invest in land, thus helping to stimulate the land market.[62]

Some women looked to Redlands as a growing city, ideal for long-term investments in real estate. Mrs. L. M. Ragin of Picacho, California, wanted information on real estate investment opportunities with a view to securing an investment that would provide future income for her young daughter. Mrs. Ragin was interested in long-term investment. She wanted "an investment which will grow in value as she [her daughter] grows to maturity."[63] She thought the best opportunity for such an investment would be in a suburban tract that would, in a few years time, be a desirable building section. She did not wish to build a home for herself at the present time. Rather, she wanted a building to sell in the future. Mrs. Ragin clearly followed an asset-building strategy of economic security that fit the strategy of the Redlands elite. She thus received an enthusiastic response from the chamber of commerce.

Some women sought work for their husbands without their husband's knowledge. Mrs. C. E. Blunk of Lima, Ohio, sought employment opportunities for her husband, either in a shoe repair business or in a custom shirt factory. Mrs. Blunk was quite concerned with the moral standing of the city in addition to the economic opportunity available. She wanted to know about churches and schools as well as about the general business climate. In addition, she wanted to know if there was "anything to keep growing boys busy."[64] Mrs. Blunk's concern for the moral and social activities available in the city is indicative of the concerns governing many moves in the early twentieth century. Economic opportunity could be found in most cities. What set a city apart was its potential for growth as well as its social, moral, and cultural attributes.

As with letters written by single women, letters written by women with families provide evidence of the class composition of Redlands. Furthermore, since Redlands sought to maintain a position of affluence through attracting families, replies to married women were enthusiastic. Family values, defined by church attendance and support for public schools became a defining feature of the middle class in the early twentieth century and are strongly in evidence in the chamber's letters. Here we see class formation, the operation of the city growth machine, and the successful dissemination of the capitalist class vision across the nation and across gender lines, at its finest. As with wage earning women and single investors, married women retained a strong degree of economic independence as the bearers of information about cities, real estate, and business opportunities, and as independent investors. Married women and single women thus participated in the California city growth game both as buyers and as sellers.

The letters between women and the Redlands Chamber of Commerce indicate that California's urban growth coalition (including both men and women) sought to preserve community identity by discouraging mere job seekers and encouraging those with investment potential. The records of the Redlands Chamber of Commerce provide the strongest evidence of the desire to exclude those of limited potential for contributions to the local economy and those who did not share in the asset-building strategy of economic security pursued by the Redlands elite. Furthermore, the inclusion of letters from women in the chamber's public relations files suggests that gender was not an issue in the growth and development of Redlands. Women with income and assets were encouraged to emigrate, whereas women with limited means of support were discouraged, just as men were. Thus, the development and preservation of a capitalist class identity appears to be the key element behind the growth machine in Redlands and, perhaps, across California and the West.

In addition, the letters from women to the Redlands Chamber of Commerce demonstrate that women had strong economic motivations propelling them into the public sphere. These letters suggest that for middle- and upper-class men and women, class identity and property interests were compelling factors motivating them to cast aside Victorian standards of acceptable behavior and to enter the economic arena. Taken as a whole, these letters, along with earlier evidence of women's property ownership and business ownership, advance the theory that California women both bought and sold the city as part of the process of capitalist class formation and as part of the California city growth machine. The evidence also highlights members of the growth machine as real people interested in quality-of-life considerations in their public behavior, not just greed.

CHAPTER TWO

Clubwomen and the Growth Machine

An apprenticeship in property provided women with their qualifications for membership in the growth machine, but how they fulfilled their role as members prior to the 1920s was constrained by the social and political dictates of the Victorian era. Women thus joined the growth machine in the 1880s and 1890s in a unique and socially acceptable manner—they created women's clubs which quickly moved beyond the stage of mere social club to become, in many cities, powerful civic players. Just as the chamber of commerce might create the vehicle through which the male elite cast off their disagreements, women's clubs provided a forum in which women could create a coalition designed to enhance the overall wealth of the city. Women's clubs became the means through which women evolved as members of the growth machine. They became the forums in which women shared their knowledge with other women and in which women gained confidence in themselves. In addition, as noted in the life of Elizabeth Eddy Fisk, women's clubs provided many members with an apprenticeship in public speaking and public activism.

Over the past twenty years, the remarkable collection of records kept by the nation's women's clubs have provided a wealth of information about the experiences of middle- and upper-class women. Women's historians have used these records to identify and illustrate the power and influence women have had in society even prior to attaining the franchise. As part of the process of both identifying women as having a history and the search for feminism in the past, much of the research agenda has focused, in Karen Blair's words, on "the clubwoman as feminist."[1] In this vein, clubs were far more than safe enclaves in which women could escape undesirable influences. Notably, as corroborated by the experience of Elizabeth Eddy Fisk and her contemporaries, they "served as a vehicle of entry into the main stream of public affairs." Across the nation, once women had established themselves as public players, they came to influence the direction public affairs would take. What drove these women into the public arena? Did the impetus come from "an emotional need to express one's identity and make a lasting contribution, . . . [or] a more authentic self-expression"?[2] Did the drive come from a need of women to express their own function in life distinctive from men?[3] Or did it emerge from a subsumed capitalistic impulse of women to protect their own wealth within the socially constrained bonds of womanhood?

Nationally, women's clubs expressed their public work most frequently in terms of the socially acceptable terminology of "municipal housekeeping," a concept that would become the central tenet of the Progressive movement. These astute women created the rhetoric of what Daniel Smith has labeled "Domestic Feminism" in order to enter the public sphere by embracing and expanding upon the concept of the Cult of Domesticity. Women thus used social stereotypes to their own ends of creating highly successful public careers. As the culture as a whole began to reevaluate theories of women's proper role, women themselves began to augment acceptable and traditional duties and responsibilities by forcing the duties of motherhood into the public eye. Women sought recognition for motherhood as an appropriate public role. Men also had to participate in this reevaluation of women's work. In terms of the club movement, men continued to express a certain resistance to changing gender roles and accepted women's clubs if they expressed their design in terms of social welfare and humanitarian reform, whereas they censured women's clubs designed solely for intellectual self-improvement. Karen Blair sees the women's club movement culminating in 1914, when men admitted that women's clubs were a desirable force in society. By this time, women had moved beyond mere literary clubs to civics programs, indicating the successful social saturation of the ideology of Domestic Feminism.[4]

In addition, by conferring social status and distinction on their members, clubs also affected the class composition and class identity of the community. They helped define communities and neighborhoods through what Darlene Roth has labeled "turf identifications" and created lifestyle variations through their specific civic activities. Furthermore, they created occupations for women and contributed to the marketplace; they "perpetuated the value systems" and encouraged women to assert their interests in the public arena.[5]

Owning a clubhouse became the key to permanence for the nation's women's clubs. By becoming "women of property," they staked a claim to their accomplishments in the name of the city without turning them over to male organizations. Far more than protecting the image of women and domesticity, or asserting a feminist agenda, clubs and clubhouses represented social and cultural asset building and increasing community wealth through real property ownership.

Women clearly used the concept of women's special moral mission to enter the sphere of public service. Their promotion of services—orphanages, schools, playgrounds, and protective legislation—did express women's special moral mission. Nonetheless, it also expressed women's contributions to city growth. The rapid evolution of clubs from social to civic groups places them in the context of the growth machine. In addition, clubs provided a social vehicle through which members could assert female moral authority as a tool in the growth machine arsenal.

Exploration of women's clubs as elements of the growth machine indicates that the moral and domestic agenda of these clubs was more than an expression of feminism; it was an expression of capitalism and the growth game. California women's clubs did work for cleanliness, sanitation, and education projects, many of which were also supported by local men's organizations. Thus, they appear as investments in social overhead and as tools in the arsenal of promoting city growth. For women club members, as with male city boosters, morality and economics became inextricably intertwined.

Indeed, it is imperative to explore the rise of California women's clubs in the context of the state's urban history. The 1880s mark the beginning of rapid and sustained urbanization in California, fueled heavily by the real estate boom of Southern California. Within only a few years of incorporation of many California cities, women's clubs were established. Santa Barbara women founded their first club in 1889, Riverside in 1890, Los Angeles in 1892, and Redlands in 1893. These local clubs were organized at the state level into the Woman's Parliament of Southern California in 1892 and the California Federation of Women's Clubs (CFWC) in 1900. Clubs also affiliated with the General Federation of Women's Clubs (GFWC) founded in 1890. In essence,

The Contemporary Club House, Redlands, ca. 1904. From the Archives of the A. K. Smiley Public Library.

women's clubs grew with their cities, and the interests of club members also followed the evolution of cities and city growth strategies. It was common for women's clubs to be founded as literary and social clubs, but by 1910 all California women's clubs had shifted their focus to civic issues. As early as 1898, the statewide federations were encouraging this at their annual and biennial meetings.

While assuredly many women joined clubs simply as a social and moral outlet, club leadership came mostly from business and professional women and property owners who were consciously aware that the creation of women's clubs would contribute to the attractiveness of their cities. In Santa Barbara, the Fortnightly Club was founded in 1889 by Mrs. Alfred Poett, Mrs. Barclay Hazard, Mrs. William Eddy, and Mrs. George Oliver. Three years later, Santa Barbara women also created the Santa Barbara Woman's Club. Many Santa Barbara women were members of both clubs, including Frances Baxter, president of the Woman's Club from 1892 to 1899. Baxter ran a successful boardinghouse behind her home on Bath Street, and as a proprietor of rental accommodations, she was fundamentally concerned with the city's ability to attract tourists. She thus participated in expanding the interests of both clubs to issues of politics, economics, and contemporary social issues. Special topics in the early years included "What Women Have Effected in the Way of Organization" (1889); "Should Women Enter Politics; Not as Voters, but to Influence Their Fathers, Brothers and Husbands" (1891); "Immigration and Naturalization" (1891); "Japan as a New Commercial Rival" (1897); and "The Uses of Waste" (1897). Recognizing their clubs' contribution to the city's tourist attractions, they also offered a limited number of memberships to women who were only temporary residents or "half-members" (those who lived in Santa Barbara only during the club season—October to May).[6]

Early membership of the Redlands Contemporary Club also provides evidence of the property interests of club members. Like the city's other booster organizations, such as the chamber of commerce and the Merchants and Manufacturers Association, the Contemporary Club drew its membership from the city elite: those citizens who held a personal investment in the city's growth through individual or family property ownership. Giving ample evidence of the close link between the citrus industry, the business community, and the Contemporary Club, the club's membership rosters read like a Who's Who of the Redlands citrus and business elite. Members who owned their own rental property, for example, included Jennie E. Davis, Blanche Holmes, Mabel S. Morrison, Mary Prendergast, Katherine Otis, Francis C. Wells, and Dia Lehman. Other members, such as Elizabeth Fisk, owned their own property. Still others, such as Helen Kimberly, wife of J. A. Kimberly of Kimberly/Clark paper products, managed their ill husband's affairs. Along with their booster husbands, these women stood to gain personally from their efforts to enhance the appeal of Redlands for tourists and future investors. Bringing general prosperity to the city, tourists patronized local businesses and purchased land.

At the state level, the Woman's Parliament of Southern California and the CFWC also reflected the business and property interests of clubwomen. However, while women asserted their capitalist priorities in these organizations, they did so within the acceptable bonds of Victorian society. For many of these women, this was a matter of expediency. According to the social mores of late-nineteenth-century society, women's public work would be accepted if it were in terms of social welfare and humanitarian reform. If it was designed for intellectual or economic self-improvement, it was less likely to gain the backing of the male sphere. Clubwomen therefore walked a fine line of maintaining traditional femininity in their public appearances. The women leaders of the Woman's Parliament thus engaged in both charitable volunteer work and careers that would provide them with economic security. In describing the president of the Woman's Parliament in 1898, the editor of *Land of Sunshine* noted that Dr. Belle Reynolds of Santa Barbara was "a woman of fine presence and profound intelligence; combining the methodical exactness of the business woman with the gracious tact of a woman of the world."[7] Social mores dictated that Dr. Reynolds and women of her class maintain the appearance of traditional femininity regardless of their nontraditional public economic interests.

Dr. Reynolds was joined on the board of the Woman's Parliament by another Santa Barbara resident, Emma Hardacre. In addition to her work as corresponding secretary for the parliament, Hardacre continued to pursue her career as a newspaper writer. Before moving to Santa Barbara, she had previously worked as Washington correspondent for the *Chicago Times*, the *New York Herald*, the *Chicago Tribune*, the *Louisville Courier-Journal*, and the *Cincinnati Commercial-Gazette*. Moving to Santa Barbara from Ohio to join her daughter and to enjoy the more healthful climate of Southern California, Hardacre became secretary and director of the Santa Barbara Cottage Hospital, local press superintendent of the Women's Christian Temperance Union (WCTU), and vice president of the Santa Barbara County branch of the Women's Press Club of Southern California.[8] Like Reynolds, she devoted time to traditional women's charitable activities at the same time she engaged in a nontraditional public career path that would ensure her economic independence.

A large body of literature attests to the role of newspaper owners and editors as members of the growth coalition, and particularly to their pervasive role as civic boosters.[9] The *Chicago Tribune* and the *Cincinnati Commercial-Gazette* both contributed to the boosterism of their respective cities from their inception. Emma Hardacre must have been aware of this as a newspaperwoman, and it is illogical to suggest her work for the papers represented a separate sphere of activity. Here was a woman who could speak the language of capitalism and of morality, who found a coalition of like-minded women in the Woman's Parliament.

Many women's club members came from the ranks of newspaper writers and editors, some working independently, like Emma Hardacre and Clara Foltz (who worked for a year as editor and publisher of the

San Diego Daily Bee), and others working alongside their husbands, like Mary Lynde Craig. Bella E. Bodkin, who presented a paper titled "The Duties of Ministers' Wives" to the 1898 Woman's Parliament, brought to her club work twenty years of experience as a minister's wife and two years of experience as business editor of the *California Independent*. Bodkin perhaps represents the "typical" clubwoman. She worked with her husband in terms of moral and social uplift as a minister's wife, yet she also demonstrated her skill and understanding of the language of capitalism as a newspaper business editor.[10]

Bodkin's story is particularly enlightening for an analysis of the growth machine. The *California Independent* was founded in Los Angeles in 1896 by P. H. Bodkin with the purpose of creating a newspaper to serve "the interests of Evangelical Christianity."[11] Here was a newspaper with an unabashed moral purpose that still found it important to retain a business editor. Christianity and capitalism have been strange bedfellows in the United States since the time of the Puritans, when John Winthrop attested that God had ordained mankind to be divided by class but that class conflict could be avoided by the application of justice and mercy. The business articles in the *Independent* reflected that same attitude almost three hundred years later. Bella Bodkin made sure that her writers did not merely inform the community about business matters but that they tried to mitigate the competitiveness of pure capitalism by introducing a measure of compassion and social justice into their business dealings. Thus, while the Bodkins supported the goals of the growth machine, they were far from willing to allow that machine to run amok. As property and business owners, they expressed a commitment to growth that would benefit all mankind.

The moral language of club work also influenced "traditional" club members. Santa Barbara resident and nonprofessional property manager Gertrude Griffin McCurdy became the treasurer of the Woman's Parliament. Working within her Victorian social role, McCurdy's local club affiliations included the Santa Barbara Woman's Club, the Hospital Association, and the Fortnightly Club. While contributing to the literary and intellectual pursuits of these clubs, however, she also possessed an astute business sense, gained from her experience as administrator of her family estate.[12] McCurdy represents another type of clubwoman—the single woman with the economic security to pursue philanthropic interests because of her family's wealth. Women such as McCurdy could afford the luxury of engaging in charity work, yet as managers of family wealth, they also recognized the economic value of serving the poor and promoting clean, beautiful, and healthy cities.

Some women club leaders were able to break the bonds of Victorian womanhood and become crusaders for women's property rights. In addition to Clara Foltz and Mary Lynde Craig, Elizabeth L. Kenney, a Los Angeles attorney, became the most prolific advocate for women's property rights through the Woman's Parliament and the CFWC. Graduating with a high school diploma from Sioux Falls, Dakota, in 1893 Kenney moved to Los Angeles, where she read for the law for two years with her uncle W. H. Shinn. She completed her education at Stanford and Northwestern, where she received her LLB. In 1897, she was admitted to practice before the Supreme Court of Illinois, the Supreme Court of California, and the U.S. District Court and Circuit Courts. She specialized in probate law and property rights for women and children. Within a year of returning to California, she presented a paper to the Woman's Parliament entitled "The Legal Status of Women in California."[13]

Beginning in 1905, Kenney offered her expertise to the CFWC by helping with the preparation of a condensed form of the California Civil Code relating to women's rights. Researched by Kenney, William Chambers, and Willoughby Rodman, the 1910 codebook included sections defining a woman's legal status vis-à-vis her husband and her children, property rights, contract rights, widow rights, rights to bank accounts, and penal laws. This book and pamphlets like it were distributed to local clubs at regular intervals.[14]

Business and professional women such as Reynolds and Kenney were joined in leadership positions by the wives of business and professional men. For example, Lu Wheat of Los Angeles, while not a professional woman herself, gained insight into women's legal issues through conversations with her husband. *Land of Sunshine* reported that "her husband, Thomas H. Smith, was a lawyer of early California days, and being a poor sleeper, he read and talked law to his wife at night. In this way, as she had a legal mind, she gained some knowledge of this knotty subject."[15] This knowledge she passed on to other women through a paper presented at the 1898 Woman's Parliament, "Law Versus Justice."[16] Wheat's relationship with her husband was probably not atypical. Many women discussed business and financial issues with their husbands and gained insight into legal and market mechanisms that enhanced both family and community wealth. Through marriage, upper- and middle-class women could complete another phase of their apprenticeships in the language of capitalism. Choosing to return to her maiden name following the death of her husband, Wheat demonstrated her personal liberation and independence from Victorian social mores. She could command the language of capitalism as an independent woman.

The combination of moral and capitalistic concerns of these California clubwomen can be interpreted in terms of the moral reform rhetoric that underlay late-nineteenth-century municipal reform efforts. Responding to Gilded Age municipal government corruption, preachers of the Social Gospel—and later, Progressive reformers—found a citizenry ready to listen to moral arguments, particularly those aimed at corrupt machine politics.[17] City boosters, both men and women, recognized the value of selling their cities as morally superior cities freed from the corruption of big city machine politics. Socially defined as the "guardians of public morality," women found greater legitimacy as public players by invoking the language of morality rather than the language of capitalism.

As the "moral guardians" of the city, most upper- and middle-class women in California, including Elizabeth Eddy Fisk of Redlands, came under increasing pressure from both men and women to serve on the boards of charitable groups such as the ladies auxiliary to the YMCA and the Redlands Contemporary Club. As the widow of a minister and as an avid churchgoer, Fisk found herself in a position familiar to many who came to Southern California. On the one hand, her indoctrination as a Christian taught her to be selfless and to contribute to all charitable activities. On the other hand, her practical experience as a property owner and businesswoman encouraged her to pursue self-interest. Her inner conflict was evident in a diary entry for November 19, 1888, referring to the time commitment involved in serving on the board of the YMCA's ladies auxiliary: "So much time wasted—had to come home without doing my errands."[18] Her frustration with the ladies auxiliary prompted her to refuse a board seat on the Contemporary Club in 1897.[19]

In part, Fisk's reticence to serve on an executive board also stemmed from her inexperience as a public speaker and from fear of assuming a public role of leadership. This she slowly overcame as her membership in the Contemporary Club exposed her to women speakers and to discussion topics in which she was interested. For example, when the club discussed women in business in January 1898, Elizabeth recorded in her diary, "I tried to talk. Didn't say much."[20] Three months later, she served as a delegate and hostess to the meeting of the Woman's Parliament of Southern California in Redlands. Gaining valuable experience as a public speaker and leader, over the next four years she regularly served as Redlands' delegate to district and statewide meetings of the CFWC.

Any questions regarding the inclusion of women's clubs in the growth machine can be answered by noting the lack of gender distinction in booster rhetoric. Writing in 1904, for example, L. A. Ingersoll, a San Bernardino County historian, praised the ability of Redlands' citizens to transform the desert into a modern city complete with strong cultural, social, and economic foundations:

> The story of the inception of Redlands reads like a made-to-order illustration of applied knowledge, clear foresight, and unyielding perseverance in the face of great obstacles. Nature had done much; but to evolve the city of today, 1904, within less than a quarter of a century, required the intelligent application of brains, industry and money; it demanded a spirit of broad-minded liberality, on the part of the founders of the colony; it required energy, public spirit, culture and wealth, on the part of every resident. All of these things have contributed to make Redlands.[21]

Ingersoll emphasized contributions "on the part of every resident." He made no distinctions between men and women, thus suggesting that successful community building was not a "male" pursuit, but one requiring the support and participation of all residents. He further noted the importance of "public spirit, culture and wealth" as contributing factors to city growth. Greed and speculation could not build a city of permanence.

In Redlands, investment in property alone was not enough to build the city envisioned by the elite. That relied on an investment in social overhead, through social clubs, both gender-specific and gender-neutral. In 1887, the *Redlands Citrograph* reported on "a typical real estate deal" demonstrating the vast investment potential for both men and women in citrus and the importance of reinvesting profits into the social services of the community. In this article, the male elite not only countenanced women entering the real estate market but suggested that men follow the example of a woman investing in both land and a social organization:

> Last winter a lady, who was stopping here for the benefit of our invigorating climate, had the good fortune to find a twenty-dollar gold piece in the street.

> Inquiry was made for the owner but he failed to appear. The lady then secured an option on ten acres of land in Crafton at $175 an acre, paying down the twenty dollar piece aforesaid. The property was placed in the hands of John P. Fisk, Jr., one of our live real estate agents, for sale. Before the time came around for the payment of the first installment on the land, it was sold for $235 per acre, clearing a cool $600 on the transaction. The lady then purchased seven acres between here and Crafton for $300 per acre, paying the $600 cleared from the former transaction down. This piece has just been sold for $375 an acre, making the net gain from the original find of $20 just $1125. Filled with gratitude at her good fortune the lady has contributed a "tithe" to the Y. M. C. A. building fund, or fifty-five dollars. Should any of our successful real estate speculators wish thus to testify to their feelings they will probably find the Y. M. C. A. ready and willing to receive their thank offering. "Go thou and do likewise."[22]

The city elite sought to create a community that was morally upright as well as economically strong. They were convinced that investment in social services promoted an educated citizenry who would stay in the community and reinvest in the city, and they saw women as the leaders in that movement. They built upon traditional roles for women and traditional concepts of women's duty to the community. Women were regarded as the moral and spiritual leaders of the community, and the city's male elite recognized the economic value of that leadership.

The city of Santa Barbara pursued a similar model in its growth strategy. As early as the 1870s, the city and the region began to define itself in terms of its environment, its past, and its social amenities. Perceiving that Santa Barbara could not compete with Los Angeles for regional dominance, the city elite chose to pursue a growth strategy based on the exploitation of the newly emerging tourist industry rather than through industrialization.[23] Unlike the East Coast, where tourists arrived after the cities were built, in Southern California tourists often preceded cities or participated in their growth and development. This was indeed the case in Santa Barbara. In 1876, W. W. Hollister chose the city as the site for the Arlington Hotel, one of the most famous tourist hotels in California. At the time, Santa Barbara was little more than a dusty village on the old Spanish El Camino Real. But Hollister envisioned a seaside resort that would cater to affluent visitors from the East. Laying the foundation for tourism to become the major industry of the city, he built a social and cultural life around the hotel.[24]

Carey McWilliams argues that tourism in Southern California stripped the region of any sense of frontier life. "In large part, the tourist influx and the tourist hotels account for the curiously incongruous spectacle of Shakespeare Clubs, oratorio societies, lecture forums, and academies of science in a region that was still in a frontier phase. They were responsible for the circumstance that, in Southern California, 'Boston culture over-lapped the *dolce far niente* of the Mexican.'"[25] In Santa Barbara the intersection of Bostonian and Mexican culture was most clearly evident as the elite sought to develop an alternative version of what California offered in the way of the good life. They looked to a romanticized Hispanic past of ranchos and leisure to symbolize the good life. The Southern California elite embraced its Mexican past in order to appear as cultured and refined. Santa Barbarans centered their cultural identity around a Hispanic past of mythic proportions. In the process, they imitated eastern efforts to appropriate a glorious and patriotic past that defined the Bostonian, the New Yorker, and the Philadelphian as the heirs to America's cultural identity. The heritage of the Spanish and Mexican Dons offered the closest thing Santa Barbara had to a patriotic and glorious past. The city thus embraced its Hispanic past in order to create a civic identity as the home of an elite heritage.[26]

Late-nineteenth- and early-twentieth-century Santa Barbara thus created a unique environment in which women found both the opportunity and the motivation to participate in the growth coalition. Creating a resort economy on the Central California coast required the equal participation of men and women in building both an appropriate infrastructure and an appropriate cultural milieu that would attract affluent tourists and residents. In addition to building beautiful luxury hotels such as the Arlington and the Potter, the city elite embraced its Hispanic past and encouraged the development of "refined and cultivated homes," social clubs, and educational facilities.[27] By 1900, these attributes had established Santa Barbara as one of the premier tourist cities in the country.

Although open only to women, California women's clubs did not exist in the exclusive separate sphere that Darlene Roth has found for Atlanta clubwomen. Club members and club priorities were not limited to "women's issues." They reflected concern with the growth and development of the community as a whole. Thus, all clubs worked with men's organizations, including the city council, the chamber of commerce, Rotary, and Kiwanis, in order to implement a vision of growth designed to enhance economic opportunity. Indeed, women's political issues and a feminist consciousness, rarely, if ever, appear in club minutes. What does appear frequently both in club minutes and in newspapers and booster tracts, is a heavy dose of clubs as cultural assets to the city. Clubhouse openings offered city boosters an excellent opportunity to sell club life. In Santa Barbara, the *Morning Press* even compared the impact of the opening of the Santa Barbara Woman's Clubhouse to that of the opening of the new Arlington Hotel.[28]

The Redlands Contemporary Club provides an excellent example of the evolution of women's clubs from social or literary societies to civic players of the growth game. Founded in 1894 primarily as a ladies social club, the club quickly expanded its interests to become a force in civic affairs. It invested in social overhead, such as the physical beautification of public property, and in the intellectual expansion of the community through its support of lyceums and club discussion sections. In 1896 the club began to discuss enlarging its work and its membership beyond mere literary considerations and to consider issues relevant to city growth.[29]

As the club made its presence known in the city, it addressed subjects that traditionally have been seen as an extension of women's domestic concerns: curfew ordinances, sanitation, and simple beautification projects.[30] At a club meeting in 1900, Margaret F. Noble outlined the role of the Contemporary Club in a paper entitled "The Contemporary Club as a Civic Factor in Redlands." Addressing the emergence of women in public affairs, Noble persuaded her fellow club members of the importance of the club asserting itself in civic issues. The club responded by creating a committee on civics with members appointed by the president. Subtopics for this committee included sanitation, compulsory education, public benches, and schools. The club demonstrated its public concerns by addressing petitions and resolutions to the city board of trustees regarding these issues.

Harriet Shepard became the backbone of the civic committee in its early days and worked to make it the most important committee for the club. The role of the civics committee expanded as the women demonstrated their success in petitioning the board of trustees. Shepard was particularly concerned with the cleanliness of the city. She encouraged club members to participate in city cleanup days and to demand that the city provide adequate street sweeping. Addressing the club in 1903, she insisted that "it was better to clean a city before beautifying it." She also recommended that the ladies promote the creation of neighborhood improvement associations, especially in the business district, as these would ensure clean streets and alleys.[31] She eventually convinced the club to petition the board of trustees to create a "Civics Day" for general street, alley, and property cleanup. She believed that property owners should be held responsible for the condition of alleys and backyards. While municipal housekeeping appeared to be the cornerstone of Shepard's civic committee, she also demonstrated a concern with the structure of city government. In the fall of 1904, Shepard arranged to have F. G. Horn address the club on a proposed new charter.[32] Although women could not vote at this time, they clearly were concerned with politics and with the apparatus of city government.

As an investor in social overhead, Shepard supported programs that would produce an educated consumer base. Beginning in 1902, she turned her attention to initiating the next generation of Redlanders in the ideals of civic-mindedness. Turning to the public schools, she insisted that children be taught civic responsibility from a young age and worked with the schools to get children to pass petitions for projects such as city waste cans and playgrounds.[33] These projects were supplemented in 1910 with the creation of the Contemporary Club civics prize for the best essay written by a high school senior on a civic issue. Through the 1930s, a ten-dollar cash prize was awarded annually to a graduating senior. Following Mrs. Shepard's death in 1911, the prize was named in honor of her work in this area.

Educating the youth of the city about the ideals of the Contemporary Club became a prominent feature of the club. While the civics prize was an overt example of this, club members worked more subtly by initiating their daughters into club life as young women and by creating a Junior League for girls from ages ten to eighteen in 1916.[34] The Junior League was the brainchild of Helen Kimberly, and she acted as leader of the league until her death in the late 1920s. Most of the young women who became leaders of the club in the 1920s and 1930s had served an apprenticeship in the Junior League before becoming full members of the club and had learned the value of club work toward civic improvement.

Redlands women were shrewd coalition builders. They understood the political realities of the day and the importance of having the support of men's organizations in their efforts to provide the city with improvements such as parks and playgrounds. In 1906, Nellie Suess, the new head of the civics committee, addressed the club regarding the purchase by the city of a plot of land known as Peffer Park. Suess thought the location on Church Street near Lowell School would be ideal for a children's playground. Since the club would not have to pay for upkeep, club members decided to petition the city for this project. The ladies thought it prudent to include the names of two or three prominent men on the petition who would eventually have charge of the project.[35]

The civics committee's area of interest fluctuated with the interests of its leader. Under the guidance of Mrs. Shepard from 1900 to 1906, the committee pursued work in line with cleanliness and sanitation issues by petitioning the city trustees to enforce ordinances and invest in municipal housekeeping. From 1907 to 1909, Nara E. Merriman turned the attention of the committee to outdoor art, playgrounds, and a day nursery program. In 1909–10, the committee returned to direct work with the city trustees. Under the leadership of Jennie Davis, who also represented the club on the City Tree Commission, the club turned its attention to the needs of a new city charter, as well as to the growing City Beautiful movement. Recognizing that most club members were still constrained by the vocabulary of Victorian womanhood that limited women's public activities to moral issues, Davis presented her argument for a new city charter in terms of civic beauty, not in terms of economic benefit.[36]

Believing that cooperation would be to the advantage of all, Davis increasingly brought the club into contact with the leading men of the city. In her effort to make Redlands a "City Beautiful," she drew upon the knowledge of the city's leading merchants and real estate developers and invited them to address the club on this issue. Regarding women's support as crucial to the success of City Beautiful projects, and thus to the enhancement of personal wealth, E. G. Judson, Kirke H. Field, and John P. Fisk, all local realtors and husbands of club board members, agreed to address the club.[37] Inviting the Riverside City Tree Warden to speak to the club, Mrs. Davis also saw to it that club members understood the economic as well as aesthetic value of tree planting and city beautification. J. H. Reed discussed municipal planting and care of trees, emphasizing the commercial and economic value of trees. He advocated municipal control as the only way to secure actual development and public satisfaction.[38]

Throughout the 1910s, the club's civic interests turned toward city and county planning, yet the club was slow to adopt language that demonstrated its understanding of the economic value of the improvements they sought. As late as 1919, the club could not bring itself to discuss the building of a tourist hotel in terms of the economic value it would bring the community. Clearly, the only purpose in building a tourist hotel is to attract people who will contribute to the economic welfare of the community, yet there is no evidence of this in the club's resolution of support:

> Whereas: A timely and feasible plan for building a beautiful tourist hotel upon some vantage point of the Redlands Heights, has been brought before the people of Redlands, and
>
> Whereas: The practicability of such a project, inasmuch as the natural advantages for a hostelry far surpasses any other point in Southern California, is known to every member of this organization and,
>
> Whereas: It is also known that a successful first class hotel can truly be of special and lasting benefit to this community, as well as the surrounding territory, and
>
> Whereas: A plan of this character must receive individual and collective support of every person and organization in this city, both in moral and monetary means,
>
> Therefore: Let it be resolved by the Contemporary Club of Redlands, that we shall lend every force possible in forwarding this project to a successful determination, and
>
> Let it be further resolved, that we, as individuals, shall advance every effort in rightly advertising the above plans in its campaign to raise the needed funds.[39]

The evolution of the Redlands Contemporary Club reflected the changing interests of women's clubs across the state. Statewide meetings increasingly encouraged discussion of civic issues in the 1890s and 1900s. By 1910, the Woman's Parliament turned its attention toward the issue of city promotion through city planning. In 1911 Riverside mayor and primary proponent of city planning legislation S. C. Evans addressed the twentieth annual session of the Woman's Parliament. He asked the women to help promote and develop Southern California. Women's clubs throughout the area responded to this plea by turning their attention to activities designed to beautify their cities, attract tourists, and sell land.[40] The parliament's shift in emphasis to civic issues reflects the second stage of middle-class women's apprenticeships. By 1911 they were increasingly entering into apprenticeships in city planning, in which they further refined their command of the language of capitalism and solidified their place within the growth machine.

The CFWC also encouraged its affiliated clubs to discuss specific civic concerns such as municipal growth and planning. By 1913, clubwomen showed increased concern with how they could exert an ever-widening scope of influence on city issues. At the San Francisco district convention of that year, clubwomen exhibited their understanding of the principles of municipal bonded indebtedness by passing a resolution in favor of restricting voting on bond issues to property owners. *The Club Woman* reported that "the kernel of this resolution is that the qualified electorate in a bond election shall be restricted to property-owners in the district affected."[41] At the same meeting, the women further demonstrated their concern with city growth by endorsing the construction of the Hetch Hetchy reservoir, which would bring Sierra Mountain water to San Francisco. Without a vast and pure supply of water, San Francisco and the Bay Area would never grow to be regionally dominant over Los Angeles.

Their concern with limiting voting on bond issues to property owners is particularly enlightening. Within a year of gaining the vote, upper- and middle-class women were trying to limit the application of suffrage to others. As property owners themselves, they recognized the connection between rising property values and the ability of the city to repay its debt. Thus, they believed that only those people who owned "stock" (in the form of property) in the city corporation should decide whether the city should become indebted. Through the CFWC then, women demonstrated their knowledge of the city growth machine and their concern with ensuring protection for all property owners.

Attempts at limiting suffrage were not unique to the clubwomen of California. In the early twentieth century many municipal reformers considered limiting suffrage as a means to control machine politics. For example, the Tilden Commission's investigation of the Tweed Ring scandals in New York recommended in 1887 that suffrage be restricted to property owners, and in 1907 a municipal reformer in Newport, Rhode Island, argued that universal manhood suffrage denied property owners political power commensurate with their economic power. This reformer proposed a system that would give majority representation to the city's wealthiest landowners. Suffrage restrictions did not succeed in the municipal reform programs of the early Progressive Era in part because "democratic principles and universal white male suffrage were too deeply entrenched."[42] The fact that women shared in the movement to restrict suffrage indicates that class overshadowed gender considerations in property issues.

As women became involved in economic activities, Victorian standards of acceptable behavior gave way to new standards and a new vocabulary that not only allowed women to enter the public sphere but encouraged them to do so. Thus in Oakland in 1908 the city's male boosters could argue that women's clubs worked as "a most effective agency in the creation of a cleaner, bigger, a better and a busier Oakland" and call for an expanded sphere of influence for women.[43] If women could help Oakland win the competition for regional dominance, they should be encouraged to do so. Hence, the Oakland male elite extended its support to women who participated in economic affairs and bought and sold Oakland without regard for outmoded social restrictions. Women were encouraged to engage in municipal housekeeping and social reform as part of the city plan to promote urban growth. In doing so, however, these women were concerned with their own personal economic gain as much if not more than they were concerned with "morality."

Women's coming of age as economic players in Oakland is perhaps most apparent in the records of the Business and Professional Women's Club (BPWC) of Oakland. Officially organized in 1917, the BPWC grew out of the woman's bureau of the chamber of commerce, which had been organized in 1915. Under the leadership of successful businesswomen such as Gladys L. Barndollar, Alice T. Burnell, and Bessie J. Wood [Gustason], the BPWC became one of Oakland's leading booster organizations and a forum in which Oakland women could fully express the language of capitalism and participate openly in the growth machine. Although the club lost cohesion during World War I as women joined the war relief effort, the women regrouped in 1920. In 1923, the club developed to the point that it could afford to publish a weekly newsletter, the *Business Women's Herald,* edited by Zannette W. Porter.[44] The BPWC was designed as a forum in which business and professional women could come together to foster their collective goals through organization: "The purpose of our organization is to make us more intelligent citizens by impartial consideration of civic matters as they arise; to become an organized force for good in the community; to assist and encourage younger women entering business life, setting higher standards of efficiency and personality, and finally, to furnish the opportunity for business women to meet socially women in their own and other lines of endeavor."[45]

As it did for their male counterparts in Rotary and Kiwanis, membership in the BPWC provided members with a neutral arena in which to offset the competitive tensions of the capitalist marketplace. It also offered women of all classes the opportunity to embrace the language of capitalism and to share in the planning and selling of Oakland. For women excluded by class rank from the more affluent women's clubs, the BPWC offered an alternative club environment in which to share in the process of creating and fostering community identity and civic pride. Open to all business and professional women in Oakland and containing on its membership lists store clerks, beauticians, small shop owners, and corporate executives, the BPWC reflected the multiclass character of Oakland.

As a booster organization and a proponent of city planning, the BPWC took an avid interest in the development of the city's waterfront and harbor. In 1923, Mrs. J. E. Reid, Dr. Cassie Morehead, and Marion McElrath were named as a committee to formulate an official position for the club on the harbor. Noting that waterfront development was crucial to the growth of the city, the leadership admonished the committee members that "this is an important issue to all of us as business women. Give it your careful consideration."[46] Throughout the 1920s, the BPWC turned its attention to civic issues and often worked in concert with other local women's clubs to oversee important projects. In 1923, the club also joined with other clubs to discuss the issue of further railroad expansion in the city and invited J. P. Potter of the San Francisco–Oakland Terminal Railway Company and Leon Gray, Oakland's city attorney, to present the two sides of the issue to the women.[47] Demonstrating a vision that was quite advanced, the BPWC was also interested in the development of air transportation in Oakland. Citing a report that in the next five years air transportation would make or break a city, in 1926 the BPWC encouraged Oakland to develop its airports. Cities without adequate airports would not be "on the map." Any city wishing to compete needed to develop airmail service and commercial passenger service and recognize that air transportation was the wave of the future. Cities that wished to win the interurban rivalry "will look to aviation to solve their transportation problems as readily as they now depend upon the automobile, the railroad and the steamship."[48]

The BPWC's interest in the planning and development of Oakland was reflected in its use of the language of capitalism, and particularly in its adoption of booster rhetoric. As businesswomen, BPWC members relied for economic stability on the growth of the city and thus entreated all members to share in selling the city as they would sell the products and services of their businesses. Reflecting their command of booster rhetoric, poems often appeared in the *Business Women's Herald* encouraging the booster mentality:

Boost your city, boost your friend;
Boost the lodge that you attend,
Boost the street on which you're dwelling
Boost the goods that you are selling.
Boost the people 'round about you;
They can get along without you,
But success will quicker find them
If they know that you're behind them.
Boost for every forward movement,
Boost for every new improvement,
Boost for the man for whom you labor,
Boost the stranger and the neighbor.
Cease to be a chronic knocker,
Cease to be a progress blocker,
If you'd make your city better,
Boost it to the final letter.[49]

Club president Bessie Wood Gustason encouraged club members to become involved in any project that would sell the city. In the fall of 1923, she informed club members that the Dairymen would hold their annual convention in Oakland that year and that this provided the women with a great opportunity to advertise the benefits of the city, particularly to the spouses of convention attendants. Noting the importance of conventions to Oakland's growth, Gustason argued that "this is our chance to SELL OAKLAND direct."[50]

The women of the BPWC found sanction for their activities in the male leadership of Oakland, particularly from the Oakland Real Estate Association. F. F. Porter, president of the association, praised the work of the BPWC as a booster organization and encouraged the women to participate in the building of Oakland both as club members and individually. He suggested three things that the women could do to enhance the value and reputation of Oakland: (1) undertake a comprehensive survey of the city and the harbor; (2) campaign for the passage of a zoning law; and (3) work for the improvement of the waterfront to draw business and industry to the city. He argued that with the application of a little "horse sense" Oakland could become "one of the leading cities on the Western Continent."[51] His recognition of the contributions of the BPWC indicated that Oakland women had matured as capitalists. They could and should be treated as equals in the strategies of city growth and no longer treated as existing in a separate sphere. They could speak the language of capitalism, and they could share in the implementation of a vision of growth based on the premise that Oakland could attain Pacific Coast dominance.

In the 1920s, California's women's clubs increasingly moved away from relying on moral and domestic arguments to blatantly economic ones. For the Contemporary Club of Redlands, this in part reflected a growing number of members in business for themselves and the creation of an evening auxiliary to the club for business and professional women.[52] At the same time, the club began serving monthly lunches to the Rotary Club and dinners to the Merchants and Manufacturers Association. The club further demonstrated an increased interest in the city planning movement by inviting the chamber of commerce to hold city planning meetings in the clubhouse. The board also extended an invitation to the secretary of the chamber, A. E. Isham, to present a program on city planning at a general assembly.[53] In 1923, the board voted to offer the chamber of commerce its cooperation "in one thing, for example City Planning which the club feels is necessary."[54]

At the same time that the Contemporary Club was pushing for a new zoning ordinance, it was encouraging club members to invest in a new tourist hotel. Kate G. Pohl presented the club with a plan for individual investment in building a hotel on the Fisher property. "This plan permits members to put $10.00 each into bonds of the $100.00 denomination and states that the club shall take each $100.00 it is received and purchase said bond and hold it as agent in the transaction." Believing it would provide a handsome return both to individuals and to the community, the club decided to invest in this plan.[55] This project demonstrated women's understanding of real estate investing and was designed to encourage small-scale investing by pooling resources. Within a month, the club had secured $1,000 for hotel bonds.[56]

This investment in a new tourist hotel induced the club to take a more active role in advertising the city. In 1925 the board endorsed a project by the *Los Angeles Times* to advertise California when writing eastern friends. This project was also embraced by the *Redlands Facts*, which offered a prize for the best letter written by a Californian to an eastern friend on "the advantages of living in California."[57] At the same time, Jane Taltavall announced that the Redlands Realty Board was offering two prizes of $5.00 and $10.00 for the two best essays of five thousand words or more on "how to advertise Redlands." The winning essay was written by club member Ruth Eddy Sargent, daughter of Elizabeth Fisk.

Ruth's essay deserves special attention. In many respects Ruth Eddy Sargent represented a typical clubwoman and a typical citizen of Redlands. Ruth had majored in English in college and returned to Redlands, where she taught high school for a few years before marrying Arthur M. Sargent. Following her marriage, however, she maintained separate financial arrangements from her husband, as had her mother, Elizabeth. In addition, Ruth entered into a business relationship with her stepfather as an independent property owner. In 1917 she sold John Fisk two lots in the city along with five shares of capital stock in the Redlands Water Company. She also held the promissory note on this deal and charged her stepfather 6 percent interest over the four years she held the note.[58]

Ruth and her husband, Arthur, both became active in gender-appropriate social clubs and in the chamber of commerce. In this context Ruth wrote her essay, "Publicity Problems of a Small California Community (as Exemplified by Redlands)."[59] Although she perceived her primary role in life as a homemaker, the content of this essay indicates the depth of her knowledge of and interest in the importance of careful advertising for the city. It demonstrates that even women who were not business owners understood the economics of the city growth game.

In her essay, Ruth expressed her understanding of the importance of proper advertising in selling any product from mouthwash, to automobiles, to cities. She suggested that in order for cities to sell themselves as successfully as General Motors sold cars, or Metropolitan Life sold insurance, they must model their advertising campaigns along the lines of these companies and develop the same degree of name recognition. But before cities could advertise themselves, they needed to discover why people chose to live where they did and then use testimonials to describe the advantages found in that community. Noting that "disillusioned people make poor townsfolk," Ruth emphasized the importance of factual advertising.

Using Redlands as her case study, Ruth suggested that city boosters had failed in their advertising campaign to sell local economic opportunities other than citrus. "Did you know that forty per cent of the wealth produced in our end of the valley comes from something else than oranges? . . . I still do not know where that forty per cent comes from. Poultry, honey, canned fruits, and dairy products are doubtless part of it. May it be increased? Is it worth advertising? What new discovery lies just around the corner?"[60] Ruth recommended that city boosters investigate these opportunities and promote investment, particularly in those industries that would produce goods for both local consumption and for export: planting of persimmons and deciduous fruits for shipment east; harvesting of eucalyptus for furniture and interior finish; planting of pomegranates and cork oaks for grenadine and cork production; and developing silk culture, animal husbandry, medicinal herbs, and arts and crafts.

While Ruth understood the importance of industry attracting residents, she also attributed city growth to the quality of life that Redlands provided: "A chance to earn a living and have a good time, is what most Americans want. So far we have advertised the living more than the good time, and yet Redlands combines the two in rather useful fashion. Vacations at small cost are within easy reach. We lie between the mountains and the city; midway between trout fishing and the Philharmonic. We are in a little city; and yet in Friendship Village. Why not mix some of these human values with citrus culture and real estate, in our advertising?"[61]

To promote these nonindustrial features of life in Redlands, Ruth proposed developing a series of illustrated pamphlets to be presented to tourists in hotels and auto courts. She recommended that they advertise such diverse attractions as the health benefits of Redlands sanitariums, opportunities for family entertainment, diversified agriculture, strong public schools, and opportunities for recreation and culture. Unified under a banner such as "Redlands in the heart of all this interesting country, is a city of opportunity," or "this is the way you may live in Redlands," these pamphlets would find their way to communities across the country and expand Redlands' name recognition.

By stressing the unique features of life in Redlands, Ruth demonstrated an awareness of the failures of traditional advertisements based on city services alone. Although she understood the importance of city services in selling the city, she recognized that in the 1920s most cities provided the basics of gas, electricity, sidewalks, and sewers. It was a town's individuality that would attract new residents: "Every town worth the name has them [services]. And one California town keeps its eye on its neighbor; swimming pool, Junior College, municipal auditorium—thus competition keeps us stirring. But competition can be carried too far. If all towns are exactly alike, none is interesting. If one advertising campaign duplicates another, its value is lost. Redlands must cultivate individuality."[62] Hence, if the service city were to continue to grow in the mid-twentieth century it had to expand its services into the realm of culture and recreation.

Ruth proposed a program to enhance the individuality of Redlands. She recommended that the city discover its personality through "better coordinated activity; a city center better planned and regulated; cooperative marketing; vocational direction; forums and classes for adult education; more expert architectural guidance; and improved city plan with fewer jogs in the streets of new subdivisions."[63] She did not recommend developing a city festival to attract visitors, because this form of advertising had become too common to be effective. Summarizing her program, Ruth proposed five steps to successful advertising: (1) study and implement new and successful advertising by emulating corporate advertising; (2) set the goal of presenting a truthful picture of life in Redlands; (3) discover and exploit the diverse possibilities of life and industry in Redlands; (4) infuse human interest into the presentation of facts; and (5) create more community spirit.

Throughout the 1930s and 1940s, the Contemporary Club and its members continued to assert their interests in city planning and city advertising and to act as a forum for discussion of all issues relevant both to city growth and to women's economic well-being. By the late 1920s, not only had women in Redlands staked their claim to "stock" in the city, they had helped to implement a vision of economic growth in which the City Beautiful, city services, and public education all played a role. Far from participating in the greedy plunder of the speculative growth models, the women of Redlands invested in their community. They believed in the unlimited potential of future growth. These were also not women relegated to separate spheres. Redlands clubwomen were property owners and community builders who cooperated with their fathers and husbands to build a citrus mecca in the midst of the Southern California desert.

Through property ownership, club membership, and business and professional careers, California women slowly adopted the vocabulary of capitalism that more accurately expressed their economic behavior than the vocabulary of Victorian womanhood. As they participated in city growth through their club affiliations, they acquired an understanding of the tools of the growth machine: petitions, resolutions, planning, and zoning legislation. At the same time, they received sanction of their efforts from their male counterparts, further eroding any sense of separate spheres for men and women.

The completion of apprenticeships in property and public activism and the spread of knowledge about property ownership emancipated middle- and upper-class women economically before they became enfranchised politically. This did not represent the "domestication" of politics as the domestic sphere expanded into the public.[64] Rather, it represented a reaction to the encroachment of the public sphere into the domestic concerns of women who owned their own homes and businesses. As club members and property owners, women entered civic affairs to protect or enhance personal wealth. Although the language of Victorian womanhood continued to influence their public discourse, the vocabulary of capitalism slowly replaced it throughout the early twentieth century.

CHAPTER THREE

Women and the Chamber of Commerce

They talk about a woman's sphere
As though it had a limit;
There's not a spot on sea or shore,
In sanctum, office, shop, or store,
Without a woman in it.
—*Oakland Enquirer*, April 15, 1909

Published in 1909, this promotional piece from the Oakland Chamber of Commerce put into words a reality of life for many California women that dated back to the 1880s. For nearly three decades, California women had gained economic experience outside the domestic arena, and this statement by the Oakland Chamber of Commerce indicates that the state's male business elite finally intended to recognize the contributions of 50 percent of the population to the development and marketing of cities. Women could be found working as residential and commercial property owners and managers and as owners and operators of their own businesses. In addition, even "traditional" nonemployed women had gained experience in the business of city growth and development through gender-specific social and civic clubs. There were no limits to the woman's sphere.

In the process of exploring their role as capitalists, many women found that individual work, or work through women's clubs, did not provide them with enough of a voice in the city growth process. In increasing numbers after 1890, they joined chambers of commerce either as full members or as members of ladies' auxiliaries. While some of their activities as chamber members or associates continued to fall along the lines of women's traditional domestic roles, women chamber members showed increased interest in the economic activities of the chambers and in working as city boosters, a key component of growth machine activities. One of the earliest examples of women's booster activities can be found in Redlands, California, where in 1888 the chamber of commerce supported the creation of the United Workers for Public Improvement (UWPI), a quasi-auxiliary organization. In 1890, the San Diego Chamber of Commerce created a Ladies Annex, upon which Los Angeles modeled a similar organization in 1891. For those women dissatisfied with an auxiliary role, full membership in chambers of commerce was possible in Los Angeles as early as 1893 and in Santa Barbara in 1904. Women members became increasingly common throughout the state in the 1910s and 1920s.

As women moved into the public arena of city development, the language they employed changed from one grounded deeply in Victorian moralism and domesticity to one shaped profoundly by the aspirations of late-nineteenth- and early-twentieth-century capitalism. In a unique blending of the two languages, California women helped convince their male colleagues that morality and business could proceed hand in hand. Even without the political power of the vote, they managed to convince city officials of the economic value of clean and beautiful streets, health and hygiene programs, and a strong public education system.[1] Throughout the state, chambers of commerce embraced this blended language of morality and capitalism to attract new investors and thus to win the city growth game.

Traditional histories of women's involvement in civic affairs suggest that women would not be found in chambers of commerce or engaging in booster or investment activities.[2] Women's historians posit that the separate-spheres mentality of the Victorian era consigned women to domestic roles or to social or moral reform movements. In addition, they argue that by creating female networks and gender-specific clubs, women often chose consciously to exclude themselves from male organizations. This may or may not have been the case elsewhere, but middle- and upper-class women in California did not fit this traditional model. Through their work with chambers of commerce, and as property and business owners and investors, women capitalists shared with their male counterparts in the work of building and selling their cities. They believed that California's urban growth and development offered unlimited potential for economic prosperity that could be realized through the careful marketing of a California Dream. They saw a place for women in this dream as both owners and managers of real property. Chambers of commerce provided a second social and economic vehicle through which both men and women could sell the dream and their cities and thereby increase the value of their property investments.

Evidence to support the economic motivations of women in civic work can be found in most California cities. Women members of the UWPI in Redlands were either independent businesswomen like Lucy Foote or partners in business with their husbands like Agnes Sloan. These same women were also founding members of the Redlands Contemporary Club. The second generation of Redlands women to join the chamber of commerce included women like Helen Kimberly, Jennie Davis, and Blanche Cannon. All were members of both the Contemporary Club and the chamber of commerce, and all owned property in the city. Jennie Davis even sat on the board of trustees for one of the local banks. These women had an economic stake in the growth and development of the city, and their membership in the chamber of commerce indicates they understood the economic value of selling the city. In terms of moral motivations, both the men and the women of Redlands were concerned with promoting their city as a healthy, morally upright, and economically viable city. The chamber of commerce sought to achieve greater cooperation among the men and women of Redlands "for a higher moral tone, for more civic pride and a keener appreciation of our city."[3] As city boosters, members of the chamber of commerce, regardless of sex, recognized that good morals were good business.

Male-dominated chambers of commerce throughout the state were concerned with city morals, a move that in part reflected a backlash against Gilded Age municipal government corruption and in part reflected the intensity of interurban growth competition in California. In the age of city boss politics, scandals involving franchise kickbacks, monopolies, and graft ruined many cities' reputations and could prove lethal in the competition to attract new residents and city investors. Progressive Era politicians and boosters invoked the language of moral reform to separate themselves and their cities from the taint of corruption.[4] Oakland tried desperately to separate itself from San Francisco's reputation as a city of corruption run by boss Abe Rueff. Responding to San Francisco's attempt to create a consolidation of Bay Area cities into one government in 1907, J. W. Dutton, an Oakland booster argued,

> They tell us if we consent to be annexed, absorbed by them, that we will not lose our identity. That talk is fallacious. We would cease to be Oakland and become at once but a tail to San Francisco . . . graft and corruption would be likely to infest our fair city. Let us not do it; but let us unite all the cities and towns here from Richmond to Hayward into one great city and county.[5]

City boosters, both men and women, acknowledged the value of moral superiority as a strategy in the city growth game. Socially defined as the "guardians of public morality," women could often find greater legitimacy as growth machine members by invoking the language of female moral authority rather than the language of capitalism. Nonetheless, as members of chambers of commerce, they clearly understood the language of capitalism even when they chose publicly to avoid that language. As was true for their male counterparts, their choice of argument was most often guided by their intended audience.

To increase the overall wealth of the city, chambers of commerce were designed to sell the city to tourists and potential residents. A woman's membership in a chamber of commerce offered her the chance to express herself with the language of capitalism and to participate in the process of selling her city. Clearly, women were concerned with promoting healthier, cleaner, and morally upright cities, but as members of chambers of commerce they were also interested in promoting their communities, and hence individual, family, and class economic growth. They were intent upon shaping the urban process, not just reacting to it.

Loosely defined, chambers of commerce represent the interests of local business and professional men and women and are concerned with improving the business environment to ensure the growth and prosperity of their communities. In the late nineteenth and early twentieth centuries, chambers of commerce throughout the United States began to expand their activities beyond merely advertising commercial opportunities to social welfare work as well. Recognizing the link between public and private economic well-being, they became, in the words of Marc Weiss, "community builders."[6] Because they sought to build a consensus among the community's elite, chambers of commerce became integral to success in city competition both as booster organizations and as mediators of civic problems. They became the mainspring of the growth machine. In cities throughout California, they could make or break a city plan.[7]

In the current debate over twentieth-century western urbanization, the contributions of chambers of commerce to comprehensive city planning laws have been overshadowed by those of real estate developers or merchants. This reflects the reevaluation of western urban development away from a speculative model with its emphasis on booster rhetoric and monopolistic land practices. Newer work argues that western urbanization proceeded along an investment model in which growth occurred in terms of controlled and planned development.[8] The contribution of chambers of commerce, however, should not be ignored, especially when placing women into the story of western urban growth.

Chambers of commerce drew their membership from both real estate developers and merchants, as well as from local entrepreneurs and small property owners. As representatives of a cross-section of city property and business owners, the activities of chambers of commerce thus reflect the vision of growth pursued by city government as well as the overriding consensus behind that vision. Thus, when responding to inquiries regarding opportunities in their cities, chamber leaders were careful to encourage those who would invest locally and to discourage those who appeared to be job seekers with little or no ability to enhance economic opportunity for the city as a whole.[9] The contributions of women in responding to inquiries and in developing promotional literature provide evidence that women shared in the vision of city growth. Women chamber members also provide evidence of the economic motivations propelling women into the public sphere and of women's role in the process of planning and selling cities in California.

Entrance into the male-dominated public sphere of California chambers of commerce did not occur without incident or debate. In the 1880s and 1890s, even those women's auxiliaries that pursued traditional "feminine" projects were not successful or self-sustaining. The UWPI pursued such a course but was abandoned within two years of its founding.

Established in 1888 and modeled after the Los Angeles Chamber of Commerce, the Redlands Chamber of Commerce sought to ensure Redlands a share of the emigration from the eastern United States to Southern California.[10] Early officers of the chamber represented the city's citrus, real estate, and business elite. S. J. Hayes, C. R. Paine, E. G. Judson, H. L. Sloan, Curtis Wells, and L. W. Clark all had a personal economic stake in the ability of Redlands to beat Riverside or San Bernardino in attracting tourists and new residents. E. G. Judson, for example, owned most of the land in the original city limits, and H. L. Sloan ran the city's main hotel. Like their colleagues in Los Angeles, these men recognized that the city needed to be sold on cultural and social grounds as well as in terms of business and investment opportunity. Turning to the city's women for assistance, the chamber created the United Workers for Public Improvement. These women, wives of chamber officers and leading independent businesswomen, dedicated themselves to improving the aesthetic side of life in Redlands as part of their effort to lure emigrants.[11]

The call to arms for a women's improvement society came primarily from the city's male leaders, especially the city's leading booster, newspaper editor Scipio Craig. While Craig encouraged the beautification of the city, he did so not from a sense of moral uplift, but out of a sense of the economic value beautification could bring to the community. He looked to the examples of the work done by women's improvement societies in other cities and concluded that beautification projects would turn Redlands into a premier tourist town:

> The town of Stock[b]ridge, in Mass., has the name of being one of the most beautiful villages in New England. What has made it so? The Laurel Hill Improvement Association, organized by the ladies of the village who transformed an unsightly mound near the center of the town into a lawn of beauty, cleared up the sidewalks, made personal appeals to every resident to beautify his own premises and thus transformed an ordinary country town into an ideal rural village. As much might be said of Williamston, where Cyrus W. Field gave $10,000 on condition that the front fences be removed, and of scores of other cities and towns throughout the east. We glory in our new city and claim with good reason that for beauty of situation and grandeur of surrounding scenery its equal cannot be found if we look the whole state over. Let us then so improve every spot within our borders that Redlands will be the mecca town toward which the steps of all wandering pilgrims may be turned.[12]

By turning to women to do this work, Craig demonstrated a traditional view toward women's public work, but he also argued that this type of public work was essential to the economic growth of the city.

The UWPI first met in the winter of 1889. Leadership came from the city's elite women, including Emma S. McConkey, manager of the Windsor Hotel, Mrs. John Dunham, manager of a furniture store, and Eliza Agnes Sloan, wife of chamber founder H. L. Sloan and co-owner and manager of the Sloan House Hotel. Other members were the wives or daughters of chamber members: Mrs. Fred Griffing, Mrs. B. B. Parkhurst, Mrs. C. E. Owen, Mrs. I. N. Hoag, and Miss Mary Sloan. As property owners and entrepreneurs, all of these women had a stake in the growth of the city, and their efforts at beautification reflected more than a desire for "self-expression."[13] They stood to benefit from their improvements just as all citizens would.

Over the three years of the UWPI's existence, the women chose to emphasize two specific beautification projects. First, in the spring of

1889 they began the process of raising funds for erecting street signs and lamps in the downtown area. They also sought funds for erecting an ornamental fountain at the intersection of Cajon, Orange, and Citrus streets that would designate the center of the downtown district. When the local newspaper failed to give the women credit for their work, Mrs. Griffing responded indignantly:

> I have an idea that since Christopher Columbus surprised the North American Indians! no class of people have been so astonished as were the "United Workers for Public Improvement," to see in the last *Citrograph,* that the neat little sign-posts now being placed by them at the intersection of our streets, were the work of the "city authorities." Now good Mr. Editor, while we have done other work that we do not care to vouch for, we ourselves thought these posts not only a great improvement, but a necessity, and we claim all the honor there is in it, except what is due to the brethren who made them, and, for us, placed them in position.[14]

The UWPI did not limit itself to simple beautification projects. Soliciting the support of the city trustees, the women worked to enhance the image of the community as a metropolitan center and not a rural backwater. To this end, it petitioned the city trustees for a law prohibiting the hitching of horses to street signposts and the staking out of livestock on streets. The city trustees passed an ordinance to this effect in the spring of 1889.[15]

By the winter of 1890, it became evident that interest in the UWPI was waning. In part, this reflected the fact that much of the work done by the group was duplicated by the Redlands Horticultural Improvement Society. This organization, open to both men and women, sought to improve Redlands through horticulture. Speakers were particularly interested in the planting of ornamental and shade trees along the main boulevards of the city and using plants and shrubs to improve property frontages. At first, the UWPI considered joining the Horticultural Society as an "annex."[16] However, by April 1891, interest had so waned that the ladies decided to disband and join the Horticultural Society independently.

For the UWPI, the choice to disband most likely reflected the desire of the Redlands elite to pursue a rather subdued growth strategy. In contrast, Los Angeles pursued an aggressive growth strategy, and its male elite struggled more with the contradictions inherent in women working with the chamber of commerce at a time when social mores dictated they remain in a separate sphere. The public behavior of the

Woman's Annex to the Los Angeles Chamber of Commerce came into increasing conflict with the social imperatives of Victorian womanhood. On the one hand, in recognition of women's interest in business matters, Los Angeles men encouraged women's public work by creating a chamber of commerce auxiliary. On the other hand, these same men struggled to define an appropriate role for the women's group once it was created. Conflict occurred when neither the men nor the women could agree as to what that role ought to be.

In 1891, the chamber created a women's auxiliary to take advantage of a growing number of women in business who were interested in boosting the city. Problems arose, however, when it became apparent that the men of the chamber and the ladies of the annex disagreed as to the proper role of the women's group. Basing their assumptions on Victorian definitions of social roles, the men expected the women to serve as the "gracious hostesses of Los Angeles," by providing fresh flowers for the chamber, greeting visitors, and arranging receptions. Many women, in contrast, expected to participate on the same footing with the men. As members of the economic and business community, they perceived themselves as boosters, equal, not subordinate to, their male counterparts.[17]

Membership in the Ladies Annex indicates that the "ladies" had broader interests than mere moral reform of the municipality. These women understood the need for a city to grow through new businesses and public services. For direction, they looked to the example of the San Diego Annex, where seven hundred members "had under way a public park, a free market-house, a watch factory and many other matters of public importance."[18] While the women of San Diego still felt compelled to decorate the chamber building as part of their duties, they were extending their public work into the economic realm. They understood that if the chamber were to attract new residents it must present an aesthetically pleasing outward appearance in addition to providing information on investment and business opportunities. In this early stage of California's city competition, beautification complemented industrial development as a means to attract people.

From its inception, the women of the Los Angeles annex struggled to define a suitable role for themselves. They created committees on immigration, visitors and reception, home industries, sanitation and public improvement, law and legislation, exposition, township, county advisory, and arbitration; these women sought work that would make them part of the city's commercial life. They also adopted a constitution modeled on that of the chamber of commerce. In their meetings, the women demonstrated their interest in and knowledge of the economic factors of city growth. They discussed the feasibility of starting a silk or tea industry in Southern California, the success of the citrus and grape industries, and the employment opportunities offered by the fish cannery industry.[19]

Their first real project, however, was the creation of a bureau of information. Its purpose was "to help reduced gentlewomen, strangers especially, to obtain work and reliable information on almost any subject appertaining to Southern California." For a small fee, the bureau would provide information on housing, business opportunities, chaperones, carriages and tour guides, musical and literary talent, artists and photographers, shopping services, real estate investment opportunities, servants, and medical and health services.[20] The bureau was designed to meet the various needs of women moving to a new city. It reflected women's continued concern with protecting a woman's reputation by providing chaperones. At the same time, it indicated a growing desire among women to pursue nontraditional activities by providing information on business and real estate investment opportunities. After a six-month trial, the bureau failed to become financially independent, so it was abandoned. Yet the innovative attempt to create such an institution documents women's commitment to developing financial independence. In addition, it demonstrates that while women were concerned with traditional "feminine" interests, they recognized that women did often enter into their own investment and business ventures.

The demise of the bureau of information led to a growing disagreement among the members of the annex. Although some members were content to serve as hostesses for the chamber, two women in particular raised their voices in protest and sought a more activist role for the women: Alice Moore McComas, an officer in both 1890 and 1891, and Sophia Knight, a committee chair in 1891. Together, these two dissenters set off an explosive debate within the annex that eventually led to its dissolution. McComas and Knight first suggested that the organization broaden its activities through a coalition with the city's other women's groups in support of a women's suffrage amendment. In addition, McComas recommended that the annex join with the Woman's Exchange to promote industrial development.[21]

Sophia Knight, however, encouraged the annex to develop into an independent body, separate from the chamber of commerce. First, Knight believed that the annex should pay rent to the chamber because "we are not a charitable organization." These funds should be raised by charging dues, which Knight believed was the proper course of action for "a legitimate business body of women." Second, Knight urged the women to change the name of the organization to reflect their new independence. She suggested "Women's Branch of the Los Angeles Chamber of Commerce" or "Women's Commercial Union." Knight argued that the term "annex" carried with it connotations of inferiority and thus unworthiness.

> No strong institution in the world is designed as a "ladies" society. Let it rather be a "woman's" association. Another thing I object to is the term "Annex," which indicates that we are annexed to something. I never knew any reason why we took that name, anyway, unless it was because San Diego named theirs that, and we never aped San Diego in anything else. Although we have gained some fame as the Ladies Annex through the orange carnival at Chicago, we have gained just as much disrepute. Another point: the social element has no part in this organization, and I suggest that we do not give public entertainments for the purpose of increasing our funds; rather let us raise our money by dues, as a legitimate business body of women should do.[22]

Knight suggested that in the future the annex should promote local industry by compiling statistics and publishing pamphlets. This would be seen by both men and women as valuable and would introduce women to the industries of Southern California and the central issues of the growth machine.[23]

McComas and Knight dreamed of the annex becoming a respected partner of the chamber and, most important, a means of making women an integral part of the city's economy. However, the two women faced many obstacles in implementing their plans. They were caught in the growing debate between profit and social good that permeated all groups interested in city growth at this time.[24] Many members found it difficult to loosen the "bonds of womanhood" to the extent that McComas and Knight suggested. They were willing, however, to take a first step and enter into the business of boosting local industries by writing pamphlets, as Knight had proposed. Chamber members, in contrast, found it even more difficult to accept broader roles for women, and they refused to treat the annex as anything other than a subordinate organization.[25]

At the end of 1891, tensions over the role and relationship of the annex to the chamber developed into a heated public debate. The immediate cause of the dispute was a perceived "snub" involving a chamber tour of a Chino sugar factory from which the ladies of the annex were excluded. Several members felt that the Chino incident was one of many instances of chamber insensitivity. "We've waited on them enough already," stated one irate member. The *Los Angeles Times* reported that the women generally agreed that "the Chamber had failed to recognize the annex many times previously and had not extended proper courtesies to them, had given them no recognition whatever, had utterly ignored them, except when there was any decorating to be done, then they were glad to call upon the ladies, but when it came to a question of importance the annex was 'not in it'"[26] Annex members believed that annexation to the chamber implied equality with it, and thus the failure to include them in chamber activities indicated a general lack of regard for the women's contributions. By disbanding, these women demonstrated their dissatisfaction with a secondary role in the development of the city and their desire for public recognition of their capitalist interests and abilities.

Tensions had been smoldering for some time over other issues as well. One instance that particularly angered the annex involved a reception sponsored jointly by the annex and the chamber. The chamber expected the annex to cover half of the expenses for the event. Although the women did authorize payment to the chamber, they questioned the fairness of financing a reception at which no women were allowed to speak.[27]

This was one of many instances in which the chamber consigned the women to a subordinate position. The Chino snub provided the "last straw" and led to the dissolution of the annex. It took another two years before the chamber opened its doors to women members. In 1893, Tessa Kelso, the city librarian, and Harriet Strong, a successful rancher, were admitted to the chamber. Regardless of the outcome, however, the existence of the annex demonstrates women's growing insistence on recognition of their participation in the city growth process. In this early, halting confrontation with capitalism, the members of the annex had proved their interest and ability. They expressed their command of the language of capitalism and their refusal to limit their lives to domesticity and moral guardianship. The experiences of the Ladies Annex to the Los Angeles Chamber of Commerce provide a glimpse into the commercial interests of California women. They also demonstrate the difficulty women had in pursuing those interests in a male-dominated public sphere.

The creation of ladies auxiliaries such as the UWPI and the Ladies Annex to the Los Angeles Chamber of Commerce provided California women with a clearly male-sanctioned opportunity to promote city and regional development. While experiences in auxiliaries differed from city to city and depended on the extent of cooperation and shared goals of the men and women, cooperation with chambers did offer women a chance to learn to express themselves in the language of the urban growth machine and to sell not only their city but their own real estate. The existence of ladies auxiliaries and their activities that went beyond providing flowers for chamber rooms, indicate that many women sought more than moral improvement or self-expression in public action. Women who joined the chamber of commerce or its auxiliaries perceived themselves as vital members of the community intent upon participating in the promotion of their city and their region.

Increasing urban rivalries at the turn of the twentieth century appear to have provided the catalyst for the changing relationship between women and chambers of commerce. By 1900 California cities had embraced the concept of "bigness," and city leaders would pursue any and all avenues to success. For chambers of commerce, this meant extending memberships to women and to including women in promotional activities. The unfettered capitalism of the western city growth machine broke down Victorian social mores and helped women achieve economic emancipation before they achieved political emancipation through the extension of the franchise.

Before women could participate successfully as boosters, they had to learn the business of city promotion. For the women of Los Angeles, San Diego, and Redlands, this had been partially achieved through the auxiliary organizations created in the 1890s. For other cities, however, a public education campaign had to be initiated, and newspapers provided access to a broad citizenry. Perhaps no public education campaign was as blatant as that undertaken by the Oakland Chamber of Commerce in 1910.

The *Oakland Enquirer* became a leading proponent of advertising the city and provided the chamber of commerce with almost daily publicity. *Enquirer* articles suggest the emergence of a capitalist consciousness among middle- and upper-class women in Oakland. Demonstrating both the confidence men had in women's abilities and the development of women's knowledge about chamber activities, in 1910 the *Enquirer* assigned Gladys Genevieve Adams as its correspondent to the chamber of commerce. Adams admitted that prior to writing an extensive article about the chamber, she had been woefully ignorant of its operations:

> Do you know what a Chamber of Commerce does? I confess I did not when I received a detail from the city editor to visit that august body and write a good, long article concerning the work of the city's great commercial league. I had a hazy idea that a Chamber of Commerce had something to do with shipping statistics, bank clearings, publicity, and promotion. . . . The busy click of typewriters answering correspondence impressed one that here is organized activity in behalf of a big corporation—the rapidly growing city of Greater Oakland.[28]

In her article, Adams reported in detail the workings of the chamber of commerce. She noted the importance of chamber exhibits in visually representing the variety of products and scenic beauty of Alameda County to visitors. In addition, the chamber provided maps, posters, booklets, and pamphlets—"portable exhibits." Adams was impressed by the chamber as a "great bureau boosting the city" and as a clearinghouse of information on Oakland and the East Bay. She wrote, "the Chamber of Commerce is a place where all questions are expected to be answered—questions about industry, questions about finance, questions about agriculture, questions about land values, questions about transportation, questions about employment, questions about taxation, questions about cost of living, and questions about climate."[29] The chamber not only advertised the city but also solicited businesses to relocate to the area. Adams concluded that without the chamber of commerce, Oakland would not be the prosperous and growing city it had become. Thus, she encouraged the citizens of Oakland to join the organization and work for the promotion of the city.

Oakland women readily responded to the appeal for help. In 1910, they signed up to staff a booster train advertising the trading opportunities Oakland could provide for its agricultural hinterland—the San Joaquin Valley. They joined the Progress and Prosperity Committee of the chamber as it planned for the opening of the Panama Canal. They also participated in the *Enquirer's* "Why Oakland" booster essay contest.[30]

The "Why Oakland" contest elicited many responses from women who understood the importance of attracting home seekers to the city.

One woman sent in a "letter" to a friend encouraging her family to relocate to Oakland. She began by stating that "Oakland is an ideal place to settle." The city enjoyed a mild and healthful climate, abundant churches, libraries, and women's clubs (including an equal suffrage society), charitable organizations, parks and playgrounds, a strong public school system, and proximity to the state university at Berkeley. She noted that her "friend's daughter" would find a musical conservatory "equal to any in Europe." In addition, Oakland was a city of homes and gardens in which both flowers and fresh fruits and vegetables flourished. Most important, however, Oakland was a modern city with a strong industrial economy: "When our new charter is completed our city government will be most modern. Oakland is the best site for Frank's Corliss engine factory, as, with our deep harbor and railway terminals, our shipping facilities are excellent, and there is no better place to invest that legacy of yours. Oakland property is rising steadily."[31]

This woman understood that in order to attract families, a city must provide not only economic opportunity but also social, recreational, and spiritual outlets. A city needed to have those attributes that would provide resources and entertainment for the entire family. She also understood that the decision to relocate was not always imposed upon the family by the male head of household; the female head of household also needed to be convinced of the benefits of relocation. Although Fred A. Campbell won the "Why Oakland" contest, the many responses from both men and women give evidence of the interest of all citizens in the business of city promotion and city growth. It is particularly important to note that four women were among the honorable mentions: Mrs. W. H. Edwards, Laura M. Hyland, Rosalie Smith, and Helena Smith.[32]

As in Oakland, the business of advertising Redlands became increasingly important to the city's women in the 1910s and 1920s. Many Contemporary Club programs reflected this interest, and so does the increased presence of women on the membership rosters of the chamber of commerce. Throughout this period, several women contacted the chamber regarding its advertising practices and offered suggestions for more effective city promotion. Offering ways in which Redlands could lose its image as a sleepy, rural town, Fannie Lockwood sent her paper "What They Do in a One Man's Town" to the chamber.[33] Mrs. Lockwood argued that far from being a one-man town, Redlands, with the growth of population and the breadth of interest of the citizenry, was a complex, metropolitan center that required the participation of a variety of professionals and civic groups:

> Not even the Los Angeles Trust Companies can run it alone,—we are to have increased capacities. Nor could a lawyer run Redlands alone. He would give us divorces without contest, which would make it dull and uninteresting. Our mills and legal papers he would draw up in his favor. So he needs competition to handle the increased population which manufacturing and wholesale distribution brings to Redlands. We have all and more of these trades and professions and each has much competition which gives a town human powder so we have struck the match and let's all join the Chamber of Commerce and keep the fire of enthusiasm burning in Redlands until our sister towns will be green with envy instead of saying we are asleep. So come on men and women! Three cheers for our home town—Redlands![34]

In 1923, Janette L. Sturges wrote to the chamber of commerce suggesting an advertising campaign that would emphasize the beauty of Redlands' homes. She thought Redlands could outdo an advertisement by Pasadena that she had seen in the *Saturday Evening Post*.[35] In 1924 Mrs. Milo Smith of Redlands wrote to the chamber of commerce suggesting that every citizen of the city put a slogan selling the city at the top of every letter sent to the East.[36] In 1926, Jane Taltavall sent a copy of Ruth Eddy Sargent's award-winning essay on city advertising and encouraged the chamber of commerce to adopt some of her plans. The chamber secretary agreed with Mrs. Taltavall and contacted the realty board to put Mrs. Sargent's plan into action.[37]

By the end of the 1920s, Redlands' women had established themselves as members of the chamber of commerce. Their names appeared on ballots for board of directors positions; they were increasingly called upon to represent the chamber at state and national conventions; and their suggestions for city advertising campaigns were implemented. The work of women in both Oakland and Redlands with the chamber of commerce suggests that in California communities men and women shared a vision of city growth that was designed to enhance business, social, recreational, and spiritual opportunities. For the men and women of Redlands and Oakland, community identity and shared goals were clearly more important than gender difference in shaping the course of development the city would follow.

Throughout the 1910s, women statewide came to understand the in-

Redlands' booster Jane Taltavall at home. The gentleman is not identified, ca. 1900. From the Archives of the A. K. Smiley Public Library.

tensity of interurban rivalries and sought to participate in them. Promotion of the Panama-Pacific Exposition in Oakland served as another opportunity for women to enter the public world of the chamber of commerce. In addition to supporting a postcard campaign designed to inundate legislators with support for giving San Francisco the exposition, the city's clubwomen met regularly with the chamber of commerce to discuss strategy. Mrs. Zoe Greene Radcliffe joined the Progress and Prosperity Committee in 1910 and enlisted the aid of Mrs. Charles J. Woodbury of the Ebell Society, Mrs. Thomas P. Hogan of the Catholic Ladies' Aid Society, Mrs. W. Mira of San Leandro, Mrs. R. D. Holmes, Mrs. S. Peters, and Mrs. W. A. Brown of the Alta Oakland Club, and Mrs. Florence B. Langworthy. Working in conjunction with the city's men's organizations, these women club leaders designed a campaign for women to persuade the voters in their families to vote yes on amendments 52 and 33 to the state constitution in the November election. Amendment 52 provided state aid to the exposition, and amendment 33 enabled San Francisco to issue bonds for the fair. At the suggestion of Mrs. Charles J. Woodbury, the committee decided to send to every clubwoman in Alameda County a circular letter encouraging her to influence her family's voters to support the exposition. The letter read as follows:

> Dear Madam: Will you use your influence with the voters in your family and the voters with whom you come in contact to vote "yes" for constitutional amendments 52 and 33 which will bring the Panama-Pacific Exposition to San Francisco? No. 52 is for state aid. No. 33 is to enable San Francisco to issue bonds for the exposition. This is not a question of personal politics. This is a case of California against New Orleans. Will you, as a representative clubwoman, use your influence in this campaign?[38]

These women did not have the political power of the vote at this time, yet they found that the social vehicles of women's clubs and the chamber of commerce provided them with a voice in public affairs. They demonstrated a keen awareness of the importance of attracting a world's fair to their region as part of national urban competition. By working with the chamber of commerce, they manifested a commercial interest that went far beyond traditional domestic concerns. Women were clearly more than "gracious hostesses."

In addition to the Panama Canal rivalry of San Francisco and Oak-

Opening day of the Panama-Pacific International Exposition, 1915. Courtesy of the Oakland Public Library, Oakland History Room.

Women pose in a citrus grove for a local Board of Trade photograph, ca. 1903.
From the Archives of the A. K. Smiley Public Library.

land, Southern California cities battled for supremacy. The battlegrounds extended from within cities themselves to national magazines and conventions and fairs. Women increasingly offered their services to represent cities in these fairs. In 1908, the Redlands Chamber of Commerce considered paying for Myra Kingman Miller of Long Beach to represent the city at the Alaska-Yukon Exposition in Seattle. Mrs. Miller clearly spoke the language of capitalism and the urban growth game. In her letter offering her services, she inquired if Redlands would advertise at the exposition. She strongly encouraged the city to do so, "as many of your surrounding cities will do." The exposition, she believed, would be a "great harvest for Southern California and Redlands especially." She suggested that the exposition would attract "the representatives of wealth, energy, industry, and capital, the very people we want to interest and who will come if our section is properly represented to them." Noting the location of the exposition in the Pacific Northwest, Mrs. Miller argued that the event would attract gold mine owners and lumber moguls, the "kings of industry," who were the very class of people a city like Redlands sought to attract. In addition, Mrs. Miller offered her services at a rate lower than a man would charge. She noted that the cities of Imperial and Beaumont had already contracted for her services and that she had extensive experience as a city booster under contract:

> I will represent three cities there which do not conflict with each others interests and thus each one of them can get a remarkable value for a trifling sum. I enclose some copies of testimonials which speak of my representing several cities at the St. Louis Exposition. This experience is of value as I will know just how to go about to get the best results. . . . For my services I will charge the trifling sum of five dollars per week.[39]

While it is unclear from the records whether the chamber sent Mrs. Miller as its representative or not, her proposal represents an active interest in the business of city promotion from women throughout the state. In addition, it demonstrates that women understood what type of people cities like Redlands sought to attract and were willing to work to sell the city to a specific class of emigrants.

Mrs. Miller's request to represent the chamber was not unprecedented. Throughout the early 1900s, chambers of commerce turned to women to represent them at state, local, and national fairs and conferences. Redlands was no exception. In the same year in which Mrs.

Women members pose for an Oakland Chamber of Commerce membership drive, ca. 1920. Courtesy of the Oakland Public Library, Oakland History Room.

Miller sought to represent the town at the Alaska-Yukon Exposition, the chamber sent a woman delegate to the Trans-Mississippi Commercial Congress in San Francisco. Mary Lynde Craig agreed to attend the congress even though it would take place while she was on vacation. Her willingness to attend such an event, as well as the chamber's confidence in a woman's ability to represent its interests, indicates that Mrs. Craig agreed with the vision of city growth pursued by the men of the chamber of commerce.[40] The chamber continued to solicit women to represent it at conferences throughout the 1910s. In 1914, it asked Isabelle Carpenter to represent the city at the National Irrigation Congress in Denver.[41] As chamber representatives, women fulfilled their role as capitalists intent on affecting the process of urban growth and development rather than reacting to that process.

Beyond advertising the city, California women joined chambers of commerce in exploring the issues of developing comprehensive city plans emerging in this period. The city of Oakland helped lead the way. In 1915, as Oakland became concerned about an inundation of emigrants with the opening of the Panama Canal, the City Planning Committee of the chamber of commerce pushed for passage of a city planning law. Working with city and county officials, representatives of improvement, civic, and women's clubs, and representatives from the State Commission of Immigration and Housing, the City Planning Committee met to discuss the importance of better housing and city planning. In 1919, the chamber of commerce appointed Aurelia Henry Reinhardt, president of Mills College, to chair the City Planning Committee and oversee the direction planning in Oakland would take.[42]

A. S. Lavenson, vice president of the H. C. Capwell Company and chairman of the City Planning Committee from 1916 to 1919, personally groomed Reinhardt to succeed him. He entered into a detailed correspondence with her immediately following her appointment to the presidency of Mills regarding plans to improve access to the college. Noting the intimate relationship between the growth of Mills and the growth of Oakland, Lavenson argued that any street improvements made in the vicinity of Mills would encourage "a scheme that cannot fail to be most advantageous for both your institution and the city. . . . The more accessible and convenient for visiting we make our noteworthy institutions the more fame accrues to the community and to the institutions." He encouraged Reinhardt to sell Oakland just as she sold Mills to prospective students and their families.[43]

Lavenson was joined in recruiting Reinhardt for chamber of commerce work by George W. Fitch, president of the chamber's advertising bureau. Echoing Lavenson's sentiments as to the economic value of the college to the city, Fitch invited Reinhardt to speak to the bureau on planned improvements to Mills. Reinhardt accepted the invitation. Early in her presidency, she became aware of the value of developing a relationship with the city's businessmen. Not only would she be able to advertise the educational strengths of the college; she would begin to develop contacts with the city elite for future endowment fund-raisers. Reinhardt wrote to Fitch:

> I have been so busy this fall I have not come in touch with the Oakland business world as I believe it would be wise for Mills College to do. Certainly, Mills College is an asset to the community, an asset larger than is generally realized. If you think that your organization would be interested in hearing of the work of the college, of our plans for its future and its certain development within the community, I shall accept with pleasure the invitation you give me.[44]

As a widow personally responsible for her family's economic security, Reinhardt understood that her future was intimately tied to that of both Mills and the city of Oakland. Selling the city and selling the college ensured her financial security. Throughout her tenure as president of Mills (1916–1946), Reinhardt frequently agreed to speak to the chamber of commerce on topics ranging from education, to sanitation, to comprehensive planning.[45] She recognized the connection between city services such as education and public health to the city's ability to attract new residents and to her college's ability to attract new students.

Along with requests to speak at meetings of the Oakland Chamber of Commerce, Reinhardt received many requests from chambers across the state. She most frequently accepted invitations to speak to Berkeley and San Francisco groups such as the Retail Furniture Association of California, the Western Fruit Jobbers Association, the Commonwealth Club, the Retailers Credit Association, the San Francisco Chamber of Commerce, and the Foreign Trade Club. She also accepted invitations to speak to the Atascadero, San Jose, and Ukiah chambers of commerce and to the Advertising Club of Los Angeles.[46] At most of these meetings, local women's groups were also invited to attend. The fact that a woman was solicited to speak to these "commercial" organizations and that women were invited to attend as listeners indicates that by 1920 women as capitalists had reached a level of equality with their male counterparts. Members of the male elite were interested in exploiting the vision of women because they believed it complemented their own. The ascendance of a woman like Reinhardt to a position of influence among the male commercial elite demonstrates that women spoke the language of capitalism, not only within the domestic sphere but also in the public sphere of the chamber of commerce.

Finding women in the records of California chambers of commerce provides evidence of an area of public work for middle- and upper-class women heretofore undiscovered. It offers an opportunity to reevaluate interpretations of women's public work away from models stressing gender identity, moral and social reform, and political activism. Instead, at least for the capitalist women of California, community identity and property interests were equally compelling factors motivating them to enter the public arena. Clearly, the job of selling the city was shared by the men and women of the city elite. In California, middle- and upper-class women believed that urban growth and development offered unlimited potential for economic prosperity that could be realized through the careful marketing of a California Dream. Through chambers of commerce, the city elite created a cross-gender alliance designed to sell that dream and their cities and thus ensure individual, family, and class economic security.

CHAPTER FOUR

Apprenticeship in Politics

The records of chambers of commerce draw a picture of California's second- and third-tier cities as idyllic enclaves where wealth and opportunity abound in wholesome and morally erect communities. Readers see the dream in these communities, the vision of what these cities hoped to be. In contrast, the day-to-day operations of city government reveal the true nature of a city's character. Eric Monkkonen has said that a city's daily political business reflects its priorities.[1] Indeed this is so; so too, a city's daily political business reflects the citizens' priorities. It is in the mundane, daily business of petitions and resolutions sent to city councils where we can find evidence of individuals who belonged to the growth machine and of how that machine sought to operate without regard to expected class or gender distinctions. Through the city council, middle- and upper-class residents in cities like Redlands, Oakland, and Santa Barbara, could fulfill the dream of their chambers of commerce, and thus protect their economic investments in the city.

The business of city government also permitted women to gain experience as political players and to influence city growth and development before they were extended the right to vote. While women's clubs and chambers of commerce may have greased the wheels of the California urban growth machine by serving as coalition builders, it was in local politics where women truly expressed their command of the game and their vision of sustainable growth. In some respects, women's interactions with city government provide the strongest evidence of their inclusion in the growth machine, for it was at the level of city government where the vision and plan of the growth machine was actually implemented.

Most Americans, whether property owners or renters, experience the impact of municipal government every day. Whether it be a matter of feeding coins into a parking meter, paying an additional quarter to 0.5 percent sales tax on purchases, riding mass transit, or simply turning on or off the lights, decisions made by local government shape our lives. The direct impact of municipal decision making on individuals has varied over time and place, but by the 1880s, the concept of the municipal corporation filling the role of "service city" was firmly in place. Americans had come to expect that city government would provide the basics of sanitation systems, paved roads, public utilities, and public transportation projects. As the service city evolved, Americans came to take both the services and the governmental body that created them for granted. With the national economic crisis of the Great Depression, and local government unable to handle the crisis, Americans further removed themselves from municipal issues and came to believe that government from Washington held the greatest significance for their daily lives.

Based on modern perceptions of voter apathy and the sense that citizens are disaffected from government, it is difficult to believe that there was a time when politics mattered, particularly local politics. But the period from 1880 to 1940 in California was such a period. It was a period when major decisions were made by local government, and citizens, regardless of their enfranchisement, took the time to have a say in those decisions. Although a variety of issues were discussed, city councils primarily made decisions affecting property and property interests. Whether creating park and recreation districts, tree commissions, or public utility franchises, all city council decisions came down to a consideration of how the expenditure of public monies could affect growth and thus property values. For historians of the Left and sociologists, this focus has given rise to both the growth machine thesis and the social control thesis. A coalition of land-based elites manipulating city government is central to this perspective; however, it is not accurate to argue that this group sought to control nonpropertied interests or to collectively hoard the wealth of the city in a monopolistic frenzy. At least in California's second- and third-tier cities, city council minutes reflect a sincere concern with responding to the concerns of individual property owners and creating a more livable city for all.

Some form of city government has existed in California since the arrival of the Spaniards, but in the American period, state government set out to increase the number of local governments in order to disperse power across a vast territory. The California Constitution of 1849 granted the state the right to issue charters for municipal incorporation, although debate continued through the constitutional revision of 1879 over the powers the state held over cities, particularly in regard to granting cities the right to tax real property. The Cities Act of 1850 required new cities to have a minimum population of two thousand residents and a limited geographical area of four square miles. The Towns Act of 1855 allowed smaller settlements with a population of at least two hundred inhabitants and a maximum area of three square miles to incorporate. In addition to the right to a small tax on real property, town governments could also regulate bars, levy a six-dollar annual tax on dogs, and elect a town recorder to judge infractions of local ordinances.

In the thirty-year period of the first state constitution, from 1849 to 1879, the state also granted 133 special charters of incorporation to seventy-three cities. Typical powers in these special charters included the ability to make ordinances and determine penalties for violations, prevent and remove nuisances, license and regulate businesses, construct and maintain public buildings and areas, regulate building construction, organize and maintain school systems, provide for city elections, borrow money, incur indebtedness, and levy taxes to a limited extent.[2] These powers for special charter cities also became the foundation for general-law cities. The key difference between a general-law and a charter city revolves around the size and makeup of the city council. A general-law city is permitted a city council of five members and a city manager or commission form of government. A charter city, in contrast, is permitted to expand its council from five to fifteen members and to elect a mayor.

The California Constitution of 1879 altered the power of state government over local government. The result, Article XI, clearly limits state legislative powers over cities and codifies home rule for charter cities.[3] Prior to 1879, the state legislature had assumed powers to enact special legislation for cities, including placing excessive tax burdens on property owners for support of local functions. In some instances this required residents to accept paying for railroad bonds without a citizen referendum on the issue. Article XI expressly prohibited such legislation. The new constitution also took away the capriciousness of state-level municipal legislation by requiring all laws to have general application. Finally, the constitution prohibited cities from receiving state funds to support local government. With these new protections of home rule in place, the state created 269 new cities between 1880 and 1950.[4]

The concept of home rule became a powerful force in California cities and perhaps is responsible for the empowerment local citizens experienced in dealings with city councils. Indeed, there are clearly documented cases where a powerful corporate elite dominated local decisions, especially in the history of Los Angeles, where decisions made by the Department of Water and Power and the Southern Pacific Railroad profoundly shaped the development of the city. The same thing can be said of the development of Orange County, where the Irvine Ranch Company has clearly dominated local government.[5] However, in the second- and third-tier cities of Oakland, Riverside, Redlands, and Santa Barbara, the local citizenry retained a substantial amount of control over city growth, particularly in each city's early development. In these cities, it becomes clear that the growth machine is not monolithic. Whenever growth policies became counterproductive to quality of life, new coalitions would form to fight back. Thus, the growth machine could succeed only when it considered all facets of the city, not just expanding corporate property developments.

In examining the daily business of city government, two things become abundantly clear. First, besides the provision of basic services, the biggest concern of city government and its greatest power lie in the control of land use. Through its planning powers, city government determines how and where the city will grow. Second, decisions on land use provide the catalyst for property owners to become engaged in the political process. Thus property ownership, by its very nature, is a political activity.

Home ownership ties the average citizen to local government in a direct and significant way—namely through the payment of annual or semiannual property taxes. In the United States, the availability of cheap land has made it possible for members of all classes, and in California for both genders, to purchase property and thus gain stockholder status in the city corporation. This accessibility to property ownership for the poor and the pervasiveness of the city growth mentality has helped ameliorate class conflict. In addition, because the growth machine could include all property owners regardless of the size of their estate or their social or occupational status, city government could not be controlled to the extent that the growth machine thesis would have us believe. Thus, the city growth machine is less an agent of social control and more an expression of the capitalist class sympathies of the majority of American city property owners.

Property ownership clearly drew women into the local political arena in California. Beyond their collective voice found in club resolutions, individual women property owners became active in city politics through petitions to city councils. Whenever they became concerned that a city project might damage their property value, women quickly emerged from their "separate sphere" to demand that they be heard.

From Redlands' incorporation in late 1888, the women property owners of Redlands became an integral force in charting the course of development for the city. As historian Larry Burgess has argued, they became "the connecting skein" in the city, helping to mold a community that would grow both economically and socially.[6] Although denied the right to vote on incorporation, within a month of the vote the women of Redlands had organized the United Workers for Public Improvement and began actively working to influence the business of the city. Although essentially an auxiliary organization to the chamber of commerce, this group regularly petitioned the city trustees on a wide array of issues, all of which were designed to enhance "the growth and beauty of this valley."[7]

Individual property owners also found a voice before the city trustees. Ellen B. Seymour, whose Prospect House Hotel relied on continued city growth for its own success, became a regular petitioner before the city council. Seymour's contact with the city trustees, however, extended beyond her income-producing property to her personal property as well. In late 1887, Seymour, along with eighteen other investors, began construction on a development of twenty homes above Highland Avenue. Within a year of completing construction, it became clear that the property was being damaged by storm drainage. Proving that gender was not a limitation in power before city government, Seymour led this group of property owners in a request to the city trustees to place a drainage culvert on Highland Avenue. The trustees agreed to the request; however, Seymour and her neighbor Leon Benson ended up absorbing the cost of construction of the culvert, owing to the city's financial weakness in its early years of incorporation.[8]

For other Redlands women, their first experience with city government came not in a personal petition to the trustees, but in an order from the trustees to make improvements on their property. Elizabeth

Eddy learned the hard way that property ownership is a political issue when she was informed by the city trustees that she would be responsible for paying for a wastewater diversion channel in front of her property. The trustees had received a petition from C. H. Baughman and others asking the city to address the problem of wastewater flowing into Fern Avenue between Center and San Mateo streets. This group of property owners wanted the water conducted into a large arroyo on Fern Avenue. The city trustees agreed with the petitioners and notified both Elizabeth Eddy and her neighbor E. J. Waite that as abutting property owners they would be responsible "to at once provide a way at their own expense for conducting said waste water to said arroyo."[9]

The issue of water runoff seems to have been a key concern for Redlands in its early years of incorporation, and the city trustees regularly attended to requests for culverts and gutters to be built on major streets. This makes sense in light of the geographic features of Redlands. The city is situated on the eastern edge of the Los Angeles basin, with an average annual rainfall of thirteen inches. When rain does come, it often arrives in large doses, and hence drainage is a major consideration. Erosion, not only to residential property but to valuable citrus property, could lead to significant financial loses. In general, when women or men petitioned the city trustees to build or maintain such systems, the city agreed.[10] As might be expected, however, property owners did not always agree with decisions made by the city trustees in terms of actual construction of these projects. In 1890, for example, Mrs. Squires complained to the trustees that a gutter they had erected on Chestnut Avenue in front of her home was too high.[11]

In addition to dealing with drainage issues, Redlands was also busy grading and paving new streets and extending streets into outlying areas. Once again, the women property owners of Redlands were actively engaged in this process through petitions to the city trustees. In 1891, the city responded to women's requests to improve State Street with sewers and paved streets and to extend Stillmen Avenue. This second project would have required the city to engage in eminent domain proceedings since the proposed street extension would require taking property from Lura Spoor Hubbard, J. G. Hale, and D. B. Alverson, among others. Expressing their understanding of this process and giving tacit support for the project as a property-enhancing maneuver, all of the property owners deeded the necessary right of way to the city and signed a subscription paper indemnifying the city against the cost of opening the street. The number of women involved in this process is significant. Once again, although they were denied the power of the vote, these women were behaving in an inherently political manner.

Riverside women, too, found a voice in city governance prior to 1911 and demonstrated their knowledge of key issues in city growth. Founded in 1870 as a utopian colony dedicated to education and culture, Riverside did not really prosper until after 1873 when the first navel oranges were planted by Luther and Eliza Tibbetts. The city then enjoyed a real estate boom in the 1880s fueled by investment in citrus. By 1882 there were more than half a million citrus trees in California, almost half of which were in Riverside. The profits attainable from even a small grove established Riverside as the wealthiest city per capita by 1895. Nonetheless, as the city entered a new century, it found itself engaged in an intense competition with Redlands and other surrounding citrus cities for continued growth. As with Redlands, the city trustees found themselves debating how best to provide the services that would make the city more attractive to investors than its neighbors. And, also like Redlands, one of the proposals on the table in 1900 was the concept of planting shade trees on public streets.

As a desert city, Riverside enjoys beautifully mild winters and blazing hot summers that begin early and end late. Temperatures begin climbing in May and can stay in the nineties and hundreds through October. While mild winters made Riverside an ideal winter tourist destination, the summers made retaining year-round residents more difficult than in a milder climate like that found in Los Angeles or Santa Barbara. An intensive shade-tree-planting campaign thus became a valuable part of Riverside's growth strategy.

To complete this project, Riverside hired J. H. Reed to fill the post of city "Tree Warden." Reed became one of the city's most visible and vocal proponents of street tree planting as a growth strategy. He wrote regular articles in the newspaper proclaiming the moral, health, and economic virtues of planting shade trees in the city. He also agreed to speak to the women's club and any other city organization that would have him on this topic. Eventually his fame spread so that competing cities also asked him to speak. Reed became a one-man crusader for urban tree planting, and his successes can be seen in the many beautiful trees that still line the major streets of Riverside, Redlands, and San Bernardino.

Mary Elizabeth Darling and Kate Greenleaf Locke became two of Reed's most ardent supporters in the tree-planting movement. Both wrote regular articles for the *Riverside Daily Press* extolling the benefits of tree planting. Although this project could be perceived as a product of municipal housekeeping or pure aestheticism, these women understood that this was a matter of Riverside winning its competition with other citrus cities.[12] In 1905, Locke wrote a series of four articles on tree planting and landscape architecture. Her fundamental point was "to prove to the fair-minded practical man of business, that it is to his interest to beautify his city." Essentially she argued that property would rise in value if beautified.[13]

While the planting of street trees seems an obvious and relatively inexpensive way to improve property value for the city, not all residents agreed with Reed, including some women property owners. In January 1900, Reed presented the city trustees with a proposed ordinance to facilitate street tree planting. He recommended that the city narrow streets by building boulevards and sidewalks to accommodate new trees. Mrs. Maynard, a property owner on Ninth Street, became the public voice of other property owners who objected to this proposal. She argued that such a plan would be disadvantageous to the city because "to vary the width of sidewalks on the same street . . . would make unsightly jogs." More important, she stated that she had put down 769 feet of curbing and 5,000 feet of asphalt, among other improvements to her property, and she did not want to have the city destroy that investment. In case her personal plea should happen to fall on deaf ears, she also argued that Ninth Street was a major traffic route that carried heavy teaming and trucking. Narrowing the street in order to facilitate planting trees would thus interfere with commercial traffic. Lastly, Mrs. Maynard argued that "we did not want narrow streets, darkened and made gloomy by large shade trees, we need more sunlight."[14]

Mrs. Maynard was not shy about addressing the city trustees or advocating for her own property interests. She also clearly held capitalistic sympathies. When a city project was approved in front of her property, she, along with neighboring property owners, appealed to the city council to bid out the work to a private contractor. In March 1900, the city authorized her and her neighbors M. C. Paxton and J. T. Jarvis to explore such a possibility. While it is unclear from the records whether this contract work was carried out, it is interesting to find a woman in such a position. Here is a clear case of a woman not only "speaking like a man" but behaving like a man as well.[15]

Maynard knew how to speak to the city trustees, and she understood the nature and responsibilities of city government. When she wished to put a cement curb on her Mulberry Street property between Ninth and Tenth streets, she requested that the city water company substitute a pipeline for an open ditch on the block. In her request she reminded the city trustees that it was the "purpose of the city to improve streets."[16]

While Mrs. Maynard proactively used the city council to serve her own property interests, other women property owners in Riverside went on the defense when they perceived city projects would damage their property value or force them to pay exorbitant assessments. Such was the case in 1903 when Twelfth Street property owners S. B. Brinkerhoff, C. A. Trimby, J. C. Glenn, Marie Hayden, and Martha E. Hewitt were faced with paying for improvements to their street. For some property owners, like Mrs. A. McCrary of Cypress Avenue, even rumors of proposed changes could bring them to address the city trustees, as she did in 1903 and again in 1905. Concerned that the city intended to abandon a road that cut through her property, she informed the trustees that such a move would "leave a big gulch in front of [my] property and destroy its value."[17] Emily Fales, owner of a block of property on Twelfth Street, was far more vociferous in her complaint to the trustees regarding a proposal to lower the grade of the street. In a strongly worded letter to the trustees she wrote, "You are further notified that I shall expect to be reimbursed for any damage I may sustain to my said property by reason of any change in the grade of said street."[18]

Like their counterparts in Riverside and Redlands, Oakland women, too, felt confident in asserting their rights before government officials when the city's growth strategy appeared to threaten rather than enhance the value of their property. In the spring of 1906, residents of the middle-class neighborhood of Fruitvale petitioned the Committee on Franchises of the County Board of Supervisors to protest railroad development in their neighborhood. Fruitvale property owners were concerned that in the process of building the road, property would be damaged with no guarantee of compensation. In a carefully worded resolution, Fruitvale residents requested that the Western Pacific Railway be denied a franchise to build in their neighborhood:

> Whereas we, the undersigned have been informed that the Western Pacific railway (a corporation) has applied to your honorable body for a franchise permitting it to lay a broadgauge track and to operate a steam train through and upon Putnam street from Fruitvale avenue to High, situated in Fruitvale, Alameda county, California; and
>
> Whereas, the granting of said franchise and the operation of trains upon said Putnam street by the said Western Pacific Railway will greatly depreciate the value of property fronting upon said Putnam street, and greatly injure and damage owners of the same; now, therefore,
>
> We, all of whom are property-owners, owning property fronting on said Putnam street, and on all cross streets between the Southern Pacific Railroad and Putnam street, respectfully request your honorable body to with hold [*sic*] the granting of said franchise until such time as the said Western Pacific Railway has made reasonable compensation to each and every property-owner on said street for damages which will inevitably accrue, and for depreciation of property by reason of the operation of said road.[19]

Among the signers of this petition were Mrs. M. J. Schwand, Mrs. M. Osegueda, Mrs. Leonora M. Harrison, Mary Nelson, Mrs. A. Jacobsen, and Lucy E. White. These property owners were concerned that the arrival of a second transcontinental railroad would decrease residential property values because of an increase of train traffic through residential streets. By signing this petition, these women demonstrated their grasp of the language of capitalism and city growth. When growth appeared to threaten their personal financial well-being, women, like men, used the political system and the vocabulary of growth to protect their investments.

The same year as the Fruitvale petition, property owners in the working-class Wood Street neighborhood filed a similar petition with the Oakland City Council. Leading the fight, Augusta Wilson took charge of circulating petitions calling on the city council to refuse the request of the railroad. "Steam roads on Wood street would mean a great depreciation in property values," she claimed. "For that reason we are opposed to the grant of franchises. All the property in this district would be affected. Even though the roads pay us for our homes the amount received will not reimburse us for our losses. This is our home and the City Council should not hand this district over to the railroads over our protest."[20]

Demonstrating its interest in the development of residential property for all classes, the *Oakland Enquirer* threw its editorial support behind the Wood Street protest. The *Enquirer* believed that industrial and commercial growth of the city at the expense of any of the residential sections would be unwise. The editor noted that Wood Street was a narrow street of small working-class homes, unsuitable for rail traffic. Building a railroad, thus, would "greatly depreciate, if not destroy, the value of all property thereon for residential purposes." He argued that Oakland was a city of homes, and if the City Council permitted the franchise on Wood Street, it would send a message to other property owners that their homes were not safe in Oakland:

> Oakland ought to encourage the building of small homes within her boundaries. The more of them we have, the better we are off. It will be little encouragement to the small home-builders, such as live on Wood street, to permit their property to be destroyed and the slow and painful savings of years to be swept away, as would be the case if the franchise in question be granted without compensating the property-owners.

The editor continued to argue that this was a class issue, suggesting that the council would not consider a franchise through a neighborhood with more valuable property.

> If the Western Pacific, Santa Fe or Key Route, or any other road should ask for a franchise through Jackson street, it is very safe to say that the council would refuse to consider it, and the reason given would be that the passage of a railroad through that street would destroy much valuable property. . . . We want homes in Oakland; and the council should not unnecessarily destroy any of those we have. The mechanic's humble home on Wood street should be just as sacred in the eyes of the council as the more pretentious homes on Jackson street. . . . The Enquirer is heartily in favor of doing anything in reason to aid the Western Pacific, Santa Fe or Key Route, but it does not believe that it is either reasonable, necessary or just to sacrifice a hundred humble homes on Wood street to save money for a rich corporation.[21]

Unlike the Redlands elite that sought to exclude working-class residential development, the Oakland elite viewed the working class as an essential element of the city. The fact that working-class residents could also speak the language of growth indicates that the capitalist class had succeeded in spreading its worldview beyond its own circle.

Indeed, in their study of North American housing trends, Michael Doucet and James Weaver found that members of the working class shared in the asset-building strategy of economic security pursued by the middle and upper classes. Home ownership was a goal shared by all North Americans because it represented freedom from the bonds of tenancy. Buying a home signaled success to peers and to the community at large. It gave working-class families autonomy to pursue their vision of the California Dream. When that dream was threatened, as in the case of the Wood Street residents of Oakland, working-class residents, like their middle- and upper-class neighbors, could employ democratic mechanisms of protest to the city council to fight to preserve that dream and the security found in home ownership. They could invoke the language of the city growth game to convince the elite to protect all residential property values in the city.[22] They, too, could become a part of the growth machine.

The Wood Street residents continued to petition the council and eventually gained not only the support of the *Enquirer* but support from members of the Alameda County Progress Club and the merchants' exchange as well.[23] By the end of May 1907, opposition to the franchise increased to the point that the city council agreed to amend the railroad franchises granted down Wood Street to protect the rights of property owners. As part of the compromise worked out between the city, the railroads, and the property owners, the railroads were permitted to lay their tracks, but they were expected to make all necessary street improvements, protect all sewer construction, and agree to recognize their liability in the event of damage to property on or adjacent to Wood Street.[24]

In addition to women petitioning city government regarding specific property interests, city government also cultivated women as political actors prior to endowing them with the power of the vote. As the California interurban competition intensified after 1900, city officials made regular visits to women's clubs to address the concerns facing their cities, especially when bond issues or charter revisions were at stake. Perhaps one of the most overt cases of this occurred in Oakland in 1906 and 1907 when Mayor Frank K. Mott undertook an appeal to Oakland clubwomen for assistance in passing a million-dollar bond issue designed to implement Charles Mulford Robinson's comprehensive city plan for Oakland. Regarding women's support as crucial to the success of the plan, Mott attended several meetings of both the Home Club and the Women's Civic Club, where he personally explained both the purpose and the goals of the newly emerging comprehensive planning movement and the specifics of the Robinson plan for Oakland. According to the social dictates of the day, Mott sought to influence the women by appealing to domestic and maternal concerns. He argued that "woman's voice . . . is potent in the domestic life and these plans for parks and boulevards in Oakland bear directly upon improved civic conditions which create the environment of the home."[25] Although women did not have the political power of the vote, Mott valued their ability to influence their male relatives enough to take time from his busy schedule to oversee their indoctrination into the principles of comprehensive city planning.

Mott's appeal to Oakland women in terms of domesticity should not be used to argue that women entered the public arena to "domesticize" it.[26] Rather, it should be seen as a political expedient. Historian Mansel Blackford credits Mott with the leadership behind the Robinson plan and with the vision and drive behind Oakland's growth.[27] A consummate businessman and real estate developer, Mott was motivated by a desire to see his city accepted as a serious rival for Pacific Coast dominance. He believed that Oakland could not attain metropolitan status without the physical trappings of a first-class city: parks, boulevards, museums, and attractive public buildings. He also understood that bond issues were inherently political issues, and he learned to use the political system to shape the city's future along his vision. Because social language in turn-of-the-century America painted women's public activities in terms of domesticity, it made sense for Mott to use these arguments when campaigning with women and more economic arguments when campaigning in the newspapers and to men's groups. However, in light of the compelling evidence of women as property owners cognizant that personal fortunes based in real property were dependent on city growth, we must not discount economic motivations for women by relying solely on public discourse.

During this period, Oakland also grew by annexation. Between 1897 and 1910, Oakland annexed the communities of Temescal, Linda Vista, Peralta, Claremont, Fruitvale, Melrose, Fitchberg, and Elmhurst. Selling annexation in terms of government efficiency through limited bureaucracy, Oakland sought ultimately to consolidate the entire East Bay into a city and county of Oakland. At the same time, however, San Francisco began to clamor for consolidation of the entire Bay Area into a Greater San Francisco. When the tables were turned on the Oakland elite in the annexation game, it cried foul. Oakland's defeat of the Greater San Francisco movement in 1911 represented its emergence as a powerful competitor for regional dominance. The city no longer identified itself as a suburb of San Francisco and was unwilling to accept incorporation into the city.

As part of the annexation fever sweeping the United States at this time, Oakland's consolidation plans were not unique. They did, however, provide the city's women with a chance to participate fully in urban politics. Throughout the early 1900s and into the 1910s, Oakland's civic organizations worked to consolidate East Bay cities into a city and county of Oakland. According to editorials in the local newspaper, the annexation movement began in response to a perceived threat of expansion from both Alameda and Berkeley. Noting the growing agitation for annexation among the city's improvement clubs, an editorial in the *Oakland Enquirer* suggested that "from now on consolidation or annexation should be the paramount issue in Oakland . . . as both Berkeley and Alameda are reaching out for more territory, and unless Oakland enlarges its boundaries this city will soon be a slender slice of territory, like the ham in a sandwich, between Alameda and Berkeley and take rank with Emeryville as one of the minor municipalities on this side of the bay."[28] This writer invoked arguments that consolidation of the cities of the East Bay into a city and county of Oakland would ease "the double-headed and expensive system of city and county government which is imposing a tax burden of $2.76 per thousand in Oakland." Consolidation would eliminate repetitive services and bureaucracy and cut the cost of government in half. In part, the Oakland consolidation movement drew strength from merchants who sought to maintain Oakland's new status as a commercial center following the 1906 San Francisco earthquake.[29]

At the same time that Oakland sought growth through annexation, San Francisco implemented a similar yet larger scheme of annexation designed to consolidate the entire Bay Area into a Greater San Francisco under one government. Like Oakland, San Francisco argued that consolidation would ease the tax burden for all citizens. In early April 1906, the Greater San Francisco Association was formed, "the objects of which are a city of a million population within a decade, adequate railway facilities; improved public utilities; suburban expansion; urban improvements and ideal homes in the outlying and unpopulated districts which are now waste places and have few advantages and fewer attractions for the home seeker, owing to their inaccessibility."[30] Some Oakland merchants supported the Greater San Francisco movement, arguing that only through Bay Area consolidation could any of the Northern California cities remain competitive with Los Angeles, Portland, or Seattle following the devastation of the April earthquake.[31]

The majority of Oaklanders, however, favored consolidation of the East Bay over the San Francisco plan, yet they needed the support of San Francisco and Los Angeles legislators to change state laws regarding city consolidation. Throughout 1906, Oakland boosters joined with Los Angeles boosters to push for legislation that would facilitate city and county consolidation. Building upon the expansion boom created by the earthquake, Oakland boosters began an impressive campaign to expand the city's boundaries. Arguing that the earthquake had deluged Oakland with new businesses and an increased population for which current city services were inadequate, the elite sought relief through expansion. "These conditions result in new civic obligations which this city must be prepared to meet. In order to do this it is necessary that Oakland enlarge its boundaries and augment its available resources in the matter of taxable property. Only a big city can do great things in the way of public improvements." Oakland wanted the state legislature to pass a law that would permit a division of Alameda County and the consolidation of Oakland and its surrounding communities into a single city and county unit. It looked for support from Los Angeles, a city constantly looking for ways to expand, and from San Francisco, which, one writer argued, needed to expand territorially "in order to meet the demands for rebuilding the city."[32] However, when the measure came up for a vote, it received strong opposition from three of the four Alameda county delegates as well as from Southern California and San Francisco.[33]

In addition to needing state legislative support for expansion, Oaklanders felt the need to draw up a new city charter to meet the needs of the proposed Greater Oakland. Beginning in 1907 and 1908, men's civic clubs, improvement clubs, and the chamber of commerce began a campaign to encourage Mayor Mott and the city council to authorize a new charter. In a 1907 letter to the mayor, the men of the Alameda County Progress Club set forth the arguments for a new charter that included the claim that the present charter was inadequate in meeting the needs of a rapidly expanding metropolis.

> We believe the time has arrived, and is now quite opportune, that this influential and rapidly expanding city, should keep pace with the requirements of its metropolitan character, and we voice the wishes of its citizens, when we affirm, that the present charter is, practically, obsolete and antiquated, and wholly unfitted for the city's present needs. A new charter is demanded, arising from altered conditions, on account of the city's expansion, in both increased population and commerce.[34]

In creating a new charter, the elite reached out to the city at large. The members of the Alameda County Progress Club, for example, argued that a charter committee should include delegates from all of the civic organizations and the trade unions, in addition to representatives of the city council. Suggested reforms included the right of recall, payment of members of the school board, civic control of the public library, a complete system of streetcar transfers, a free municipal market, free schoolbooks, competent inspectors, a practical health board, and a new city hall. All of these were considered services expected of any metropolitan center that wished to beat its rivals for regional dominance.[35] The Alameda County Progress Club believed that consolidation of the city and county of Oakland could not and should not proceed until a new charter was enacted. This was particularly urgent in light of the movement developing in San Francisco for consolidation of the entire Bay Area into a Greater San Francisco. In the fall and winter of 1907, the major commercial bodies of Oakland formed the Consolidation League to fight annexation to San Francisco and to create a city and county of Oakland. "The best and quickest way to end all this agitation for the consolidation of the cities on this side of the bay with San Francisco is to at once set plans in motion for the formation of the city and county of Oakland."[36]

As the debate over a Greater Oakland or a Greater San Francisco intensified, Oaklanders began to draw sides. On the one hand were arguments in favor of a Greater San Francisco put forth by J. Mendenhall. He argued that East Bay cities did not have the national name recognition that San Francisco had that attracted both tourists and new residents. "At the final analysis, what we would get would be a good advertisement, and men would learn where we live. . . . Covered by the aegis of the greater city, our town lots would have a ready sale, people headed from the East would cease to go astray, and we would have all the benefits of the advertisement." Counter this with the opposing view of John P. Irish, who argued that Oakland had single-handedly managed to retain the bay as the commercial center of California following the 1906 earthquake and had thus reached a level of equality with San Francisco. Annexation would imply inferior status.[37] The members of the city council agreed with Mr. Irish's position and in December 1907 officially expressed its disapproval of the Greater San Francisco movement. The council supported a Greater Oakland consolidation of East Bay cities but emphatically opposed annexation to San Francisco.[38]

As San Francisco stepped up its campaign for consolidation, the women of Oakland organized both to defeat the San Francisco movement and to campaign for a Greater Oakland movement. In the spring of 1908, the women of the Oakland Club sent a petition to Mayor Mott asking him to take steps necessary to call for an election of freeholders to rewrite the city charter. Led by Mrs. A. A. Denison, wife of the secretary of the chamber of commerce, a resolution was signed by a long list of clubwomen and presented to the city authorities.

The request of the women for a new city charter was greeted with respect and renewed calls for women's suffrage on the part of the *Oakland Enquirer*. It was, an editorial stated, another example of the outstanding work women did for the city of Oakland and provided more evidence that women should have the right to vote on issues that affected them directly. The editorial noted that over 75 percent of the women petitioners were city taxpayers and that the city owed it to these women to listen to their petition. It credited Oakland women with building the public library; raising the funds for a city ambulance; installing public drinking fountains, streetlights, and waste cans; and publicizing the faulty construction of public buildings. In addition, the editor pointed to the many instances in which the city's male leadership had turned to women for support of public projects:

> It was to the women of Oakland that Mayor Olney appealed in his campaign for the beautifying of Oakland by the planting of trees upon its public streets. . . . It was to the women of Oakland that Mayor Mott and the health department appealed for support and active co-operation in the clean city campaign. . . . It was largely through the influence of women that the movement for public playgrounds was initiated in this city. Even Mayor Mott has conceded the courtesy to women by proposing to name three of them upon the advisory board for the improvement of the public playgrounds of Oakland. Women have served the city of Oakland with conscientious fidelity and ability on its Board of Education and upon its Board of Health. Women are employees of the city and interested in the municipal administration as employees of the school department, as employees in various offices in the city hall, as employees in the free public library, as employees in the health department, besides the larger interest which every woman has in the clean, honest and efficient administration of municipal affairs. Representatives of this large, intelligent and influential body of Oakland's citizens have requested the City Council to permit the framing of a charter which will insure a clean, honest, efficient and progressive government for Oakland. They may not have the votes, at present, to enforce this demand, but they have an influence in municipal affairs which no man or body of men can afford to ignore.[39]

Although the Greater San Francisco and Greater Oakland movements appeared to be a dead issue in 1909 and 1910, they took center stage again in 1911 when San Francisco legislators tried to pass the Wolfe amendment through the state legislature. The amendment sought to amend section 7, article 11, of the state constitution relating to the formation of consolidated city and county government. It was designed to allow consolidation of cities or cities and counties or any part thereof into a single government. Although this was the design of the Oakland elite in their own consolidation bid of 1906–7, when turned on them by San Francisco in 1911, the elite rebelled.

Throughout the winter of 1910–11, advocates on both sides of the issue rallied to gain supporters for their side. In Oakland, both men and women turned out to fight the Greater San Francisco movement. In February 1911, at a rally of both male and female antiannexationists, the general feeling was that "we like San Francisco and are willing to concede her worth. We are willing to be friends with San Francisco, but we do not want to join with her. There is no reason for it. And there is no excuse for it, and this Wolfe bill is political theft!" The speakers believed that passage of the constitutional amendment "would operate to the detriment of Oakland's interests and destroy the industrial and commercial welfare of this side of the bay; would work a hardship on Oakland people by forcing them to shoulder, in addition to our own bond issues, a share of San Francisco's bonded indebtedness." Serving as chairman of the rally, W. E. Gibson argued that if Oakland consented to consolidation with San Francisco, its citizens would become "minority stockholders" in a "political corporation whose principal place of business and power of control lies beyond the confines of our county." Oaklanders, he asserted, would lose control of their own commercial and industrial activities just as they were propelling the city into metropolitan status. H. C. Capwell argued that if San Francisco annexed Oakland, "San Francisco would again make us the 'bedroom' of that city, which we once were, but which we are no longer." The men and women present at this rally signed the following resolution to send to the state legislature:

> Whereas, Amendment [*sic*] to the State Constitution are pending in the legislature having for their object the consolidation of a large part of Alameda county with San Francisco, and
>
> Whereas, One of said amendments proposes that said territory to be consolidated, including San Francisco, shall vote as a whole, the majority of the whole vote to decide; and

> Whereas, San Francisco having a majority of the whole vote, will have the power to make virtual conquest of the bay cities of Alameda county, regardless of the will and wish of their people, and in violation of the sacred principle that governments derive their powers from the consent of the governed; and,
>
> Whereas, The second of said amendments provides that the municipal debt, bonded and otherwise, of San Francisco, shall rest as a lien upon all of the territory and its taxpayers of the proposed consolidated district; now, therefore, be it
>
> Resolved, By this assembly composed of representatives from all the cities and sections of Alameda county that said proposed constitutional amendments are un-American in principle, unjust in purpose, and keenly antagonistic to the high interests of Alameda county and its cities.
>
> Resolved, That Oakland has no desire to override her neighboring cities of Alameda and Berkeley to annex them or to destroy their autonomy, but rather to furnish to them an example of civic enterprise, prosperity, commercial growth and greatness that will stimulate their individual efforts and enterprise to the same purposes, to the end that these east bay cities shall grow in an atmosphere of mutual enterprise and mutual respect, until they achieve such commercial greatness.[40]

As the Wolfe bill went to committee in Sacramento, Oaklanders sought to rally as much public opinion against the bill as possible. Although women did not yet have the vote, the *Oakland Enquirer* sought their support against the bill and asked women to mail in "ballots" stating their stand on the bill. These ballots, the newspaper would forward to the state legislature. In calling for a female "straw vote," the editor stated, "Recognizing the fact that the voice of womanhood in California is rapidly becoming a great factor in public affairs and that the proposed consolidation of the cities about the bay with San Francisco is a matter which concerns women as much as men, The Enquirer desires to secure the opinion of Alameda County women upon the measure."[41]

Alameda County women eagerly responded to the *Enquirer's* balloting of their opinion on the Wolfe amendment. Not only did they return the ballots from the newspaper; many wrote letters and telephoned their opinions. The paper printed the names of all women who voted against the amendment, and some of the letters. Anna A. Cannon included a note with her ballot suggesting that the councilman who favors the amendment should be sent across the bay. Frances E. Gannon wrote, "both my sister and I shall continue to speak against it [the Wolfe amendment] on every opportunity. We have lived nearly ten years in California in general and Oakland in particular, so of course, we are deeply interested in Oakland's splendid harbor, so are naturally opposed to the Wolfe bill. We doubt some of the other women who are down as favoring the bill, for I cannot understand any one living on this side of the bay doing so."[42]

Frances Gannon's thoughts were echoed by an eighty-two-year-old woman who wrote to say, "If I made a mistake in filling out a woman's ballot, I am very sorry. I have lived in Oakland forty-eight years, and have seen it grow from third to sixty-sixth street. I have never patronized San Francisco. I am 82 years old next Thursday, and would be ashamed to go back on my home I love so well."[43]

Other women registered stronger complaints against the amendment. Emma Benedict wrote, "I cannot resist saying a few words of protest. Horror takes hold of me when I think that Oakland should be annexed to San Francisco. I feel that in that event it would be seriously important that I sell all I have and follow the command that God gave Lot—'Escape for thy life; look not behind thee. Neither stay thee in all the plain. Escape to the mountain lest thou be consumed.'"[44] Although stated in moral language, Mrs. Benedict clearly feared that both her community and her property would lose value if Oakland became tied to San Francisco and its reputation of depravity. For her, Oakland's main asset was its moral value system and its reputation as a city of homes.

Some women's responses read like booster tracts. Jessie K. Dorn of Fruitvale wrote in her protest against the Wolfe amendment, "Oakland, First in name, First in Deed, first in the thoughts of Native Daughters and Sons—Oakland Forever." Mona Whalen, a twenty-five-year-old native Oaklander, wrote what could be used as a booster tract in her denouncement of the Wolfe amendment.

> Oakland! Essentially a city of homes, churches and schools, where good predominates and our boys and girls are shielded from the courser [sic] sights found in a more congested metropolis. Oakland! The City Beautiful—'the Athens of the Pacific'—looking toward the Golden Gate, and with its world-famed sunsets gilding every spire and eminence and lighting the western windows into torches of golden flame, on her left hand shimmer the blue waters of the bay, on her right rise the beautiful Piedmont hills, faintly green, with darker blotches of timber. If Oakland—improbable as it seems—should consolidate with San Francisco what will she gain? More business? She will get that anyway. San Francisco can only grow so far—she lies between the ocean and the bay—and she has pretty nearly reached the limit. But Oakland!—all east is hers and even now she is reaching out and smoothing down the foothills for her choicest home-lands. Then what WILL Oakland

> gain. She won't gain much of anything but what would come to her eventually. She will lose, tho'. Lose her individuality, lose her greatest source of wealth—the control of her waterfront—but more than all the rest, she will lose her fame; for being KNOWN as San Francisco is as bad as BEING San Francisco. So Oakland, think well before you give over your civic rights to a city that is known as the 'toughest town on the Pacific Coast.' Think of your open ways and streets, think of your freedom from crime and THINK OF YOUR BOYS AND GIRLS.[45]

As the *Enquirer*'s campaign against the Wolfe bill wound down, the newspaper lauded the support of women as equal players in political affairs. On the last day of its straw vote, the paper reported receiving over six hundred votes from women opposed to annexation and only thirty in favor. Once again, the editors commended the women's public awareness. Even after the paper had closed its straw vote, women continued to send in ballots.[46] The language employed by these women provides evidence of a transition phase for women in acquiring the language of capitalism. On the one hand they expressed themselves in terms of growth and local control, but on the other, they still relied on moral arguments and a desire to see Oakland homes and children protected from the evils of San Francisco. Women were emerging as capitalists but were still constrained by Victorian morality.

Throughout the 1920s and 1930s, Oakland, Riverside, and Redlands continued to compete in California's urban rivalry. Incorporating the tools of comprehensive city planning and zoning, along with traditional booster rhetoric, each city presented itself as a viable alternative to its competitors as both residential and industrial cities of metropolitan status. It is the story of women's involvement in the planning and development of these cities that provides insight into both the vision of the growth machine and the emergence of a new vocabulary that identified women as equal partners in that vision.

CHAPTER FIVE

Women and City Planning

As the city growth game intensified at the end of the nineteenth century, cities increasingly turned to the emerging nationwide movement for comprehensive planning to help them win the game. Growing out of efforts by social reformers, sanitation engineers, and landscape architects to create a more livable city in light of perceived increases in crime, disease, and population density, the planning profession finally gained national prominence in 1893 with the World's Columbian Exposition in Chicago. By 1900 planners had established their own professional journals and organizations and had gained a powerful influence over the direction future city growth would take.

California cities were some of the first in the nation to turn to professionally developed comprehensive city plans as a primary element in their growth strategies. Oakland and Santa Barbara turned to Charles Mulford Robinson; San Francisco hired Daniel Burnham; Riverside hired Charles H. Cheney. The greatest contribution of California cities came in 1909 when Los Angeles created the nation's first zoning ordinance. Although California cities took a leadership role in creating city plans, no plan was accepted unanimously, and no plan was implemented fully. Concerns with property rights and property taxes were usually the primary arguments against implementation.

An examination of city planning is crucial for understanding the nature of the city growth machine. Most planning historians have documented that city planning was not controlled exclusively by professional planners.[1] The social reformers who agitated for the first efforts at planning in the 1860s and 1870s did not step aside in the 1890s and 1900s. While cities may have hired professional planners to develop comprehensive city and regional plans, implementation of those plans could not occur without the support of the broader community. In this context, women found a ready opportunity to participate in the growth game. They could publicly promote their own growth agendas in the process of approval or denial of a plan. Remarkably, even before 1911 and women's enfranchisement, city leaders and planners turned to women to gain the needed electoral support for city plans.

While comprehensive city planning has been studied by a variety of scholars, the participation of women has largely been ignored. This is an unfortunate lapse. It diminishes the contributions of women to city growth and development, and it fails to fully explain the process by which cities implemented plans. In the cities of Riverside, Oakland, and Santa Barbara the contributions of women both to the development and to the implementation of plans were crucial.

One of the key reasons for this omission of women from the scholarship lies in the nature of women's contributions. Because they lacked the political power of the vote and the professional status of "planner," their work as advocates for city plans has been marginalized. In some respects, they were background participants in this process, but they learned to use their women's clubs as powerful tools to influence the shape comprehensive plans would take. All of the women's clubs in Riverside, Santa Barbara, Oakland, Redlands, and Los Angeles became involved in discussions of city planning, and many of these clubwomen eventually served as members of city planning committees and commissions. Even though the social constraints of Victorian womanhood limited women's participation well into the twentieth century, clubs built upon traditional roles for women as housekeepers and decorators to become a powerful force in the city planning movement.

Once they had established their credentials through implementation of physical beautification projects along the lines of the City Beautiful movement, women were then able to move into public discussions of zoning ordinances and the economic effects of planning. As the comprehensive city planning movement matured between 1905, when the first city plans were prepared, and 1915, when statewide zoning legislation was enacted, so too did women's participation in the movement grow. The apprenticeship in city planning that the women of Oakland entered in 1906 to help win approval of bonds for implementation of the Robinson plan was completed by 1919, when Aurelia Henry Reinhardt was named as chairman of the Oakland Chamber of Commerce

City Planning Committee. That same year, two women were appointed to the Riverside City Planning Commission. By the mid-1920s, Pearl Chase of Santa Barbara had become the de facto city planner of Santa Barbara through her work with the nonprofit Community Arts Association.

Women's historians have primarily documented the civic work of women in terms of their organized club activities and have shown that clubs evolved from social and literary organizations to more politically active groups across the nation. Robyn Muncy notes that 1890 marked a turning point for American women's clubs as they began a process of shifting away from their original focus on literary and charitable pursuits, toward the more challenging direction of increasing political activism. Karen Blair argues that this transition was completed by 1914.[2] In many respects this shift reflects the growing number of college-educated women who joined women's clubs in the late nineteenth century. Dissatisfied with their postcollegiate lives, these new members set into motion a search for innovative female roles. This search eventually led to the formation of the General Federation of Woman's Clubs, which became a national lobbying organization for women's political advancement. The question remains, was this a matter of intellectual dissatisfaction or more one of capitalist self-interest?

Muncy's emphasis on national political activism does not adequately address the reasons for the shift in women's city planning interests from city beautification to active participation in comprehensive city planning. If women's club members were property owners with a stake in the beautification and planning of their cities, then the explanations offered by city planning historians provide a more likely explanation for the shift in behavior. On the local level, the shift away from small-scale city beautification projects to involvement in larger planning projects reflected what Mansel Blackford has seen as a natural progression from the City Beautiful to comprehensive city planning as cities sought to assert regional dominance. Thus, perhaps the changing emphasis of women's clubs was not a matter of national political activism but of local city growth. In addition, the shift in emphasis for women's clubs occurred at a time when women were increasingly owning property and adapting the language of capitalism to their needs. The changes in women's clubs reflected a coming of age of women as capitalists rather than as politicians.

In the current scholarly debate over the importance of city planning in twentieth-century urban history, historians have focused primarily on defining the leadership and the goals behind the movement. Building upon the work of William H. Wilson on the City Beautiful movement, Marc Weiss argues that although the City Beautiful movement served as a preliminary step toward increasing public appreciation of civic improvement projects, city beautification must be considered distinctive from city planning.[3] Weiss contends that the impetus for comprehensive city planning came not from civic officials but from real estate developers creating and planning new residential subdivisions. The emphasis on subdivision or neighborhood planning, he suggests, contrasts sharply with the City Beautiful's focus on refurbishing and replanning the city's older business center through the construction of civic centers, municipal art projects, and street improvements.

Weiss further argues that the sponsorship of City Beautiful and city planning movements differed. With its focus on the central business district, the City Beautiful movement found support from the merchants who owned downtown commercial property. Support for city planning, however, grew from the needs of large real estate developers to ensure the current and future property values of their residential subdivisions. The developers' call for the control of private property led to the defining feature of the city planning movement: creation of federal, state, and local legislation regulating the use of private property. Weiss argues that the first step toward strong municipal control over private property came in the form of zoning legislation and ordinances. This was later followed by a call for comprehensive city management through the creation of citywide master plans. Nowhere in his study does Weiss mention the participation of women in both calling for and working on planning legislation.

Mansel Blackford challenges Weiss's distinction between the City Beautiful movement and the modern city planning movement, as well as Weiss's emphasis on real estate developers. Blackford argues that the strict distinction that Weiss makes between the City Beautiful and city planning does not hold for major metropolitan centers competing for regional dominance. He suggests that efforts at city improvements, begun as City Beautiful projects in the 1890s, coalesced into comprehensive city plans during the Progressive Era. Further, the City Beautiful movement should not be dismissed as a movement solely concerned with cosmetic work on the older inner city. Instead it should be seen as an early tool used by businessmen and boosters to sell their cities. City beautification represented one means to enhance a city's reputation and thus to heighten its appeal. "Beauty and economic growth would develop hand in hand."[4] The City Beautiful matured into comprehensive planning movements as the city elite sought to centralize and coordinate disparate improvement efforts as intercity rivalry on the Pacific Coast intensified with the opening of the Panama Canal. City planning was a means by which to coordinate efforts to lure trade, industry, people, and capital to a community. Suggesting that businessmen viewed planning as "a means to shape their urban environments both economically and socially," Blackford gives businessmen rather than real estate developers primary credit for this movement.[5]

Blackford's study of early city planning in Oakland provides some of the strongest evidence that businessmen were the strength behind West Coast city planning. But Blackford's businessmen were far from a monolithic group. Indeed, he notes that although they were conceived and developed by businessmen, the success or failure to implement the plans depended on politics. City plans could not be imposed on the city's residents. Given that bonds were needed to fund improvements, a plan was either accepted or rejected at the polls. Herein lies the fundamental issue for the city growth machine—could the elite convince the electorate to implement its vision of growth as outlined in a comprehensive city plan? Blackford notes that in Oakland the elite tried to sell its vision through the city's newspapers, its commercial clubs, and its service clubs. What he misses, however, is the important role the city's women played in the passage of bond measures, even before they were granted the power of the vote.

The history of planning in Oakland provides an interesting case study of the process of implementing a city plan and the role of women in that process. Since its incorporation in 1850, the city of Oakland has had grandiose ambitions of becoming the central metropolis for the San Francisco Bay Area, if not for all of Northern California or for the entire Pacific Coast. The ambitions of Oakland, its myriad natural advantages (good climate, natural harbor, abundant natural resources, proximity to the agricultural interior) all suggested that Oakland should become the central metropolis of Northern California rather than San Francisco, which was separated from the interior by the bay.

In most scholarly studies of California's urban development, Oakland has usually been regarded as the poor, ugly stepsister of San Francisco, if discussed at all. Scholars like Kevin Starr paint the California growth process as a competition between San Francisco and Los Angeles for state and regional dominance.[6] Starr suggests that Los Angeles won this competition in part because Los Angeles created a municipally owned water system twenty-one years before San Francisco did. Through the public water system, Los Angeles gained control of Owens Valley water and could manipulate the water resources, and hence politics and municipal growth for the entire Southland. The Los Angeles water elite used water to hold its neighboring cities hostage. It would sell water only if a community agreed to annexation. Thus, between 1913 and 1927, annexation drove growth in the Southland and ensured Los Angeles's domination over the region.

In contrast, Starr continues, once San Francisco obtained municipal control over Hetch Hetchy water, the city did not play the same annexation game that Los Angeles did. Starr implies that the failure of San Francisco to annex its neighbors through control of water relegated it to a secondary status as a core metropolitan center. Starr's Los Angeles/San Francisco dichotomy fails to give credit to cities like Oakland (within the state) and Portland and Seattle (outside the state) that also competed for regional dominance.[7] Furthermore, in Southern California, most cities had accepted Los Angeles as the core metropolis by the 1910s and 1920s, so Los Angeles could focus its competitive energies against San Francisco rather than its closer neighbors. In the north, in contrast, the cities of the East Bay, led primarily by Oakland, did not concede to San Francisco until after the Second World War, if then. In the San Francisco Bay Area, Oakland appeared to be winning the interurban rivalry especially following the 1906 earthquake that leveled San Francisco but left Oakland largely intact. The Oakland elite were unable to capitalize on the opportunity presented by the earthquake and to emerge victorious over San Francisco.

Oakland's close ties to San Francisco and its identification as a suburb of that city date from its founding in the 1850s, when the wealthy from San Francisco crossed the bay only for a few days of picnicking and camping. Several of these early visitors, including George M. Blake, F. K. Shattuck, William Hillegass, and James Leonard, eventually concluded that the East Bay shoreline held its own growth potential and settled there to stay.[8] Yet throughout the 1850s and 1860s, Oakland remained on the San Francisco periphery as a small place where picnickers and hunting parties could find and spend a pleasant day. A few business houses were scattered along Broadway Street, but the majority of Oakland residents did their shopping in San Francisco. Tourist facilities were limited to a few boardinghouses, and banking and manufacturing were largely undeveloped. All in all, Oakland appeared to be a little country village—a suburb of San Francisco.

In the 1870s, however, Oakland entered a boom period of residential development in which the population doubled.[9] Believing that Oakland's destiny lay in its suburban relationship to San Francisco, the emerging Oakland elite started the city along a path of development that would influence planning and advertising in the city for the next seventy years. This elite, led by families such as the Shattucks, Durants, and F. M. Smiths, committed itself to the cultural and intellectual growth of the city, which it perceived complimented the city's residential status. Building upon the natural assets of the East Bay (the beauty and fertility of the hinterland, the mild climate and clean air, and proximity to San Francisco), this elite undertook the construction of roads to connect the burgeoning city to the products of the countryside and to take advantage of the tourist potential in developing routes for affluent motorists. These natural assets provided evidence of Oakland's rapid growth potential and attracted new residents, businesses, and industries. Beginning in the 1880s, the opening of the harbor, the establishment of competitive steamer lines, the construction of a local railway, and the prospect of the terminus of the transcontinental railway being established in the city further supplied Oakland with the tools necessary to play and perhaps win the city growth game.

Throughout the 1880s and 1890s, the Oakland elite, content with the city's secondary status to San Francisco, pursued a growth strategy designed to maintain the city's identification as a San Francisco bedroom suburb. The board of trade advertised the city as "largely a city of homes" where "almost every dwelling is provided with an ever-green lawn and an ever-blooming garden."[10] Given Oakland's identity as a bedroom community, the elite recognized the commercial value of developing the city's natural assets through the creation of an extensive park and boulevard system. Enhancing the rural atmosphere of the city distinguished it from the urban crowding of San Francisco, and by protecting the appearance of the city, members of the elite protected and enhanced the value of their own private property.

The effort to improve upon and add to the city's park and boulevard system thrust Oakland into the modern era of city growth through comprehensive planning that distinguished urban development in the twentieth century.[11] Growth through park development also provided a natural avenue of entry for women into civic affairs. Because of their connection to child rearing, in the context of Victorian social mores, parks and playgrounds appeared to be the natural purview of women. Women could, therefore, learn the language of modern city planning and enter the public arena of civic affairs in an unobtrusive and non-threatening manner. Once they had a foot in the door and a rudimentary knowledge of the language of growth, they could begin to assert themselves publicly without relying on the language of domesticity. Thus, in 1909 women could explain the benefits of playgrounds in terms of how they would protect capitalism and capitalists rather than protecting the home. The "fair play" doctrine of the playgrounds "would result in building up solid 'play fair' business men" who would protect the capitalist class from destructive competition.[12]

Between 1890 and 1910, as the elite began to experiment with the nascent techniques of city planning that characterized Progressive Era city growth, Oakland finally began to break free of its identity as a suburb of San Francisco. The Oakland elite also developed a vision of its city as an independent commercial and financial center so that by 1906 Mayor Frank K. Mott could declare that "Oakland is bound to soon take her place as one of the great cities of the United States."[13] In addition to a continued emphasis on residential growth, the Oakland elite also began pursuing both commercial and industrial developments at this time. Harbor improvements allowed Oakland to take over much of the coastal and foreign trade that had once gone through San Francisco, until by 1910 about 30 percent of the freight tonnage passing through the Golden Gate was handled by Oakland merchants.[14] With better transportation links resulting from the improvements to their harbor and the entrance of additional railroads to their city, Oakland manufacturers were able to increase the scope of their operations and to provide San Francisco and Los Angeles with serious competition for Pacific Coast dominance.

Following in the path of its neighbor San Francisco, Oakland commissioned its first comprehensive city plan in 1906. Under the leadership of Mayor Frank K. Mott, Oakland entered a new era of city growth designed to enhance the residential qualities of the city while at the same time developing the city's commercial potential. In his annual open letter to the city, published January 1, 1906, in the *Oakland Enquirer,* Mayor Mott outlined his plan of action for the year, which included the commercial development of the harbor and waterfront, the beautification of the city's parks, and improvements to the city's streets. Mayor Mott understood that in order to win the population competition of the growth game, the city needed to be attractive to both residents and businesses, and he was unwilling to allow the city's residential neighborhoods to decline only to see the commercial sector grow. He believed that in 1906 Oakland was standing on the verge of metropolitan greatness. "Oakland is bound to soon take her place as one of the great cities of the United States. It would seem as though no human effort could thwart her progress. Oakland's destiny must be ever onward, ever enlarging, ever toward a greater end."[15]

Under the guidance and vision of Mayor Mott, Oakland began to emerge from the shadow of San Francisco. Between 1905 and 1915, when he left office, Mott's vision became Oakland's reality. Motivated by a desire to see Oakland attain her destiny as a leading metropolitan center, in 1906 Mott invited Charles Mulford Robinson to prepare a comprehensive plan for the city's future development. Building upon Oakland's existing reputation as a bedroom suburb of San Francisco and a personal commitment to the idea of the City Beautiful, Robinson's plan dealt mainly with the need for parks and boulevards. Aware of Oakland's rivalry for regional dominance with other Pacific Coast cities, Robinson argued that park development would provide Oakland with a crucial asset. Robinson's emphasis on parks reflected a growing sentiment throughout the country that parks were as crucial to economic development as to social and moral development. Parks could enhance the value of nearby private property, thus boosting the city's tax base. They could also improve a city's economic base by attracting tourists and settlers. As social tools, parks could instill certain values and ways of thinking (the corporate industrial worldview) in those who used them, especially children. Parks could, as well, serve as alternatives to saloons and street gangs. A humanitarian concern could thereby mix with an economic one.[16]

Throughout 1906 and 1907, Robinson's plan received strong endorsements from city councilmen, the *Oakland Enquirer,* and the city's commercial and service organizations. The *Enquirer* entreated "every man and woman who loves this city to get behind the movement to make Oakland the most beautiful city of the Pacific Coast." Noting the fierce competition between Pacific Coast cities, this editorial argued that "the city which offers the largest opportunity for the greatest aesthetic satisfaction and is best adapted to the adjustment of commercial and industrial conditions to the life of the citizen will have the advantage in attracting population and encouraging the investment of capital."[17] For Oaklanders, both men and women, beautification and economic development could not be separated.

As Mayor Mott sought to sell the Robinson plan to Oakland, he took his message not only to the newspapers and the men's clubs but to women's clubs as well. Throughout the fall of 1906, Mott stepped up his campaigning for the plan by visiting several of Oakland's women's clubs, including the Home Club. The women of the Home Club extended a special invitation to the mayor, indicating an interest in civic affairs that extended beyond the stated purpose of the club, namely as a forum in which to discuss issues of home and family. Since the matter affected all Oakland citizens, the women scheduled their meeting for an evening and invited their husbands to attend as well.[18] After explaining the Robinson plan in detail, Mott outlined the bond propositions that would be on the ballot and asked those present for their support. "When that is done we expect all citizens to do their duty, both women and men."[19]

Mayor Mott was also invited to address the Women's Civic Club in early 1907 on the Robinson plan. Unlike the Home Club, the Women's Civic Club was created as a forum from which women could influence city affairs. Founded in 1903, the club quickly immersed itself in the major issues affecting the city. The club oversaw street tree planting, street cleaning, and other city beautification projects before coming to the aid of the mayor in support of the Robinson plan. Like the Home Club, the Women's Civic Club opened this meeting to the public.[20] Mayor Mott urged the women of the city to work for the bonds despite the fact that they did not have the right to vote. Women "ought at least be able to exercise an influence in their own homes and stimulate their husbands and brothers to go to the polls and register their ballots for progress." Playing upon women's domestic concerns, the Mayor argued that "woman's voice . . . is potent in the domestic life and these plans for parks and boulevards in Oakland bear directly upon improved civic conditions which create the environment of the home."[21] As a good politician, Mott understood the need to temper the economic side of the city plan when addressing a female audience. In 1906, gender role constructs prevented him from recognizing a woman's public interests except in terms of domestic issues. That the women of the

Civic Club were concerned with more than just moral issues is evident from the fact that in February 1907 the club heartily endorsed a resolution by the Woman's Parliament of Southern California calling for amendments to the community property law that would provide stronger protections for women's property.[22]

Mayor Mott was not alone in seeking the support of the city's women as the election drew near. He was joined in January 1907 by Councilman Albert H. Elliot, who spoke to a meeting of the city's prominent clubwomen under the auspices of the Home Club.[23] Unlike Mott, however, Elliot addressed the women in terms of both the social and moral benefits of parks and the economic value of the investment. "The price that we pay for these lands will not be too high. Each piece has been submitted to a board of real estate experts who have placed a reasonable value upon it. If the men who own the land will not take these prices, the property may be condemned and the question submitted to a jury. The men who vote for the bonds will be protected." Elliot continued his address by urging the women to influence their husbands to vote for the bonds. "Whatever other election a man may neglect, he should never miss a bond election."[24] When the park bonds passed, Mayor Mott sent a personal letter of appreciation to the women's clubs, thanking them for their support in the campaign.[25]

Mayor Mott's recognition of the power of women in affecting the vote reflected the elite's perception of women's clubs as a cultural, social, and economic asset of the city. The elite did not consider women's clubs as frivolous or mere harmless diversions for women; rather, they were considered an essential resource to be exploited in advertising the city. All of the city's promotional literature stressed the importance of women's clubs in creating a livable and vibrant city that helped attract people of wealth and culture. The elite particularly encouraged the building of women's clubhouses, arguing that "the clubs of Oakland and vicinity are admirably housed, several indeed giving handsome architectural strength to the argument that Oakland has the qualifications for becoming California's metropolis."[26] The women's clubs, including the Ebell, the Home Club, the Oakland Club, the New Century Club, the Book Club, the Vida Scudder Club, the Women's Civic Club, and the Adelphian Club (all in existence in 1906), took it upon themselves to be aware of civic affairs and to participate to the extent possible in civic improvements.[27]

Owing to the social constraints placed on women, most of their work appeared to fall into the traditional category of municipal housekeeping. But if municipal housekeeping was part of the City Beautiful movement pursued by both men and women, perhaps there was an economic purpose beyond the stated moral purposes of women's public work. This is particularly clear considering that municipal housekeeping was not the special sphere of women. Indeed, the *Oakland Enquirer* in editorial after editorial called upon residents to clean up and beautify the city. It is difficult to believe that women were unaware of these editorials and their emphasis on the economics of cleanliness. In 1906, the *Enquirer* argued for the economic value of city cleanliness:

> Prosperity and dirt do not belong together. The glistening engine room of a great factory symbolizes the cleanliness which pays. It costs more to maintain filthy streets than clean streets—only the excess may be obscured. It consists in indirect expenses. Every tradesman in the city is compelled to increase prices in order to cover the value of the goods ruined or injured by smoke or street dust. The consumer pays the increase plus a margin for collection. Every landlord of an office building provides in rents for the excessive sweeping and scrubbing necessitated by the same evils. [28]

This is not a moral argument but an economic one. Perhaps the failure of women to embrace such an argument publicly reflects their immaturity as capitalists rather than their sense of moral superiority.

Prior to gaining suffrage, Oakland women continued to campaign for Mayor Mott's park and boulevard plan both within their clubs and through a growing association with the men's commercial and social clubs, which were also supporting park construction. In 1909, the men's Tri-City Rotary Club became involved in park and playground development. In addition to the potential of playgrounds for developing morally upright citizens who would become morally upright businessmen, they viewed parks as a substantial real estate investment. Recognizing the important role women played in both the passage of bonds and the development and protection of parks and playgrounds, the club invited several prominent women to speak on the issue. Mrs. Cora E. Jones commended the club for its support of playgrounds and noted that the key benefit derived from playgrounds was the creation of good citizens who knew how to play by "the rules." Mrs. A. A. Denison, wife of the secretary of the chamber of commerce, also attended the meeting and suggested that Oakland could achieve greatness only if men and women worked together to enhance the city's park and playground assets.[29]

Following a suggestion put forth by Mrs. G. W. Bunnell of the City Playground Commission, the Tri-City Rotary Club formed a committee of five to petition the city council for greater financial support of the city's playgrounds. John Aubrey Jones, chairman of this committee, began his appeal to the city council by pointing out the social benefits of playgrounds before turning to their economic benefits. He noted that playgrounds "constitute healthful training institutions; training of the mind, the morals and the muscles of the boys and girls who avail themselves of the advantages afforded." In addition, he argued that "for every dollar of the people's money paid for establishing these playgrounds, three dollars will come back, to say nothing of the moral betterment which accrues."[30] The city council, and Mayor Mott personally, heartily endorsed the Rotary Club's petition, indicating that men as well as women believed that moral development went hand in hand with economic development.

Women's influence on planning in Oakland remained that of the petition and of secondary campaigners in bond elections until after 1911, when they earned the right to vote for themselves on bond issues. At the same time, women were expanding their influence in the realm of business and commerce by joining the Oakland Chamber of Commerce and becoming involved in its planning program. In 1915, the chamber of commerce created a planning committee to look into and propose plans for the city's growth and development in light of the opening of the Panama Canal. In February 1915, the chamber held a Better Housing and City Planning exhibit designed to arouse interest in the future development of Oakland. Working with city officials; state representatives; civic, improvement, and women's clubs; and the State Commission of Immigration and Housing, the exhibit was designed to address the need for improving the housing conditions of the working classes. At this time, Commissioner F. C. Turner announced that he would introduce an ordinance for the establishment of a city planning commission in Oakland.[31]

The timing of this new phase of planning coincided with the opening of the Panama Canal and reflected a belief on the part of Oakland citizens that a population boom and housing shortage were imminent. Anticipating the need to control growth in order to sustain it, the chamber of commerce endorsed formalizing planning in Oakland. It believed that Oakland had everything to gain by engaging in comprehensive city management. By managing the housing needs of the population influx; increasing the city's rail capacity; planning ahead for school sites, parks, playgrounds, and main traffic arteries; and particularly planning for the financing of municipal improvements, the chamber of commerce believed that Oakland could win this phase of the city growth game. It therefore encouraged both its male and female membership to campaign for comprehensive planning, zoning, and regulation.

As Oakland entered a new phase of city planning through the creation of a city planning commission in 1914, the city's women took a more activist interest in the issue. By 1915, the vocabulary women used to express their interest in city planning issues had changed. Whereas in the early 1900s they were publicly concerned with beautification and social and moral issues, by 1915 they were openly espousing the economic benefits and drawbacks of planning and working closely with the city's male planners. Particularly noteworthy is the relationship that developed at this time between A. S. Lavenson, chairman of the Oakland Chamber of Commerce City Planning Committee, and Dr. Aurelia Henry Reinhardt, president of Mills College. The two entered into a detailed correspondence on city planning beginning in 1916, and in 1919 Reinhardt was chosen to succeed Lavenson as chairman of the city planning committee.

Although Reinhardt did not personally own property in Oakland, as president of Mills College, her job—and hence financial well-being—relied on the growth and development of the city. In addition, her mother was an Oakland property owner and boardinghouse operator. Reinhardt understood the importance of advertising both the city and the college in order to attract students, just as the city was interested in attracting new residents. Her interests in boosting Mills complemented nicely the booster plans of the Oakland Chamber of Commerce. Lavenson began to groom Reinhardt to succeed him on the city planning committee in 1918. As a member of the executive committee of the California Conference on City Planning, Lavenson made sure that Reinhardt received copies of the conference's activities, including a copy of Charles Henry Cheney's "Procedure for Zoning or Districting of Cities" (1917), which guided state zoning in the coming years. Reinhardt was thus in command of the most recent language of city planning as well as its techniques.[32] In addition, Reinhardt received direct reports from Thomas H. Reid, president of the California Conference on City Planning. He sought her assistance in campaigning for a statewide eminent domain amendment in 1918.[33]

Dr. Aurelia Henry Reinhardt served as president of Mills College, 1916–46, and as chair of the Oakland Chamber of Commerce City Planning Committee, 1919. She is shown here in her office at Mills College. Special Collections, F. W. Olin Library, Mills College.

As Reinhardt served on the city planning committee, she came into close contact with most of the city's leading planners. She frequently met with the city manager, the mayor, the park commissioner, and other male members of the city elite.[34] She received requests to write articles on city planning, such as one from the Santa Fe Improvement As-

This view of Mills College from Prospect Hill shows the undeveloped land around the college, ca. 1916. Special Collections, F. W. Olin Library, Mills College.

sociation entitled "The Need of a City Planning Commission."[35] In 1920, she was named chairman of the parks and playgrounds subcommittee of the city planning committee.[36] Reinhardt's ascendance to the chairmanship of the city planning committee in 1919 marked the culmination of Oakland women's apprenticeship in city planning. It signaled women's arrival as the equals of men as participants in the city growth machine and as speakers of the language of capitalism.

It is significant that the appointment of Dr. Reinhardt to the city planning committee coincided with the consummation of city planning as the tool of choice in the California city growth game. By the First World War, Californians had accepted the theories of comprehensive city planning as the only means by which to ensure economic stability and to engage successfully in Pacific Coast urban competition. The appointment of Dr. Reinhardt to the city planning committee highlights the important role played by women in the development and promotion of West Coast cities in the early twentieth century.

Oakland women were not alone in their efforts to shape a planned future for their city. The women of Riverside played a crucial role in the creation of a city planning commission for that city, and three women even served as commissioners from 1919 to 1921. Riverside created its planning commission in 1915 and became the first Southern California city to do so. The evolution of this commission as a powerful force in Riverside development paralleled that of other planning efforts in the state and across the nation. Although created over twenty years after the City Beautiful movement gained its first real expression in Chicago, the Riverside planning commission embraced the rhetoric of the City Beautiful movement and the booster mentality that went along with it in its early years. It was not until 1921 that the commission grew into a more activist and regulatory agency.

In the 1910s, Riverside was engaged in an intense competition with its sister citrus cities for growth. One of the obvious indicators of success in that campaign was the ability to attract major conventions. In 1914, the Riverside Woman's Club fought an intensely booster-driven battle to attract the Thirteenth Annual Convention of the California Federation of Woman's Clubs to the city. They won, in part, by arguing that Riverside was the "City Beautiful" of Southern California. With the

This view of Mills College shows the encroachment of development around the college, 1927. Special Collections, F. W. Olin Library, Mills College.

date of the convention looming, the women needed to fulfill this promise. Turning to the techniques of city planning, to which they had become familiar through a traveling exhibit on city planning and zoning prepared by Charles H. Cheney, the club organized a special meeting to discuss the club's role in the city and the possibilities of cooperative action with other women's organizations "to better aid in making the city clean and beautiful."[37] Using both the moral and economic rhetoric of the city planning movement, the women took their campaign to city leaders to clean up the city.

The 1914 convention served as a forum for both the women of Riverside and the women of California generally to come into direct contact with the leadership of early California city planning. Among the attendees was Mrs. May L. Cheney, mother of Charles H. Cheney and chairwoman of the California Federation of Women's Clubs' Education Committee. Although her main interest was in education, Mrs. Cheney also crusaded for adoption of City Beautiful ideas in all California cities and for women to spearhead such movements in their own cities. She urged all those in attendance to seek ways to implement the conference's "City Betterment" theme. Other speakers at the conference included Riverside mayor Oscar Ford, who established the city's first planning commission, and the secretary of the California Commission on Immigration and Housing, Carlton H. Parker.

Reflecting the unsteady adoption of the message of the leaders of California's city planning movement, Riverside women, like their male counterparts, did not focus their attention on the creation of a citywide plan or implementation of zoning ordinances that would separate industrial and residential uses in 1914. Still caught up in the booster zeal of the period, they instead focused on the theme of beautification. Looking for a quick fix that would help Riverside win the growth game, they were interested in getting the most benefit out of the least expense. In light of Riverside's history as a citrus city competing for winter tourist dollars, this makes sense as the path of least resistance. In addition, city beautification would be a way to avoid potential conflict over property rights that could destroy the growth coalition and the city's prospects for growth. Thus, combining their efforts with those of the chamber of commerce and the Riverside Business Men's Association, the Riverside Woman's Club chose community boosterism as its primary approach to early city planning.

By early 1915, the Riverside Woman's Club was fully involved in the creation of the first city planning commission. Like their husbands, who were members of the city's citrus elite, the women saw the commission as an opportunity to further the interests of Riverside and its citrus industry. They also followed their husbands in defining the early planning commission in purely booster terms and found no difficulty in identifying a number of city betterment projects they thought appropriate for consideration by the new commission.

Proving a direct connection between the city's women and the creation of a planning commission, the Riverside Woman's Club created a Department of Civic Welfare, which held its first formal meeting only two weeks after the creation of the planning commission. The five members of this committee represented the Riverside citrus elite and the male planning commission elite. Mrs. Bigelow, who represented the interests of one of the area's leading citrus families, served as chairwoman, and Mrs. H. A. Hammond, whose husband sat on the planning commission, served as the committee's recording secretary.

The members of this committee were not merely interested in simplistic beautification schemes. No longer would street tree planting provide the amenities that would continue to attract tourists and possible new residents. They took their time to educate themselves about the nature of problems facing the city that could be alleviated by a planning commission, and they informed themselves about the legalities of the planning commission by a careful discussion of the 1907 city charter. In addition, Mrs. DeNyse prepared a thorough presentation on population statistics and sewage disposal methods before the women identified a number of issues which they felt must be reviewed immediately by the new planning commission and the city council. Still, at the heart of their concerns for the planning commission lay a desire to add "to the attractions that Riverside already [offered] to the eastern tourist." They thus proposed the establishment of a permanent city dump site, the construction of a "public restroom needed for the convenience of the many automobile parties passing through the city each day," and the development of a proper citywide waste and sewage removal system.[39]

For these women, the city waste disposal problem appeared to be of the most concern. Over the years, no permanent location had been found for the city dump. The city routinely moved its dump site from place to place, including a location near the south end of the tourist-attracting Mt. Rubidoux. The city also had an inadequate sewage disposal system. Although Riverside had nearly forty-five miles of sewage lines, the outlet on the west side of the city was a breeding ground for mosquitoes, and on hot summer days it created an extremely offensive odor which threatened to destroy the most carefully orchestrated booster efforts. The women viewed the lack of a permanent dump site, as well as the poor sewage disposal methods, not only as a menace to the community's health but as a menace to its economic viability. It was, they argued, a reflection of "hap-hazard" organization and planning that was completely inappropriate for a competitive city.[40]

The committee's efforts paid off when in 1916 the city council voted unanimously in favor of purchasing 350.94 acres of land from the Riverside Land and Irrigation Company for a sewage farm. Land purchased for this project came from a tract owned by Senator S. C. Evans and was located west of the Santa Ana River. Sewage farms were a popular answer to disposal problems for a number of Southern California cities in the early 1900s. After a period of initial decomposition, waste materials were spread out over a large farming area and served as fertilizer for a wide variety of citrus and nut trees. Fruits and nuts harvested from these sewage farms were then sold to cover the costs of the farm's operation, with any surplus monies going back into city funds. Such farms frequently appeared in city promotional materials, as their use was considered the latest in sewage disposal techniques and could be used to advertise the city's ability to plan for future growth.[41]

In 1919 the Riverside planning commission experienced a fairly significant reorganization. First, the mayor was removed from automatic seating as president of the commission. Second, the city engineer was excluded from membership. Finally, the commission named two women as members.[42] A year later, in 1920, a third woman joined the commission as well.

All three women represented the Riverside citrus elite and the Riverside Woman's Club. Laura A. L. Turner, wife of George Turner, had been a longtime member of the Riverside Woman's Club and was involved in that organization's lobbying efforts to establish a city planning commission as well as efforts to bring a Citrus Farm School to Riverside. Sara Curtis was also a club member from 1914 to 1916. Edith Bishop, the third member, appointed in 1920, was married to John L. Bishop, president of the Highgrove Orange Growers Association and had served for a number of years as president of the Woman's Club.[43]

Unfortunately, by the time women finally joined the planning commission, the commission had entered a period of transition marked by a low public profile and relatively limited decision-making abilities. Between 1918 and 1921 the commission's only major project proved to be approval of a new city hall project to be located at the corner of Seventh and Orange streets. In a clear tie to the Woman's Club, the commission expressed "particularly their approval of the comfort station facilities" promoted by the Woman's Club. The only other significant project for this period was passage of a proposed subdivision map for the Casa Blanca neighborhood.[44]

This brief four-year period marked the culmination of a time when Riverside citizens viewed the role of the planning commission exclusively as a booster organization. After 1921 the commission began a slow but steady move away from boosterism toward the acceptance of a new role centered upon the utilization of the new zoning and planning theories espoused by consultant Charles H. Cheney.

Despite the limitations of the early Riverside Planning Commission, the appointment of women to the commission highlights the role women played in the development and promotion of California cities in the early twentieth century. As members of the Riverside Woman's Club and the local booster community, these women worked closely with their male counterparts to promote and develop their city. Because of their gender, however, they were denied full participation in the political expression of their boosterism, and as a result, urban historians have failed to recognize their efforts and contributions.

Redlands clubwomen also became increasingly interested in city planning in the 1910s and 1920s and expressed this interest primarily through the work of the Contemporary Club. In 1910, the club took the significant step of sending two representatives, Jennie Davis and Katherine Meigs, to the City Planning Conference in Los Angeles.[45] Davis returned from this conference advocating the creation of an active civic league or improvement league to be formed within the club.[46] Within a year, the club's interest in city planning had extended to the point of discussing a subscription to the National Municipal League's *National Municipal Review*.[47]

Throughout the 1920s, the club showed an increased interest in city selling and city planning. It worked closely with the chamber of commerce on a variety of projects and invited the city's advertising agent to address the club.[48] In addition, Gordon Whithall, city planner of Los Angeles, was invited to present a program to the club on some of the problems Los Angeles faced and how to "make Redlands all that her loyal citizens wish her to be."[49] In 1924, the club sent a resolution to the city trustees, the chamber of commerce, and the *Redlands Facts* calling for fair zoning to protect investments.

> Whereas, The early enthusiasm and inexperience of most small municipalities has caused great and costly mistakes, and the subsequent expensive reconstruction could have been saved by the exercise of calm deliberation and timely restrictive legislation. And,
>
> Whereas, Many cities in the United States are levying heavy assessments to raise vast sums of money to redeem valuable franchises rashly conceded, natural resources needlessly sacrificed, and building privileges carelessly granted in the confused desire and inducement to stimulate rapid growth. And,
>
> Whereas, The constant and reliable increase in population of Southern California justifies the prediction that both manufacturing and residential centers of reputation are destined to become large cities. And,
>
> Whereas, There is sufficient foundation to warrant the opinion that our well established Redlands will participate in the general prosperity of this alluring "Southland" and will in the near future be obliged to consider more extensive and varied Industrial and Housing (flats) applications and proposition. And,
>
> Whereas, We deem it not only precautionary but a civic duty to call the attention of the City Council, Chamber of Commerce, Real Estate Board, Merchants Association, and all public dealing organizations to what is being enacted in other cities to govern building operations, locations and uses. Now, therefore, be it
>
> Resolved, That we, the Contemporary Club of Redlands, take this means of urging the passage of a fair zoning ordinance, now while it can be done without cost to taxpayers or injury to individual and safeguard the investments of our citizens before contentions and influences arise to prejudice our judgment.[50]

The chamber of commerce particularly endorsed this petition, stating that "a city planning commission [should] be organized at the earliest possible time to study and propose the best means to preserve and extend the beauty of our city, as well as to preserve values and foster proper expansion and orderly growth."[51]

As the city developed a comprehensive plan in the mid-1920s, the club kept current on the issues of the day. In April 1926, Mayor Allen Wheaton addressed the club on the "needs of Redlands," and Hugh H. Pomeroy, secretary of the Los Angeles regional planning commission, discussed "what city and county planning means and why."[52] Mayor Wheaton noted improvements made in the fire department, the municipal plunge, and street repaving. He discussed the desire of the city board of trustees to create an adequate zoning ordinance, the beautification of the Zanja, and the restoration of the old mission, all of which would draw people to the area. Mr. Pomeroy, in turn, discussed the tremendous population growth of Southern California and the absolute need of keeping pace with it by planning ahead in both city and county affairs, building more and broader highways and buying up country acreage while reasonable for future parks, "thus saving enormous waste in tearing down what the past generation has unwittingly and extravagantly built up."[53]

Since Redlands was primarily a residential city, the club was particularly concerned with enacting zoning laws that would affect residential property values. As the business district began to expand into residential areas, the club passed a resolution demanding that zoning ordinances be enacted to protect property values.

> Whereas, it is the strong belief of the members now assembled in regular meeting that the opening of stores or other places of business in the residence portion of the city would detract much from its general beauty and greatly impair the value of contiguous property, Therefore, be it Resolved that we appeal to the Board of Trustees to prevent by proper restrictions opening of stores or other places of business in the residence sections of the city so that owners of homes may be saved from loss by impairment of values to their property by reason of such places of business adjacent to residences.[54]

The passage of resolutions such as these placed women firmly in the center of public affairs and city planning in Redlands. Far from representing a separate "female" vision, their demands fit with those of male planners. In recognition of their contributions, the mayor requested the club to appoint a representative to the city zoning board. In November 1926, Mary Pettibone Smith became that representative and thus the liaison between the club and the city.[55] She was succeeded by Mary K. Shirk, then president of the Contemporary Club and daughter of Helen Kimberly.[56] At about the same time, the club also appointed representatives to the Redlands Realty Board and the chamber of commerce.

Because women's historians have chosen to focus on the political evolution of women and urban historians have accepted the separate-spheres dichotomy, the contributions of women to city planning have gone unnoticed. Even with the substantive research of women's historians, we continue to take as gospel the view expressed by Alan Dawley that the early twentieth century was a "period of separate spheres, with the women involved in home and church as an expression of selfless virtue and the men involved in the market and politics in pursuit of self-interest."[57] On the surface, this may appear to be true, but an examination of the activities of Oakland, Riverside, and Redlands women indicates that particularly for property-owning clubwomen, the separation of spheres may not have been so clearly defined. In these cities, the women and men of the capitalist class came together in an informal yet highly effective partnership toward the achievement of shared goals. Economic and social freedom allowed a significant number of California women to stand on a more equal footing with their male counterparts and to expand their influence beyond the home and into the community. It is important to note that in their use of both City Beautiful and city-planning rhetoric, women's groups, chambers of commerce, and the newspapers all shared the goals of enhancing and protecting property values within the city. These goals extended the moral reform rhetoric of the Progressive Era into a movement to extend the language of capitalism and to protect the capitalist class. This is the fundamental issue of Progressive Era city growth.

CHAPTER SIX

City and County Planning in Santa Barbara

One of the primary reasons that women have not been adequately studied as members of the growth machine or as contributors to the modern city planning movement lies in their relative invisibility. Their work, as exemplified by the stories of planning in Oakland, Riverside, and Redlands, has predominantly been behind the scenes. They have been perceived as gentle agitators on the sidelines, motivated primarily by domestic and maternal concerns. In addition, because their public crusades generally came in the form of women's club petitions, they have not been situated in any obvious position of power relative to official city government. Such was not the case, however, in Santa Barbara, where real city planning took place neither in official city council meetings nor in city planning commissions, but in the private nonprofit Community Arts Association headed by Pearl Chase.

In the 1920s and 1930s, Pearl Chase took women's mastery of city planning to new heights of influence. Through her work with the Plans and Planting Committee of the Community Arts Association, Chase personally guided the development of both a city and a county plan for Santa Barbara. Building upon the City Beautiful tradition, Chase worked to make Santa Barbara the most aesthetically pleasing city on the West Coast. She recognized that the Santa Barbara tourist economy relied on developing the region's natural and historical assets rather than on industrial development. In addition, she found that by working within the context of female moral authority and domesticity she could achieve far greater influence over city growth than through political activism. She masterfully blended the language of capitalism with the language of female moral authority to realize her vision for the city and region over a fifty-year period.

Pearl Chase, ca. 1910. As a young woman returning home from the University of California, Berkeley, Chase resolved to work for the beautification of her hometown. Santa Barbara Trust for Historic Preservation.

In a city such as Santa Barbara, intent upon maintaining affluence as well as growth, the language of female moral authority became a particularly powerful tool. Women like Pearl Chase found a citizenry open to appeals to aesthetics and beauty because they would protect the lifestyle and unique atmosphere for which the elite were willing to pay top dollar. Prior to the 1910s, real estate development had proceeded primarily along the lines of large private estates rather than in smaller subdivisions. Thus, the city tended to attract wealthy retirees and eastern capitalists seeking a haven from harsh winters. In this setting a tradition of elite family involvement in city affairs developed. Seeking to enhance both personal wealth and quality of life, families like the De La Guerras, the Dens, the Fernalds, and the Storkes gave generously of time and money to civic improvements and city beautification. The women of these families found a niche for themselves in this environment as city beautifiers and charitable volunteers.

When smaller real estate subdivisions began to emerge in the 1910s and 1920s, it was natural to build upon the aesthetic tradition begun by these early families. Pearl Chase could also build upon the tradition of wealthy women property owners working for charitable city improvements. Believing that a nonprofit, nonpolitically aligned citizens' group could provide greater continuity and a stronger inducement to follow a city plan than traditional politics, Chase chose to pursue her vision in the context of female volunteerism. She could often achieve more through "righteous indignation poured on thick" than any other means.[1] Nonetheless, as the daughter of the city's leading subdivider in the 1910s and 1920s, and a property owner in her own right, Chase clearly understood the economic value of her volunteer work. Her story, therefore, represents the maturation of women civic volunteers as capitalists, visionaries, and planners, and hence as members of the growth machine.

The work of Pearl Chase, and Santa Barbara women generally, complemented the interests of the city's male elite in designing an attractive, affluent community and in building upon the city's Hispanic tradition. Santa Barbara first began to reenvision the city in terms of its Hispanic past following the centennial of Mission Santa Barbara in 1886. The value of this past was supplemented by the publication in 1896 of Sarah Higgins's scholarly study of the Aguirre Adobe and her crusade for its restoration. While little actual preservation took place at this time, the seeds of a preservationist impulse that would come to characterize the city's planning and growth strategy had been sown.

Starting in 1909, the Santa Barbara elite began to embrace the city's Hispanic past with ardor. In that year, the Civic League initiated an effort to restore the De La Guerra Adobe and create for the city a historical museum and art center. Members of the league viewed the adobe and the De La Guerra family as the prime example of the elite heritage of Mexican Santa Barbara. They pursued a preservation strategy that would create a cultural attraction unique to the city. In the process, they would demonstrate that Santa Barbara was more than a rural backwater. As a city of culture, Santa Barbara attracted citizens who embraced the past to ensure the future. During the next decade, private citizens joined the Civic League's preservation crusade. In 1917 Mrs. Gardiner C. Hammond purchased and remodeled the Hill-Carrillo Adobe into an art studio and tearoom. In 1919 Bernhard and Irene Hoffmann purchased the De La Guerra Adobe, the Casa La Aguirre, and adjacent

State Street, the major thoroughfare in Santa Barbara, ca. 1880. The Community Arts Association worked to replace this frontier architecture with a mission style more fitting to the topography and history of the city. Santa Barbara Trust for Historic Preservation.

plaza properties and commissioned James Osborne Craig to restore and construct a Spanish-style streetscape. They followed this in 1922 with the acquisition and remodeling of the Lugo Adobe to create a headquarters for the Plans and Planting Committee of the Community Arts Association. In the same year, Louise Murphy Vhay, another powerful member of the Plans and Planting Committee, restored the Ramirez Adobe as her private residence. This preservation fever was supplemented by a flurry of new construction in Spanish revival architecture for both commercial and residential buildings. Once again the elite used the Hispanic past to attract new residents and new tourists.

Santa Barbara's appropriation of its Hispanic past was not unique to Southern California. It reflected a growing movement throughout the region, commencing in the 1880s, to capitalize on the past in order to attract tourists and permanent residents. Beginning with the publication of Helen Hunt Jackson's *Ramona* in 1884, the mission legend of Southern California took shape, only to be reworked to fit the needs of specific communities. By the early 1900s, most cities held some sort of fiesta and had adapted mission-style architecture in their public buildings. Noting that the publication of *Ramona* coincided with the real estate boom of the 1880s, Carey McWilliams argues that the rediscovery of the Hispanic past supplemented the booster rhetoric of the region's real estate developers. At about the same time, the region's leading booster and preservationist, Charles Lummis, formed the Association for the Preservation of the Missions, which later became the California Landmarks Club.[2] Thus, for Southern Californians regionally, historic preservation and Hispanicization became a commercial tool to exploit as part of the city growth game.

In many respects Southern California's appropriation of history as a planning tool places the region in the vanguard of both the modern preservation and city planning movements. Nationally, historic preservation evolved from a grassroots movement led by private efforts to save individual buildings to a public policy codified in the National Historic Preservation Act of 1966. In the nineteenth century, preservation efforts were aimed chiefly at buildings in which great men had lived or in which great events had taken place. Buildings were esteemed based on associational value to the man or event, not for their architectural merit. The preservation of Mount Vernon in the 1850s set the stage for future preservation work around the country. It established a pattern of private initiative, women's involvement, and a focus on saving individual landmark buildings for patriotic purposes.[3] It was not until the mid-twentieth century that the nation began to seriously consider preservation based on architectural significance or to value historic districts as part of a comprehensive city plan.

As the twentieth century dawned, preservation continued to be dominated by an elite, which by this time was more concerned with moral decay caused by corruption and materialism than with simple patriotism. In light of perceived threats to capitalism and American society from Gilded Age excesses and a new influx of immigrants, preservationists suggested that the nation's historic infrastructure could provide an antidote to cultural decay by instilling in visitors a militant loyalty to America. At the same time, however, preservation lacked any true national scope, and it instead became a means by which regions could defend themselves against the cultural dominance of the East. Southerners and westerners thus became interested in their own histories and their own great men and to cultivate that identity as a regional selling point. This period also bequeathed to the future a limited understanding of how historic structures should be presented to the public. As part of the effort to indoctrinate visitors into a middle-class American worldview, historic house museums and commemorative plaques avoided controversy and played down any unanswered questions.

The early twentieth century did witness a few efforts at architecturally motivated preservation, particularly in New England, when William Sumner Appleton founded the Society for the Preservation of New England Antiquities (SPNEA) in 1910. Although not as successful in terms of actual preservation as the SPNEA, Charles Lummis's Landmarks Club exerted a powerful cultural influence over Southern California. By the early twentieth century nearly every city in Southern California had undertaken some local preservation of the Hispanic past. The Landmarks Club's most significant contribution, however, was to popularize Spanish-American or mission revival architecture. In a unique way Southern California developed a historical identity based on new building construction in an old style. Unlike the historic districts of Boston, Newport, or Charleston (most of which were not formally recognized until the 1930s and 1940s), in which new buildings were designed to enhance an existing neighborhood design, Southern California created neighborhood design to fit a small number of missions and to fulfill the mission legend embodied in *Ramona*. This reached its greatest expression in Santa Barbara, where preservation developed from an emphasis on restoring individual adobes to preserving a way of life, however constructed or mythological that might be. The Santa Barbara vision of preservation sought to "remake" the city, not as a shrine to the past, but as a city of the future grounded firmly in the past through architectural control.

In Santa Barbara, the Hispanic identity achieved its first token of official recognition in 1909, when Charles Mulford Robinson designed a city master plan around the mission, the Plaza De La Guerra, and the Potter Hotel. He envisioned Santa Barbara as a resort city and recommended that the city avoid industrialization. Robinson was one of the foremost American city planners in the early 1900s. As a champion of the City Beautiful movement, Robinson believed that comprehensive plans should embrace the past as well as the future. In 1903, he published what became the bible of the City Beautiful movement, *Modern Civic Art, or the City Made Beautiful*. By the time Santa Barbara commissioned a plan by Robinson, the Great White City of the 1893 Chicago World's Fair had convinced most civic leaders of the growth potential behind city planning.[4] In addition, Robinson had successfully completed plans for the Spanish-style quadrangle at Stanford University, and Frank Miller's Mission Inn in Riverside had proved the value in tourist dollars of investing in Spanish-style architecture.

Although rejected by the city in 1909, Robinson's vision and plan came to prevail in Santa Barbara politics over the next fifteen years. Under the leadership of Pearl Chase and Irene and Bernhard Hoffmann, the nonprofit Community Arts Association provided the vehicle through which the basic Hispanic vision of the Robinson Plan could finally be implemented. By building upon its nonprofit, nonpolitically aligned status, as well as upon the language of moral authority, this group of preservationists developed an incredible amount of local political power. As Kevin Starr has argued, "the Association captured Santa Barbara, politically, bringing the community under the control of a coherent group of affluent, genteel, preservationist-minded citizens who forced their will, quietly but effectively, on the community for the next two decades."[5]

The Community Arts Association began innocently enough as an organization created to enhance the cultural life of the city through sponsorship of music, drama, and art programs. Reflecting the cultural aspirations of the Santa Barbara elite, the association's membership included Edward Payson Ripley (Santa Fe Railroad), David E. Perkins (Akron Rubber), George Owen Knapp (Union Carbide), various members of the De La Guerra family, John James Hollister, Fanny Van de Grift Osbourne Stevenson, and Adele Herter. The real power of the organization, however, rested in the hands of Pearl Chase and Irene and Bernhard Hoffmann, who expanded the association's interests to include city planning and beautification.

Owing to the broader interests of the Chase-Hoffmann inner circle, the association enlarged its scope in 1922 through the creation of the influential Plans and Planting Committee. With a Carnegie Foundation grant of twenty-five thousand dollars, this organization entered into an experimental project of civic improvements designed to serve as a model for other cities. With Bernhard Hoffmann serving as chairman of the committee and Pearl Chase as secretary, the Plans and Planting Committee embarked on a comprehensive program of beautification and civic improvements that fundamentally reshaped Santa Barbara in the Hispanic tradition.[6] The success of these improvements and the moral authority invoked by committee rhetoric soon led to virtual community-wide support for association projects. The vision of the Chase-Hoffmann circle became so powerful that the Plans and Planting Committee became a de facto city planning commission. Santa Barbara thus became a preservationist-controlled city.

Throughout the early 1920s, when cities like Charleston were just beginning to create historic districts, the Plans and Planting Committee pushed through the political system its plan to redesign the entire city of Santa Barbara in the Hispanic tradition. At the same time, and at the urging of the committee, Santa Barbara established a city planning commission in 1923 and hired Charles H. Cheney as consultant. Cheney drafted a comprehensive building zone ordinance, which the city council adopted in May 1924. As evidence of the power of the Plans and Planting Committee, this measure gave the committee official authority over the city's future development. Cheney and his associates were required by law to report to the committee as well as to elected and appointed officials, treating them as coequal authorities. A nonelective, nonappointive citizens' committee now had the same power and legitimacy as the city's duly elected officials. Much in the same way as the water oligarchy of the Department of Water and Power oversaw Los Angeles's growth, the architecture oligarchy of Santa Barbara maintained tight control over that city's future development.

Pearl Chase saw no problem with the less-than-democratic nature of the relationship between city government and the citizens' group. Just as the water oligarchy provided continuity for Los Angeles policy, Chase viewed the Plans and Planting Committee as the guardian of the Santa Barbara vision. "Government officials," she once said, "are really temporary—they come and go—and this constant turnover means that many citizen organizations have far greater continuity and relative importance in community affairs."[7] Thus Chase achieved a far greater influence over community development and the Santa Barbara growth machine by remaining outside of traditional politics.

The most significant feature of the Plans and Planting program prior to a massive earthquake in 1925 was its campaign to educate the public as to the value of good building practices and architectural harmony. When the June 1925 earthquake leveled most of the buildings on State Street, this committee and many of its supporters convinced city officials of the need for an Architectural Board of Review to supervise reconstruction efforts. The success of their control effort and the personal involvement of Pearl Chase provide evidence both of the vision of the Santa Barbara elite and of the economic and commercial motivations behind a nonprofit beautification program.

Our Lady of Sorrows Catholic Church, destroyed in the 1925 earthquake, was built in an architectural style that did not fit the Community Arts Association's vision for Santa Barbara, 1925. Santa Barbara Historical Society.

Working within the context of the Santa Barbara vision, Pearl Chase quietly but effectively imposed her own vision on the city in the 1920s and 1930s. Drawing upon both her family and her community heritage, Chase's vision for Santa Barbara's growth followed a three-step process. First, Chase sought to beautify the lower-income neighborhoods of Santa Barbara that had been neglected by other improvement projects. To this end, she created a small house design program for Plans and Planting that eventually merged with the Better Homes of America contests in the mid-1920s. Second, Chase believed that architectural harmony would create a more aesthetically pleasing city that would attract more tourists and residents. She thus supported the creation of an Architectural Board of Review following the June 1925 earthquake, and she engaged in other public education campaigns extolling the economic and aesthetic virtues of good architecture. Third, Chase believed in home ownership. She crusaded for the building of more quality small homes in Santa Barbara and worked to educate the public about the entire process of home buying and building.

To attain her goals, Chase understood that she had to engage in a grassroots movement of public education and cooperation. Drawing upon her social connections, she created a network of support for her projects that included the chamber of commerce, the Real Estate Board, the Building and Loan Associations, the Woman's Club, and other members of the city elite. She also took her education campaign to the local schools and the Boy Scouts to initiate the next generation into her vision. Working within the context of her assigned gender role and employing the language of female moral authority, Chase successfully guided the development of Santa Barbara for over fifty years. In some respects, she became the nexus of the city's growth machine.

In later years, Chase would state that her interest in city improvements began while she was an undergraduate at the University of California at Berkeley. Upon a visit home in 1907, she remembered "how ashamed I was of the dust and dirt and ugly buildings here and I resolved to do what I could to improve Santa Barbara."[8] Yet Chase's interest was not entirely self-defined. She was clearly the product of both her time and her environment. While a student at Berkeley from 1905 to 1909, Chase made frequent visits to San Francisco. She witnessed first-hand the destruction of the 1906 earthquake and the subsequent efforts to rebuild. Her diaries indicate that the architecture and style of the city influenced her vision for Santa Barbara.[9] In addition, during Chase's tenure at Berkeley, the campus experienced a wholesale transformation as the state implemented Phoebe Hearst's architectural plan for the university. She thus observed a woman working to realize a vision and a comprehensive architectural plan for a community.

Upon returning home from college, Chase joined the Santa Barbara Woman's Club just as it was expanding its interest in civic affairs. As the daughter of one of Santa Barbara's leading citizens, she expected to engage in volunteer and charitable activities as part of her social training. Chase also came from a family recognized by one historian as the leading family of civic improvers of Santa Barbara.[10] In addition to the real estate subdivisions that her father and brother developed and sold, the family contributed to the establishment of a bird refuge, the beautification of the waterfront, the expansion of the Cottage Hospital, and the development of the Community Arts Association. Although her mother died in 1913, Pearl learned from her example how to work for civic improvements and the importance of women's volunteer work for community growth and development.

Becoming her father's "apprentice" after her mother's death, Pearl became intimately involved in his private business affairs. She also became the owner of the family home on Anacapa Street two years before her father's death in 1951.[11] Although she did not work in his office, her preparation of a history of the H. G. Chase Real Estate Company for the Santa Barbara Real Estate Board indicates her connection to her father's business and her sense that her civic improvement work contributed to his success.[12] Indeed, there is no doubt that Chase's volunteer civic work indirectly affected her father's real estate business. As Santa Barbara's national reputation grew through her winning Better Homes and Garden Tour campaigns, more and more tourists and settlers approached the H. G. Chase company to help them find homes.

Chase's vision of Santa Barbara was clearly influenced by her apprenticeship with her father. Her emphasis on cooperation, consensus building, and beautification emulated his business practices. During his long career in real estate, Hezekiah Chase taught both his son and his daughter the importance of cooperation and integrity in the business world. As early as 1908, Hezekiah sought to ease the threat of ruinous competition in the real estate market by organizing a Santa Barbara Real Estate Board. The board set standards for commissions, rental prices, and loan rates that helped to preserve both property values and the upper-class character of the city. Hezekiah also served as a charter member of the California Real Estate Federation and later as a director and vice president. Representing real estate, he became a charter member of the Santa Barbara Rotary Club, and in 1927 he had his firm join The Interchange, a national cooperating realty group. When Hezekiah died in 1951, he was remembered as a community builder and a "one-man chamber of commerce." He sold property in Santa Barbara and vicinity by "selling" the region.[13] From his example, Pearl learned the value of cooperation and of selling a community, not just a piece of property.

In addition to her father's example, Chase gained practical experience in cooperation through her work in the 1910s with the county Social Service Conference. As part of a nationwide Progressive movement for social and moral reform, Chase's experiences were probably typical of most middle- and upper-class, college-educated women. According to historian Roseanne Barker, this social service work, specifically with the Santa Barbara Mexican poor, provided the environment in which Chase developed her comprehensive plan for neighborhood and community development. Through this plan she could simultaneously improve the lives of the city's poor and beautify the city.[14] Under the auspices of the Community Arts Association, in 1923 Chase began her work in small house design that became her lifelong crusade. As part of this program, Chase sought to standardize architectural design for all Santa Barbara buildings, whether large mansions, downtown shops, or small homes. She believed that by making small house plans available at a reasonable cost, home builders would embrace the Santa Barbara architectural style. "One can go to an architect and secure the beauty of line in detail that is so essential for a perfect whole but the majority of persons can ill afford architectural service—or in some cases would not appreciate it if they could. This is the class we are trying to influence."[15] Chase viewed the issue of small house design in terms of class. She sought to influence the middle and lower classes of Santa Barbara to embrace her vision (the elite vision) of a city of unsurpassed architectural beauty. This would enhance the value of their property and protect both her property and class interests.

For Chase, architectural harmony and the beautification of lower-income residential neighborhoods proceeded hand in hand. At the same time that she served as secretary and chairman of Plans and Planting, she also entered Santa Barbara in the national Better Homes in America contest. Initiated in 1922, Better Homes in America was a national movement to build and improve private residences. At its heart, the program sought to extend the City Beautiful beyond the civic center and downtown business district to residential sections. Capitalizing on social mores that assigned the domestic sphere to women, Better Homes became an ideal avenue of entry for a generation of women into the city growth game. Previous historical studies of Better Homes have placed the movement in the context of the rise of women as municipal housekeepers.[16] Indeed, contemporary women leaders of Better Homes invoked the language of municipal housekeeping to justify their work and call other women to arms. Yet, if we look at the motto of the National Committee for Restriction of Outdoor Advertising, a female-headed organization that contributed to Better Homes, we find evidence of ulterior motives: "We urge the confinement of all display advertising to commercial locations where it will not injure scenery, civic beauty or *residential values*" (emphasis added).[17] This motto is not surprising considering that women were increasingly owning property in this period, both private homes and rental property. Perhaps the Better Homes movement was more an expression of women's capitalist motivations to improve the value of their property than a public manifestation of domesticity.

In addition, Better Homes can be interpreted in terms of the rise of modern subdivision development. In their study of Hamilton, Ontario, Michael Doucet and James Weaver found that the Canadian Better Homes movement was designed "to educate the average renter into the method and means of ownership."[18] Developing in the 1920s, the Better Homes movement coincided with new forms of financing for home ownership, such as the low down payment and the extended mortgage that revolutionized home ownership for the lower classes. The market had to be expanded, and people had to be convinced that buying was cheaper than renting. Better Homes fulfilled that need. At the same time, the domestic imperatives of the women involved in Better Homes ensured that as the lower classes bought property they would be introduced to the middle-class lifestyle that the middle class believed was crucial to maintaining property values. If the lower classes were to be introduced into the ranks of home ownership, they needed to be indoctrinated into the middle-class worldview.

As Chase succeeded with individual small house design in Santa Barbara, she enlarged her vision to take in both the outside of the home and the appearance of entire neighborhoods. This approach of "environmental design," as she called it, expanded her crusade to vacant lots, sidewalk repair, tree trimming, and all-round general cleanup.[19] It also placed her in the forefront of the subdivision movement to create planned communities. By the 1920s, as competition in the real estate market increased, land developers found that they had to sell services and communities as well as land. As a student of human nature, Chase observed that improving the aesthetic side of life in one neighborhood caused people in other neighborhoods to respond positively. The combined efforts of the elite working with the lower classes to clean up the city bridged the gap between the rich and poor and helped build a tremendous sense of community in Santa Barbara. Furthermore, Chase noted, well-tended homes and yards tended to discourage vandalism, which was a constant threat to property values.[20]

Roseanne Barker argues that Chase's motivation for this program stemmed from her earlier social work and her feminine domestic con-

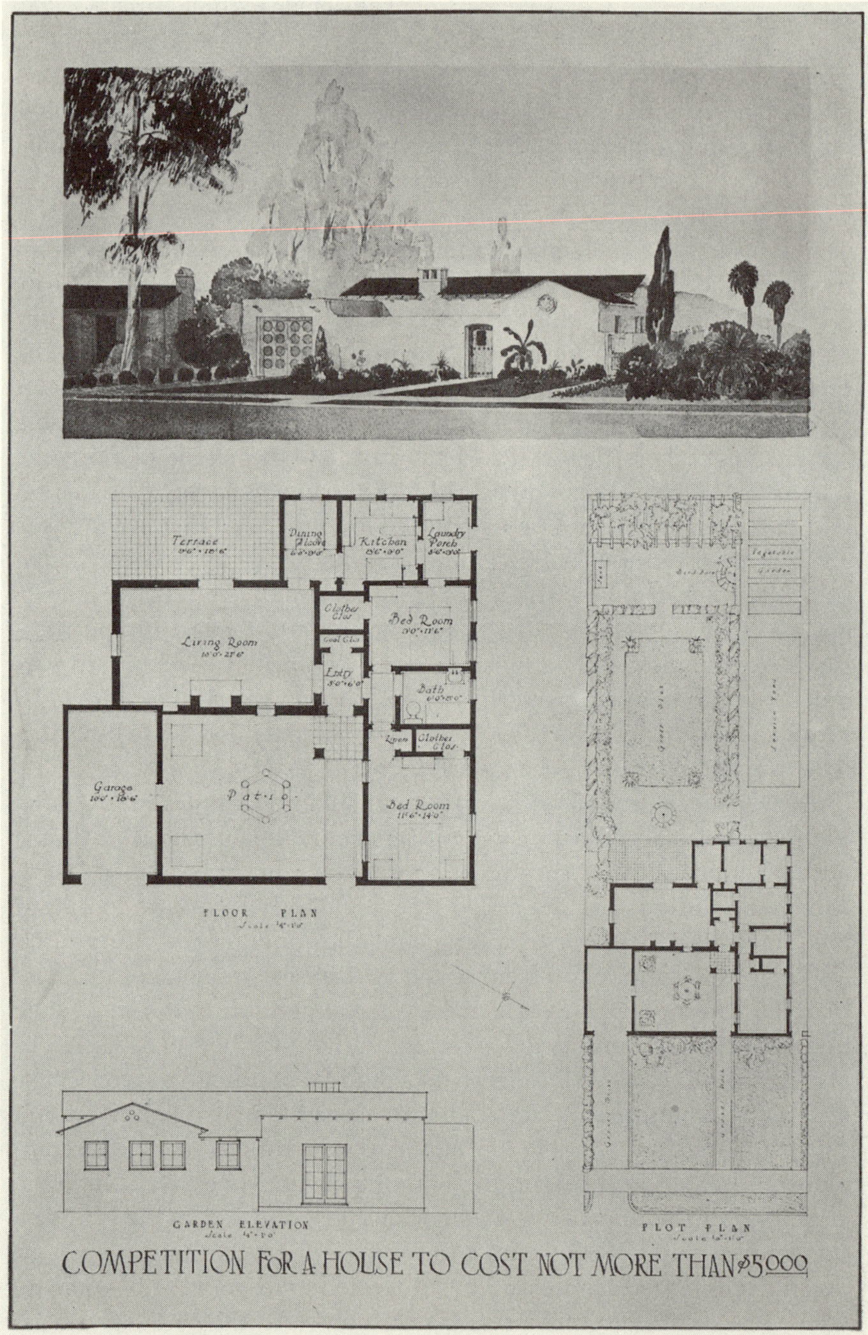

An example of the small house design competition sponsored by the Santa Barbara Better Homes in America competition. From *Report of Competition on Designs for Small Houses by the Community Arts Association, Santa Barbara*, 1923. Santa Barbara Trust for Historic Preservation.

This physician's office in Santa Barbara reflects both the scale and style of the Community Arts Association's architectural vision for the city, ca. 1930. Santa Barbara Trust for Historic Preservation.

cerns.[21] While Chase clearly recognized that as a woman she would be more accepted as a crusader for home design rather than business design, it should be pointed out that her father emphasized residential real estate over commercial buildings in his business.[22] In addition, many of the houses built for demonstration purposes in Better Homes were built in the Hope Ranch subdivision, developed by her brother, Harold S. Chase. Considering the close relationship between Chase and her father and brother, it is logical to assess her interest as an extension of their business interests and thus as an effort to enhance her family's economic security. Furthermore, the small house design projects of the Community Arts Association were not separated from the larger goals of citywide beautification. The precursor to the small house design competition of 1923 was a 1922 design contest that included both remodeled business structures and small residences. The Plans and Planting Committee sponsored the contest to "stimulate an interest in the community in more harmonious and artistic and fitting buildings and dwellings in Santa Barbara."[23] These competitions demonstrated the vision of the Santa Barbara elite that Spanish revival architecture should be *the* style for the city and should be available to all classes and income levels.

As Santa Barbara's reputation grew following its 1926 win in the Better Homes competition, Chase was well aware that the city was making a name for itself. For a city whose main source of income was tourism, and for the daughter of the city's leading realtor, these accolades were essential to growth and prosperity. Organizations such as the chamber of commerce and the Realtors' Board took note of Chase and her accomplishments and accordingly contributed to future Better Homes programs and courted Chase as a favorite speaker.

That Chase's vision of a beautiful Santa Barbara extended beyond altruism is evident in her correspondence with these civic groups. Through both subtle pressure and outright coercion, Chase convinced all of the city's major civic organizations to contribute to her Better Homes campaigns and to the work of the Plans and Planting Committee. By the 1930s, if Chase did not acknowledge publicly the economic value of her work, the city's male elite did. In 1931, the board of directors of the Santa Barbara Builders' Exchange conferred upon Chase an honorary membership in their organization in recognition of her contributions to the Santa Barbara economy.

> WHEREAS, It has been the observation of the Board of Directors of the Santa Barbara Builders' Exchange, that Miss Pearl Chase, Chairman of the Plans and Planting Branch of the Community Arts Association of Santa Barbara, has co-operated in the past with the Builders' Exchange in every way possible in helping this organization realize its aims and purposes; and has striven to further the best interests of the Builders' Exchange as zealously as if she had in fact been a member of said organization, and,
>
> WHEREAS, We have also noted, with a high appreciation, her manifold and fruitful labors for the welfare and beautification of the City of Santa Barbara, now, therefore,
>
> BE IT RESOLVED, That, in a grateful sense and in consideration of the many services which she has rendered to this organization, we hereby declare Miss Pearl Chase to be an Honorary Member of the Santa Barbara Builders' Exchange.[24]

The Santa Barbara Real Estate Board also expressed its appreciation for Chase's work in 1931. W. C. Paulton, president of the board and an agent of the H. G. Chase Company, wrote to Chase to thank her for organizing a Home Inspection Tour under the auspices of the Plans and Planting Committee. Although it was led by Winsor Soule, an architect, and L. L. Pope, the city building inspector, Chase, as chairman of Plans and Planting, had created the program. Paulton noted the value of such a program for both realtors and prospective clients, stating, "that much valuable information was obtained relative to architecture and the requirements of the City Building Department of this city. Tours of this nature cannot help but be beneficial to Realtors, as well as present and prospective home owners."[25]

Chase's expertise lay in her ability to find the right argument to convince a group of people to support her plans, and this is what made her an essential part of the Santa Barbara growth machine. When speaking to the Santa Barbara Woman's Club, she would invoke the language of female moral authority, domesticity, and the protection of home and children. When speaking to a group of businessmen, such as the Building and Loan Associations, she invoked arguments that an investment in the Better Homes campaign would be an investment in their own business. In seeking financial support for the publication of a pamphlet entitled "Model Specifications for Small House" [*sic*], Chase reminded these businessmen that they would benefit in new clients by supporting this publication.

> Your organization has had an important relation to the growth and development of Santa Barbara, and I believe that your conservative and helpful guidance of the small home owner has been of great value. Through the Better Homes in America Campaign, we have tried to foster interest in the owning of attractive small homes. There is an increasing demand upon us for advice, both within the City and by correspondence throughout the country. It is planned to publish several illustrated pamphlets, and to arrange several traveling exhibits of photographs of attractive small house plans. The first, a pamphlet now ready for publication, is called, "Model Specifications for Small House" [*sic*], and has been prepared by John Frederic Murphy and L. L. Pope, and reviewed by several small house contractors and we think will be of use to your clients. The only contributions received are those of the Plans and Planting Branch, and $100 from the Chamber of Commerce for photographs. The Committee hopes that your Board of Directors will be willing to appropriate at least $20 for Better Homes in Santa Barbara.[26]

The third part of Chase's vision, that of increased home ownership, reflected a growing movement within the United States to encourage home buying and building that eventually received concrete support from the U.S. government through the secretary of commerce, Herbert Hoover. As secretary and later chairman of Plans and Planting and the Better Homes in America program, Chase came into contact with some of California's and the nation's leading realtors, planners, and civic officials, both male and female, as she crusaded for increased home ownership. Her vision was spread to the San Francisco Bay Area through correspondence with Duncan McDuffie, that area's leading developer. McDuffie first came into contact with Chase through a general inquiry to the Community Arts Association for information on small house plans. He requested a copy of the association's small house design book be sent to a woman client in San Francisco at his expense.[27] Over the years, their correspondence grew into a friendship that included both of their extended families. McDuffie even invited Chase to visit his family while she was attending the National Conference on Social Work in San Francisco in 1929.[28]

Signifying her personal mastery of property ownership, Chase used the Better Homes campaign as the vehicle through which she could educate the general public about the entire process of home buying and building. Using her connections with the H. G. Chase Real Estate Company, Chase worked closely with W. C. Paulton, an agent of her father's company, and agents of the Ambassador Tract subdivision to purchase a low-priced lot on which to build one of her first demonstration houses in 1924. She and her committee eventually agreed to purchase lot 108 on West Yanonali Street, priced for $2,750. In a report to the Better Homes committee, Chase explained the terms of the sale, the plans to obtain a contractor, materials, and labor, and the need of a loan to pay for day labor and incidentals: "It was decided to take an option until January 15, and the following terms were secured: $2000 for cash on or before January 15, which meant that there had been subtracted a sum which more than covered 5% commission and 10% off for cash and 10% more off in accordance with the offer of the owner to the first ten purchasers building on the tract."[29] Chase held the deed for this property in trust through the County National Bank and Trust Company.[30] She thus had a personal financial stake in the outcome of the Better Homes campaign in its first year. It is interesting to note that the subdivision chosen for this first demonstration house was one billed by its developer, Earle Ovington, as "The Completely Improved and *Carefully Restricted* Subdivision" (emphasis added).[31] Although Chase espoused a philosophy that embraced the lower classes, her small house design was clearly aimed at the middle and upper classes.

When it came time to sell this property, Chase referred interested purchasers to Lloyd Tilton, Better Homes treasurer and a member of the Santa Barbara Building and Loan Association. Although he oversaw the sale, she chose the terms:

> It is suggested that bids be asked providing at least 25% cash or such other amount as would enable the building and loan to carry the balance. It is suggested that the House be offered with Lot Planted, 1) House with curtains, brackets and linoleum $9,343. 2) House and Lot as (1) plus inside furniture and furnishings not reserved (1400) $10,743. Articles reserved or included are (a) linen (b) personally loaned articles, (c) Extras: piano, radio, washing and sewing machines etc. 3) House and Lot as (1) and partly furnished, separate articles to be sold according to committees and list with consult of store owner. This figure would be between $9,343 and $10,743. The Committee Members consulted are inclined to favor No. 2 or 3 kind of offers provided the amount received for house and lot is as high as in any other.[32]

In a later letter to Norman McFadden, the agent assigned to sell the house, Chase expanded these instructions to allow for a contract purchase. "While it is most desirable that the purchaser be able to pay cash any serious offer which provides for a considerable down payment and regular monthly payments thereafter large enough to cover interest and a considerable amount on principal, will be considered."[33] Although Chase volunteered her time, she was not willing to donate the demonstration house. She did not expect to make a profit on it; that would rob her of her valuable facade of selfless interest. Nonetheless, she did expect to get back the amount of money put into the building. She also expected a rapid sale of the house and sought Tilton's assistance in dealing with McFadden. "It is of course unwise to sign up giving multiple listing an exclusive for 60 days and if he [McFadden] is unwilling to present it in any other way we will send out a letter direct to the active firms."[34]

Chase also envisioned Better Homes as a means to sell more houses, thus supplementing the for-profit work of her father's real estate business. Through the Better Homes Committee and Plans and Planting, Chase made available both a guidebook to the demonstration houses and a pamphlet entitled "How to Own Your Own Home."[35] She also worked closely with James Ford, executive director of the National Better Homes in America organization, to provide information on the entire process of home buying and building to the American public.[36] Chase's mastery of property ownership is further demonstrated by a request from the National Association of Real Estate Boards (NAREB) for her to contribute to a series of lessons in home ownership prepared by the NAREB. Chase's contributions to Lesson XI, "What Does a Family Gain From Its Home?" and Lesson XII, "Buying a House Already Built," demonstrate her ability to draw upon both the language of domesticity and the language of capitalism to convince the public of the benefits of home ownership.[37]

In Lesson XI, Chase argued that the home represents a family's expression of its self. "Planning and building a house is the largest piece of creative work that the average family ever undertakes." A home is a public expression of a family's tastes, hopes, ambitions, and interests. It is an expression of "efficient living"—a family that owns its own home will feel more comfortable and be more likely to contribute to the community. In terms of family life, home ownership creates stability, which contributes to raising morally upstanding children.

> Families which have built a home for themselves have in general a more stable life than they would otherwise have. If the family moves its residence frequently, the school groups in which the children find themselves will be constantly changing. Is it easier to make friends if you live a long while in one place or if you move frequently from one neighborhood to another? If the family feels settled, father, mother, and children will be more likely than otherwise to join fully into the life of the community.[38]

As a financial consideration, home ownership and property improvements are a valuable investment and an excellent way to save.

> If you were a banker and a man came to your bank to borrow money for a new business in which he wanted to engage, would you loan him the money the more readily if he owned his home? Would it be evidence to you that he was thrifty? Would it be evidence that he was of dependable character? If you were a merchant and a family asked to open a credit account in your store would you give preference to the family that owns its own home? The better financial standing which it gives is one of the substantial advantages of home ownership.[39]

Lesson XII then outlined the steps required in buying a house already built. First, a family should consider the region: climate, neighborhood, zoning, property restrictions, transportation, schools, shopping, and other city services. Second, a family should examine the building site: boundaries, public utilities, assessments, grading, house placement on the lot, garage, and grounds. Third, the family should decide if the plan of the house meets its needs: room number, design, location, lighting and ventilation, resale value, and construction materials. Fourth, the family should examine the overall quality of construction, the general appearance of the property, and the potential cost of maintaining the home. Finally, Lesson XII addressed the basic questions a prospective buyer should ask about the title and payments.[40] By the mid 1930s, this rhetoric became a major part of the New Deal and the Federal Housing Administration's ideology and message.[41]

Chase clearly envisioned the Better Homes campaign as a vehicle through which she could preach the gospel of home ownership, and she easily enlisted the help of the Santa Barbara Real Estate Board in this endeavor. Echoing the sentiments of the NAREB's home ownership lessons, Howard C. Gates agreed to a radio address on behalf of Better Homes Week in 1938. Gates, like Chase, adapted the language of domesticity and moral rectitude to this radio broadcast to increase his appeal. "The members of the Santa Barbara Real Estate Board stand ready to assist you in the selection of a home—and while it is true we derive our incomes from the sale and management of Real Estate—this program has no commercial connection. It's [*sic*] only purpose is for the betterment of the American family life." Nonetheless, Gates proceeded to call attention to "the many desirable lots in the Loma Media Tract, on the Riviera, . . . The Samarkand Hills and . . . The Rutherford Tract." He argued that home ownership created "a feeling of security." It developed "self respect—independence and self reliance." Property ownership created better and more productive employees and an assured savings account. For those who did not have cash available to purchase a home outright, Gates recommended financing through either a Building and Loan Association or the Federal Housing Administration.[42]

Chase's crusade for home ownership paralleled that of Better Homes in America. Far from being an altruistic or a philanthropic undertaking, Better Homes represented a clear attempt by the capitalist class to assert property interests and to preserve capitalism. This was particularly important during the Depression, when unemployment and homelessness seemed on the verge of destroying capitalism in America. Better Homes justified promoting home ownership by arguing that it would preserve the American way of life. The Better Homes leadership believed that home owners were more likely than renters to make improvements to property and to invest their savings. "The building of good homes for this reason increases national wealth and well-being." They also believed that home ownership created family and civic pride that contributed to social stability. "Through the relation to his neighborhood and to the city government, he (the property owner) acquires a keener civic interest and a greater sense of civic responsibility." Thus, home ownership contributed to character development and to social, economic, and, perhaps, political preservation.[43]

Better Homes was successful because it could build upon an American cultural ideal: "the will to possess." Americans have, since the early days of colonization, embraced the concept of home ownership as a common and uniting goal. What began as a protest against land concentration and tenancy in Europe came to be a symbol of American values. Thus interpretations of home ownership as a capitalist construct imposed upon the lower classes to stimulate consumption ignores the very powerful will to possess and the ability of home buyers to make a conscious decision to invest in an asset-building strategy of economic security. Home ownership provided owner-occupants with freedom and status, two intangibles that the Marxist approach fails to evaluate. Better Homes did not create demand and manipulate the lower classes. It simply built upon and fueled the will to possess.[44]

Home ownership, architectural harmony, and aesthetic improvement all contributed to the Chase vision. Implementing this vision required a simple philosophy: create a cooperative network of citizens to lead the public officials. Chase perhaps explained it best in a 1940 interview for *Survey Graphic.*

> We believe that volunteer committees should control the policies of private agencies and be ready to consult and advise public administrators. We know that it is better to bring about results voluntarily and by reason rather than by force of law, though the latter is often necessary. We have found hundreds of citizens willing to give time and service almost without end, others who have shared their means with extraordinary generosity. Every community is bettered if its citizens will cooperate in discussing and planning its present and future. We believe that a community can stand about four good hard-hitting committee drives a year, and no more, but they are good for it.[45]

Chase maintained her authority by working within the political and social system and by scrupulously preserving her feminine image. Her genius lay in using the power of female moral authority to construct and then implement a vision that had clear capitalist goals.[46] She never had any illusions about the perceived role of women in early-twentieth-century American society, and she manipulated that public perception to become an extremely influential, though unofficial, city planner. She understood that she could accomplish more by working in a behind-the-scenes capacity and by assigning a man to the public leadership role. Working in a close and equal partnership with Bernhard Hoffmann at the city level and L. Deming Tilton at the county level she successfully remade Santa Barbara in her own image.

The Plans and Planting Committee, along with the Better Homes program, provided Chase with the organizations through which she could implement her city plan and her public education campaign. Building upon the cooperative networks she found essential to successful planning, Chase expanded her public education program by organizing one of the first city planning conferences in Santa Barbara in April 1925. Entitled "Conference on City Beautiful," this planning conference was designed "to advise with the people means for the beautification of the City of Santa Barbara." Under the joint auspices of the Plans and Planting Committee, the City Planning Commission, the Park Commission, the Better Homes Committee, the mayor, the city manager, and the city engineer, the conference demonstrated Chase's ability to engage in public education as well as practical improvement projects. Subjects of discussion at this conference included civic art and architecture, public buildings and institutions, parks and playgrounds, roads and boulevards, and the impact of city planning and zoning laws.[47] By opening the ideas of city beautification and zoning legislation to public discussion, Santa Barbara citizens were thus more prepared to embrace a comprehensive plan following the June 1925 earthquake than their counterparts in 1906 San Francisco.

On June 29, 1925, an earthquake estimated to have measured 6.3 on the Richter scale shook Santa Barbara and became the catalyst for rebuilding a large portion of the business district in Spanish revival architecture. In addition, the earthquake thrust Pearl Chase into the chairmanship of the Plans and Planting Committee after Bernhard Hoffmann resigned to chair the new Architectural Board of Review. Although the earthquake had caused massive damage to the city, there was strong sentiment that it had been a blessing in disguise. Santa Barbara had been given the same opportunity that San Francisco had in 1906 to implement a comprehensive plan. Meeting as a general architectural advisory committee in July 1925, Bernhard Hoffmann, Charles H. Cheney, and local architects called for the official creation of an architectural board of review to ensure that Santa Barbara would learn from the San Francisco experience and engage in planned rebuilding.

Herbert Hoover was an active supporter of Santa Barbara's Better Homes in America competition. He is pictured here with Bernhard Hoffman (far right) and other Santa Barbara dignitaries, ca. 1925. Santa Barbara Trust for Historic Preservation.

> WHEREAS a very large number of the business buildings and public and semi-public structures of the city must be very materially repaired or entirely rebuilt, and millions of dollars are being made available from outside sources, placing an unusual responsibility upon the architects, builders, financiers and the Building Department of the City; and Whereas the building of a bigger and better Santa Barbara is foremost in the minds of everyone, provided it can be done at reasonable cost and without delay, Now, Therefore, Be it Resolved:
>
> That the certified architects of Santa Barbara recommend to the City Council and the general Architectural Advisory Committee the immediate establishment of an Architectural Board of Review, consisting of three trained architects and two laymen versed in matters of design and building, to be selected by the City Planning Commission and appointed by the City Council; provided that in case of vacancies, appointments shall always be made of the three architect members from a list of nominees numbering twice the existing vacancies, nominated by the certified architects of the city, of one lay member from a list of two nominated by the Community Arts Association, and of one lay member from a list of two nominated by the City Planning Commission. The ordinance should provide that no building permits be issued by the Building Inspector until a report has been received from the Architectural Advisory Committee on each application for a building permit; that if the report of this Board is favorable, the permit be immediately granted, but that if the Board recommend changes in the design or construction of the building which the owners are unwilling to accept, the matter be referred to the City Council for action; provided that the Board of Review shall be deemed to have given a favorable report if no action be taken by it for more than thirty days after the filing of application for permit.[48]

But Chase and Hoffmann had to convince the city of this opportunity and to outline a plan of attack to take advantage of it. To this end, they prepared a series of newspaper articles and public speeches for local service clubs to explain the board. Working together to publicize the benefits of rebuilding in a unified architectural style, Chase and Hoffmann drew upon both moralistic and commercial language. They argued that "efficiency and community welfare demand A Plan—Community living demands a zoning law. A law that will be elastic and can be let out even as the jacket of a growing child."[49]

The strongest argument against the Architectural Advisory Board was that it would impose a single architecture on private property owners. Hoffmann and Chase continually had to defend the board against such attacks by stressing its advisory capacity and its altruistic desire to assist rather than impose upon property owners.

> There has been added to the Building Department a Board of Architectural Review—an Advisory Board merely—but one empowered by the community to advise with every prospective builder—so he may realize his neighbors [*sic*] plans—his possibilities of contributing to the community charm while gaining for himself the advice and experience of those who are well qualified to consider architectural proprieties—harmonious relationship and beauty of design.

For those to whom this altruistic argument did not appeal, Hoffmann and Chase could alter their tactics to play up the commercial value of unified architecture:

> Commercial it may be—but surely the cry of "Beauty Pays" is heard. In Santa Barbara our "trade" is luring tourists—our Mission is a shrine, but also are our hills—and beach lines, temple settings where a thirsty soul may drink in beauty and be refreshed. Unless man offends, the charm can but attract and hold. And so the clothing of our housing needs in fitting raiment must reflect the beauty of the hills—the color of the sea—the brilliance of our sun. Our front yards and our gardens will be set with tree and vine and flower that will further add to the joy of a region that can draw on a flora that is rich in scope and possibilities. . . . The widened street will mean increased purchasing power to the merchant and enhanced appearance constitute an advertising value for the dealer and the town—each building its tile in the mosaic that will joyfully impress the visitor and constantly delight those who are fortunate enough to call the town their own. This is the opportunity.[50]

Both of these arguments appealed to the Santa Barbara Woman's Club, which notified Hoffmann of its endorsement in July 1925.[51] The Chase-Hoffmann plan also received a strong endorsement from the California Federation of Women's Clubs (CFWC). Sending a special letter of congratulations and appreciation to the mayor and city council, the CFWC praised the city for using the disaster as an opportunity for "making a great contribution to the beauty of California., by co-operating with your architects, artists and other citizens of vision, for the rebuilding of Santa Barbara under a unified architectural plan." Recognizing the economic value of beautification in terms of the tourist dollar, the letter continued, "Such a city Santa Barbara has a wonderful opportunity of becoming; and we wish to congratulate you upon your appreciation of this opportunity. The whole state will be watching the new Santa Barbara, and especially the new State street, which may become one of the famous streets of the world—a mecca for tourists, if the plans of your far-seeing architects and citizens are carried out."[52]

The Chase-Hoffmann team campaigned relentlessly in the months following the earthquake to convince Santa Barbarans of the unique opportunity the city faced. As the public voice of the team, Bernhard Hoffmann took the message to the newspapers, but before articles were submitted, Chase edited and approved them. In an undated typescript, probably by Chase, the basic argument employed by the proarchitecture faction ran as follows: "Santa Barbara has an unparalleled opportunity to profit by the mistakes of other cities and rebuild logically and well in accordance with the most modern standards in architecture and City Planning so that the new Santa Barbara will arise in fine and substantial form an object lesson to all other communities in progressive city building."[53]

In addition to approving press releases, Chase also kept copies of the minutes of meetings of the Architectural Board of Review and the correspondence of Bernhard Hoffmann. These letters provide the strongest evidence that Chase understood the commercial value of her city plan as well as its more altruistic contributions to quality of life. A letter of support from the Allied Architects Association of Los Angeles, for example, stated clearly the commercial value of unified architecture: "Beauty, like climate, is an asset of inestimable value. The citizenship of Santa Barbara heretofore has evidenced, as have few modern communities, its knowledge that beauty has a currency value. Those who have guided Santa Barbara to its present appreciation of the commercial value of beauty and distinction must and will now insist that the financing of rehabilitation must include the financing of every project planned for civic betterment."[54] Other letters echoed this sentiment. When Chase and Hoffmann felt that they had reached the limits of their advertising resources, they turned to the Coral Gables group of New York for assistance: "Our big job here is to persuade individuals to remember the economic value of charm in architecture and city planning in the reconstruction of Santa Barbara. The efforts being made by the Coral Gables group will be one demonstration and will aid on the competitive side."[55]

State Street became the centerpiece of the new and improved Santa Barbara, along the Chase-Hoffmann plan. In addition to rebuilding State Street businesses in Spanish revival style architecture, Hoffmann also proposed widening the street and erecting awnings. In a letter to the editor of the *Morning Press,* Hoffmann explained the benefits of street widening:

> Increased traffic on the street, the increased purchasing power which would result and the added dignity and charm of the buildings on such an improved street were all important factors in leading up to this recommendation. . . . Experienced business men, after careful consideration, have concurred in the suggestion that in this way they could retain business on our main thoroughfare . . . and increase the amount of effective purchasing power and prevent traffic from going to adjoining thoroughfares prematurely, thus raising property values."[56]

Not all State Street property owners, however, were convinced of the need to rebuild in a single architectural style or to widen the street. The Architectural Advisory Committee thus developed a strategy of personal appeals to individual property owners, both men and women, and to entire blocks. Among the owners in the first three blocks of State Street were Erma M. Gehl, Theresa Roeder, Mrs. G. R. Baker, and Jennie Callahan.[57] In a personal appeal to Mrs. John Kahn, an absentee landlord from Los Angeles, both aesthetic and commercial arguments were employed:

> Consider remodeling your property on the lines of Spanish architecture such as is suggested by the Architectural Board. If you do this, it will result in benefits to your property and assure values on Estado Street. If we do not improve this thoroughfare, there is a danger of other streets being improved for business. Knowing your personal interest in all of the finer and cultured things of life, we are sure that you will want to do your part in making Santa Barbara an unique and colorful city such as is contemplated on "Estado Street (State Street), following uniform plans of arcading and Spanish type buildings.[58]

As the Architectural Board of Review came under attack with a change in city government in early 1926, Hoffmann called upon his colleagues to preserve the board. It is interesting to note that one of the builders he contacted was Helen Dean Bogsa. One of only a few women builders in the state, Bogsa supported Hoffmann and the board, but she feared to state her views publicly. Although she provided Hoffmann with an article in which she outlined her support of the board, she wished to remain anonymous because "I am not at all a newspaper agitator." As a builder of "pretty houses and comfortable houses," Bogsa regarded the Architectural Advisory Board as "kindly, helpful, and generous." She related an incident in which the board had caught a flaw in one of her plans for a five-room house. She had not allowed enough head room on the stairs. She was grateful to have a second opinion on her plans because "no builder or architect is infallible." Noting the economic value of architectural control, she continued:

> Thanks to the Architectural Board's far-visioned efforts we shall in a year's time have the whole world at our gates. We have always had an unparalleled situation. Then we shall have a city conceived in one spirit, and that a picturesque one—so unique a rising [*sic*] from its ashes that it will command universal attention. The hotel men know this. Outside capital would not come in if it did not realize that Santa Barbara would shortly become a tourist mecca on a large scale. . . . The cry will go out over all the country. The hotels will be flooded because people will want to see the arcades and flower boxes and recesses which the Architectural Board is providing. And flooded hotels mean more people who finally buy and settle more prosperity for us all. The builders of this town are short sighted indeed if they do not realize that this increased, this booming prosperity for them is dependent on their continued support of the Architectural Board. Whatever we do we must work shoulder to shoulder to see that nothing uproots it. My personal commendation cannot be too great. As a builder I thank them for the particular good they rendered, and as a citizen for the inestimable good they are doing for Santa Barbara.[59]

The demise of the Architectural Board in March 1927 helped propel Pearl Chase into leadership of the architectural vision of Santa Barbara. Control reverted back to the Plans and Planting Committee on which Chase now served as chairman. Responding to the growing animosity to direct architectural control on the part of the review board, Chase turned her attention to indirect control through a massive public education blitz as part of the Better Homes campaign. Chase understood that she could achieve more at this time by appealing to residential property owners and giving business owners a respite. She believed that they would eventually see the benefits of working for an aesthetically beautiful city in increased tourist revenue and then follow her lead.

As rebuilding gave way to new building in 1926 and 1927, Santa Barbara's reputation as a beautiful and architecturally unique city gained Pearl Chase a national reputation as a city planner in her own right. Her successful Better Homes campaigns that replaced the Architectural Board of Review as the main engine for architectural uniformity brought her to the attention of the City Planning Publishing Company of Boston. Writing to Theodora Kimball Hubbard, one of five editors of *City Planning* magazine, Chase indicated that there was growing support among California realtors for comprehensive city planning. She explained that she had been invited to speak at the March 1927 conference on city planning sponsored by the City Planning Committee of the California Realty Board. In regard to the meeting, Chase declared,

> It is a very forward-looking step and as the realtors in California have a great opportunity they are being made to realize that their obligations are proportionately large and that the duty to their community as well as to the future welfare of their state, depends upon their understanding of and following the better known methods of subdivision work. There are so many subdivisions here which run from one hundred to thousands of acres, that the future of the towns and cities may be directed by the subdivider to a very great extent.[60]

Hubbard was a contributing editor for *City Planning*, the "official organ" of both the National Conference on City Planning and the American City Planning Institute associated with Harvard. Chase's primary reason for writing was to bring the topic of subdivisions to Hubbard's attention. By watching her family's real estate business grow with new subdivisions, Chase understood that the future of city growth and city planning lay in the hands of subdividers. In addition, as a delegate to the California Real Estate Association's annual meeting, Chase had recognized "that one of the strongest committees . . . is that working on city planning and the regulation of subdivision development."[61] Chase believed that subdividers were a key factor in future city planning and hoped that Hubbard might write an article to that effect.

Chase's views on subdivision and the important role of developers in city planning placed her at the forefront of a nationwide movement. A large body of literature, especially in the last ten years, has pointed to the rapid increase and transformation in subdivision activity that occurred between 1880 and 1945. Throughout this period, realtors became involved in the entire process of subdividing, constructing buildings, and marketing communities. Fully planned communities began to emerge as subdividers encountered keener competition in the real estate market and as purchasers came to expect services along with their land. Marc Weiss argues that California realtors became the national innovators "in the growth, organization, and regulation of the real estate industry; in the creation of land use regulations and planning agencies; in the extensive involvement and strong support of California realtors for state, county, and city planning efforts."[62] The relative youth of California cities and the vast tracts of available land near city cores made subdivision the leading form of urban land development in the state. Chase's awareness of this trend documents the depth of her involvement in real estate affairs and thus her grasp of the innovative tools of the twentieth-century urban growth machine.

Chase's interest, knowledge, and reputation in city planning grew rapidly in the late 1920s. In March 1929, LeRoy E. Bowman, secretary of the National Community Center Association, asked Chase to speak on city planning at the Association's National Conference on Social Work to be held in San Francisco. Chase's work had been brought to Bowman's attention by Paul U. Kellogg, editor of *The Survey.* Bowman asked Chase to attend an organizational meeting for the conference on the general topic of "city planning and social work."

> The first paper will be given by Prof. E. W. Burgess of the University of Chicago on—Population Movements and Consequent Social Disorganization. The second paper will be on Town and Country Planning—meaning the planned organization that can be effected to bring the town and country closer together. The third paper will deal with Zoning and City Planning. I have asked Carol Aronovici to talk on this last topic. I wonder if you would be willing to take ten minutes to discuss either the second or the third topic. We are particularly interested in the plans that have been drawn up by certain city planners to make the new developments complete social and neighborhood units.[63]

By attending this function, Chase developed contacts with some of the nation's leading city planners. The honor of being asked to comment on a paper by Carol Aronovici signified Chase's acceptance into the top ranks of a male-dominated profession.

Returning to her contacts with the California Real Estate Association (CREA), Chase researched the position of realtors toward city planning before speaking at the National Conference on Social Work. The CREA's general policy on city planning was "to devote itself to the large general phase of city planning activity and to keep away from city planning controversies which may arise in the various cities where planning is being carried on." Noting that some property owners would inevitably lose with the implementation of a plan, the CREA chose to pursue an educational campaign designed to heighten a sense of community rather than individuality.[64] Chase combined this strategy with her own belief in architectural uniformity to urge social workers to contribute to city planning efforts across the country.

Chase's success with implementing a city plan in Santa Barbara led her to broaden the scope of her vision to include the entire county. Building upon her father's belief that one needed to sell an entire region rather than just a single piece of property, Chase sought to enhance the reputation of the City of Santa Barbara by enhancing the reputation of the County of Santa Barbara.[65] The Better Homes campaign provided an ideal forum in which to expand the Santa Barbara vision countywide. Throughout 1927, Chase began to formulate her plan for countywide beautification as she corresponded with leading city and county planners across the country. Working in conjunction with New York City planner Harry B. Brainerd, Chase came to see the value of regional planning in addition to city planning. Brainerd sent her copies of his correspondence with Professor William A. Boring of Columbia University regarding developing a regional plan for New York that would emphasize street design. Brainerd proposed a more informal system of architectural review than that established in Santa Barbara. Believing in cooperation, he recommended that property owners on a given block agree to appoint a controlling architect for the block who would fit all exteriors into a harmonious unit. He proposed that these architects work with the architectural division of the Regional Plan Office to ensure architectural uniformity for the entire city and its surrounding boroughs.[66] Chase endorsed this plan and sought to implement a similar system in Santa Barbara County.

At the same time, Chase cultivated a friendship and an informal partnership with Santa Barbara County planning consultant L. Deming Tilton. Treating Chase as a professional planner, Tilton discussed every facet of the Santa Barbara County plan with Chase, including when and where to hold future conferences on city and county planning: "It is my personal feeling that Santa Barbara has a great deal to show in the way of city planning achievement and I would consider it a great mistake to schedule a general public conference here and find only a handful present. Can we not arrange after our county planning work gets a bit under way to invite the League of California Municipalities to meet with us, or some such group?" Chase knew that she could call on "Dem" when she needed information for public speeches on planning, and Tilton could call on her to rally public support for his plans.[67] This partnership became so open that outside agencies recognized its authority. The Automobile Club of Southern California, for example, took its concerns regarding roadside development to either Chase or Tilton, depending on whoever was available.[68]

Although lacking a politically recognized title or position, Chase wielded a tremendous influence in Santa Barbara. Tilton felt it necessary to keep her informed of threats to the beauty of Santa Barbara County, including the discovery of oil near Montecito. He also publicly recognized her contributions to planning by inviting her to a luncheon for Russel V. Black, director of the Philadelphia Tri-State Regional Planning District in 1929. Black had requested that Tilton arrange for a "selected group who are interested in city and county planning" to attend.[69]

Chase found that her most effective forum for asserting a county plan lay not in conferences but in the grassroots Better Homes in America program. Leaving the chairmanship of the city's Better Homes campaign in 1928, Chase created and assumed leadership of a county program. Redefining Better Homes in 1928 and 1929, Chase envisioned a program that would clean up and beautify the entire region. The program would embrace Chase's vision of "environmental design," in which parks, roads, public buildings, and private homes were included. Chase could build upon the cleanup and the Scenic Highways campaigns that she had initiated at the county level beginning in the early 1920s. Working with the California Roadside Council, a group dedicated to the eradication of garish billboards and signs along the state's scenic highways and to the creation of attractive roadside parks, Chase directed her efforts particularly to the entrances of cities. Because "neglect is not good advertising," she gained support in this effort from the Commercial Club, the Woman's Club, and the chamber of commerce.[70]

Although she continued to work heavily within a female network, Chase found that not all women agreed with her vision for Santa Barbara County. Early in 1928 she came into conflict with a Buellton woman who owned a particularly offensive billboard situated at the entrance to Buellton known locally as the "big, blue sign." Mrs. Buell apparently leased the billboard and collected rent for its use and was unwilling to lose money over a beautification plan. Working with the Better Homes Committee, Mrs. Buell's daughter-in-law tried to discourage her from "having such things" but was unsuccessful.[71] The rent that Mrs. Buell collected probably had a higher priority than appearances, the Better Homes women's approval, or participation in the Clean-Up Week campaign. For some women, as for some men, immediate income was more important than future potential profit.

Although Chase served as the County Chairman for Better Homes through the 1930s, the city remained her primary focus. Perhaps this stemmed from the difficulty she found in getting rural women to follow her plans. In addition to the refusal of Mrs. Buell to take down her billboard, Chase occasionally ran into conflict with her own organizers. Hazel G. McCabe, chairman of the Lompoc campaign, for example, did not "quite agree with all of [Chase's] suggestions," although she supported the overall plan.[72] Despite winning county campaigns, the organizational work involved proved a daunting and at times unrewarding task. Thus, Chase found more personal satisfaction in her city planning campaigns and is remembered today in Santa Barbara for this work rather than her county planning work.

Like so many middle-class women of the 1920s, Pearl Chase chose to assert her political and economic power through traditional "female" roles. By maintaining a public appearance of selfless virtue, she came to wield a considerable influence on local planning and politics. Believing that politicians exercised only fleeting power, Chase favored working with nonprofit, nonpartisan civic organizations. Real power, she argued, lay with citizen volunteers, unfettered by worries about reelection. Building a career on this philosophy, Chase remained at the center of the local and state power structure for sixty years.

Historian David Gebhard has argued that "Santa Barbara's image was not directly an outcome of any formal large or even small scale planning." Any structured planning that did occur was "accomplished indirectly and to a considerable degree behind the political scene. . . . The real organization, which was to transform Santa Barbara's image, was the Plans and Planting Committee."[73] Gebhard's conclusion fails to give credit to Pearl Chase as a powerful and influential city planner. While she may not have held elective or appointive office, she clearly had a vision for Santa Barbara and a conscious plan of development. As a de facto city planner in the de facto city planning commission of Plans and Planting, Chase actually served as one of the longest planning incumbents in the state, if not in the nation. Serving as chairman of Plans and Planting for forty-six years, from 1925 to 1971, her vision and plan for Santa Barbara was one of the few comprehensive plans to be executed. Her ability to engage the language of female moral authority and capitalism, her belief in public education as a potent tool for selling her vision, her organizational skills, and her network of powerful civic organizations all enabled Chase to become one of the most powerful and respected city planners in the country. Her achievement suggests that middle-class women could confront capitalism and master its tenets. They could speak the language of capitalism, and they could contribute to a successful strategy toward winning the city growth game.

Conclusion

The story of Pearl Chase's mastery of city planning in Santa Barbara offers a capstone to the story of the women capitalists in the California growth machine. As California cities engaged in a regional growth game between 1880 and 1940, middle-class women first staked a claim to the city and then asserted their rights to influence the vision and plan for city growth. With the founding of women's clubs in the 1890s, these women developed a collective voice through which to express their vision. They learned the language of capitalism and the mechanisms of city government to shape their communities politically, culturally, economically, and intellectually. They created a class alliance with their male counterparts and thus shared in the promise of wealth and sense of destiny that contributed to California's urbanization.

In the apprenticeships in property ownership and management and in city planning that they entered and completed in the early twentieth century, middle-class women successfully confronted capitalism and learned the connection between city-bonded indebtedness and property values. They became familiar with both the economic and the social and moral value of parks and beautification projects. Although they often remained bounded in their public discourse by the social mores and language of Victorian womanhood that placed their public activities in the context of domestic and maternal concerns, they behaved as capitalists. By entering into these apprenticeships, middle-class women developed the capitalist consciousness and then the capitalist vocabulary that emancipated them economically before they were emancipated politically.

As California's middle-class women asserted their capitalist interests, the separate spheres of Victorian womanhood broke down. The men and women of the capitalist class united in an informal yet highly effective partnership designed to achieve shared goals. Increasing economic and social freedom for California women allowed them to stand on a more equal footing with their male counterparts and to expand their influence beyond the home and into the community. In their use of capitalist and moral rhetoric, participants in the California growth machine shared the goals of enhancing and protecting property values within cities. These goals extended the moral reform rhetoric of the Progressive Era into a movement to extend the language of capitalism and to protect the capitalist class. This is the fundamental issue of California city growth and the driving force behind the urban growth machine as it functioned in California.

The stories of California women engaged in city growth and development provide a unique opportunity to reassess a variety of historical paradigms. First and foremost, they help us reevaluate the enduring growth machine thesis of the urban sociologists. More than twenty-five years after its publication, Harvey Molotch's theory still wields a powerful influence over urban studies. Much of the preceding study supports the theory, particularly the conclusion, that city government exists to serve property interests in a perpetual struggle to grow. The history of California's urban women, however, suggests that this growth game was not a conspiracy of the elite to impose its vision and value system on the masses. Instead, the growth machine should be evaluated as a coalition of like-minded people, from a variety of classes, who shared the "will to possess" and who sought economic security through urban property ownership. In addition, the women of the growth machine as it existed in California's second- and third-tier cities were intent on improving quality of life as they increased their property value. For growth machine members of both sexes, a moral value system was tightly interwoven into their growth strategies.

Second, the evidence presented here that women were property and business owners and active in local politics prior to enfranchisement suggests that the growth game was not a gendered game. The city's male elite could not afford to ignore women in creating and implementing their growth strategies, particularly in second- and third-tier cities struggling to woo investors to "cities of homes." Furthermore, even had members of the male elite wanted to ignore women, the women themselves insisted on being heard. Through personal and collective petitions to city councils and through membership in chambers of commerce, California women actively participated in defining a community ideal and a plan to achieve the growth goals that they shared with their male counterparts. They believed in the California Dream, and they were not shy in voicing their opinions on how that dream could be realized.

Third, analyzing women's public work in terms of the growth machine theory offers new insight into the motivations behind club work. While many women did achieve a tremendous sense of personal satisfaction and self-improvement through their club work, the compelling evidence of their personal economic interests in city growth and development sheds new light on this activity. In addition, the strong "moral" language of male civic groups suggests that such programs as parks, playgrounds, and beautification were not just about the moral rectitude of the community. Women as well as men understood that these programs would pay back in rising property value.

Fourth, the evidence of women's involvement in city boosting sheds new insight into this much-maligned aspect of city growth. Women chamber members had a significant effect on the nature of the California booster message. Unlike the boosterism of Babbitry, where inflated messages sold a myth, women boosters sought to sell reality and to make any "dream" become reality. They helped soften the booster message that focused solely on economic opportunity by adding a strong dose of morality and domesticity. They would sell their cities as places where an individual or a family could grow in mind, body, and spirit and make a buck or two in the process. Even without the political power of the vote, they convinced city officials of the value of clean and beautiful streets, health and hygiene programs, and a strong public education system that would help sell cities. Throughout the state, chambers of commerce increasingly embraced this blended language of morality and capitalism in their booster messages.

In addition, finding women referenced frequently among the records of California chambers of commerce provides evidence of an area of public work for middle- and upper-class women heretofore unrecognized. It offers an opportunity to reevaluate interpretations of women's public work away from models stressing gender identity, moral and social reform, and political activism. Instead, at least for the capitalist women of California during this time period, class identity and property interests were equally compelling factors motivating women to enter the public arena. Clearly, the job of "selling the city" was shared by both men and women of the city elite.

The coming of World War II radically altered the California urban landscape and the strategies employed by the urban growth machine. Cities that had been struggling to compete for regional dominance found themselves swept up by the population boom that accompanied the growth of wartime industries on the Pacific Coast. As Gerald Nash has pointed out, "the four years of frenzied wartime expansion compressed what might have been as many as forty years of peacetime growth."[1] This growth saw some California cities double and triple in population. More than 1 million newcomers made California their home in this period, and 90 percent of these immigrants settled in towns and cities. For some cities like Richmond and Vallejo in the San Francisco Bay Area, the influx of immigrants was overwhelming. Housing shortages led to cheaply built federal housing projects that would eventually degenerate into slum housing in the succeeding decades. Other cities, like Riverside, Redlands, Santa Barbara, and Oakland, would survive this influx in part because of their location, but largely owing to plans laid in the previous decades. Because of experiments with city planning and zoning techniques, most California cities had at least a minimal guide as to how to handle the population boom. As a result, California cities would become the model for cities nationwide in the postwar years.

The evolution of California cities prior to 1940 helps explain the state's postwar history. By adding women to the story of California's prewar urban development, we see that the urban growth machine was far more than a mechanism to make money for its citizen "stockholders." It was also a mechanism for the creation of controlled cities. The men and women who chose to use the tools of city planning and zoning to win the urban competition sought growth but not at the expense of destroying their living environment. The women who learned these mechanisms would use them to push for limitations to growth in the 1960s, 1970s, and 1980s. As long as quality of life was not destroyed by unlimited growth, women supported selling their cities and growing physically. However, when it became clear that there was a downside to growth—pollution, overcrowding, traffic congestion—women would become the leaders of the slow growth or no growth movements. Once again, these movements express themselves in terms of protection of home and hearth, but they also express themselves in the language of property values, particularly in smaller, exclusive communities like Orinda, Redlands, and Santa Barbara. Women have always recognized that growth requires more than just basic city services like sewers and water; it requires developing a high quality of life.

The study of women's entrance into the economic life of cities prior to World War II also helps explain their political successes after the war. Since 1945 women have served as mayors of South Pasadena, Santa Barbara, San Francisco, Modesto, Orinda, and Stockton, to name just a few cities. Carl Abbott attributes this to an institutional openness in western cities generally after World War II. He further suggests that middle-class women had the time and the energy to create new community ties to the massive numbers of newcomers who flooded into the West with the war.[2] Was this a mere extension of "women's work?" Certainly domestic ideology provided women with a socially acceptable avenue of entry into politics, but the evidence supporting women's claims to political power based on their status as property owners offers an alternative explanation. Domesticity may have provided a vehicle for entry into politics, but protection of property values, quality of life concerns, and economic security provided the drive.

At the heart of this story lies the influence of city planners. Most histories of California city planning have stressed the roles of professional city planners, real estate developers, and boosters. They have not adequately situated women in this story, but it is not enough merely to say they were there. The women in this study were not mere "women worthies," nor were they anomalies. They were capitalists interested in wealth accumulation through city building, municipal competition, and the metropolitan regionalization of the western economy. When one views women as capitalists and women's civic and voluntary work as more than municipal housekeeping, the many layers of the urban experience begin to come together. "Benevolence," when studied in the context of the urban growth machine, takes on a new meaning. It becomes a tool used by capitalist planners to ensure rising property values.

This is not to suggest that women were merely doing "women's work" in the public arena. That would continue to marginalize the contributions of women to the urban process. The stories of women in California cities suggest instead that the urban environment created the ideal intersection of both men's and women's cultures in the pursuit of wealth accumulation through rising property values. The key to understanding the urban experience of California is to explore the issue of ideology and how ever-changing gender roles have profound social and political implications. The ability of California's middle-class women to invoke the language of both moral authority and capitalism suggests that complex factors affect the implementation of a community or city plan and that both men and women were concerned with these issues.

It is my hope that this study will spur a new research agenda for western urban historians and for women's historians. More research needs to be done on second- and third-tier cities in order to understand their relationship to each other and to the regionally dominant cities of Los Angeles and San Francisco. What did "losing" to these major cities mean for lower cities? In the postwar years, did these cities lose their individuality and community character in light of the massive influx of new residents?

For women's historians, my hope is that this study will help move the field away from its emphasis on feminism and power relations. The women in this study were clearly constrained by the social constructs of their time, but they still wielded a powerful influence on their communities. Must we decry the fact that they did not overturn the existing power structure? Must we search for feminist consciousness in everything they did publicly? I suggest that far more important to most women than sisterhood, feminism, or political activism was creating a high quality of life in their cities and protecting property assets which provided economic security.

This study also leaves one key unanswered question that I hope future historians will tackle, namely, how prevalent was property ownership for women in California? We must engage in a statistical analysis of women's property ownership in order to more fully document their influence on city growth and development. The anecdotal evidence is compelling, but we now need to crunch the numbers found in the census, assessment records, and other tax rolls.

By exploring the means through which California women became property owners and managers and eventually reached the highest ranks of city planning professionals, I offer new insight into the effects of gender and class on the process of western urbanization and the operations of the growth machine. The evidence supports the conclusion that the unfettered capitalism of the West introduced women to the language and strategies of economic growth and in turn broke down Victorian social mores regarding women's public activities. Because women realized that their economic security depended on sustainable urban growth, they joined the growth coalition and shaped it by their own concerns and interests. City life may have altered gender roles and perceptions, but the central story here is the strength of the growth mentality in bridging the distance that once separated both men's and women's private and public lives.

REFERENCE MATTER

Notes

Introduction

1. *Santa Barbara News-Press,* November 17, 1968.

2. Harvey Molotch, "The City as Growth Machine: Toward a Political Economy of Place," *American Journal of Sociology* 82 (September 1976): 309–32.

3. Eric Monkkonen, *America Becomes Urban: The Development of U.S. Cities and Towns, 1780–1980* (Berkeley, CA, 1988).

4. Entrepreneurial capitalists were "speculative" capitalists who threatened the capitalist system because they stimulated boom and bust cycles that destroyed economic security. See James Livingston, *Origins of the Federal Reserve System: Money, Class, and Corporate Capitalism, 1890–1913* (Ithaca, NY, 1986).

5. Jeffrey A. Charles, *Service Clubs in American Society: Rotary, Kiwanis, and Lions* (Urbana, IL, 1993).

6. Douglass North, *The Economic Growth of the United States* (Englewood Cliffs, NJ, 1961). See also Albert Hirschman, *The Strategy of Economic Development* (New Haven, CT, 1958).

7. This description of Redlands appeared in many letters written by the Redlands Chamber of Commerce to prospective emigrants. For example, see Redlands Chamber of Commerce to Miss E. B. Wilmarth, February 8, 1906, Public Relations Files, Redlands Chamber of Commerce Papers, Heritage Room, A. K. Smiley Public Library.

8. Marc. A. Weiss, *The Rise of the Community Builders: The American Real Estate Industry and Urban Land Planning* (New York, 1987); Marguerite Duncan-Abrams, "The History of the Riverside Planning Commission, 1914–1928" (master's thesis, University of California Riverside, 1994); Gabriele Carey, "From Hinterland to Metropolis: Land Use Planning in Orange County, California, 1925–1955" (Ph.D. diss., University of California, Riverside, 1997); and Michael Doucet and James Weaver, *Housing the North American City* (Montreal, 1991), 99–102.

9. Monkkonen, *America Becomes Urban,* 203; Kenneth T. Jackson, *Crabgrass Frontiers: The Suburbanization of the United States* (New York, 1985), 190–218.

10. Molotch, "The City as Growth Machine," 312.

11. *Riverside Enterprise*, November 30, 1915.

12. I am indebted to Charles Wetherell and Ronald Tobey for coining this term.

13. See, for example, Kevin Starr, *Inventing the Dream: California Through the Progressive Era* (New York, 1985); Starr, *Material Dreams: Southern California Through the 1920s* (New York, 1990); William Cronon, *Nature's Metropolis: Chicago and the Great West* (New York, 1991); Patricia Nelson Limerick, *Legacy of Conquest: The Unbroken Past of the American West* (New York, 1987); and Gerald Nash, *The American West Transformed: The Impact of the Second World War* (Lincoln, NE, 1985).

14. Sarah Deutsch, "Learning to Talk More Like a Man: Boston Women's Class-Bridging Organizations, 1870–1940," *American Historical Review* 97, no. 2 (April 1992), 379–404.

15. *Redlands Citrograph*, November 14, 1891. The editor reprinted in its entirety a speech given by Mrs. Mary Lynde Hoffman, Treasurer of the Pacific Coast Women's Press Association, at an association meeting in San Francisco. Mrs. Hoffman displayed her knowledge of the history of roads dating back to the ancient Assyrians. She described the purpose of roads in city growth and outlined road projects in the major cities of both Europe and the United States.

16. *Oakland Enquirer*, May 8, 1907.

17. Mrs. W. L. Lawton to Bernhard Hoffmann, February 22, 1924, Letterhead, Better Homes Papers, Community Development and Conservation Collection (CDCC), Special Collections, University of California, Santa Barbara, Library.

18. Starr, *Inventing the Dream*, and Limerick, *Legacy of Conquest*.

Chapter 1

1. Harvey Molotch, "The City as Growth Machine: Toward a Political Economy of Place," *American Journal of Sociology* 82 (September 1976): 309–32.

2. See Paula Baker, "The Domestication of Politics: Women and American Political Society, 1780–1920," *American Historical Review* (June 1984): 620–47.

3. Peter Thomas Conmy, *The Historic Spanish Origin of California's Community Property Law and Its Development and Adaptation to Meet the Needs of an American State* (San Francisco, 1957), 1–2. It should be noted that this was not necessarily a natural occurrence. Most states in the union did not grant women this right, and the Constitutional Convention did experience a fairly lengthy argument over this law. Apparently what carried the day was an argument that protecting women's property rights would encourage single women to come to the state and, it was hoped, marry the state's many bachelors. Some married representatives at the convention argued that they should have the right to protect their wives' property. They eventually lost.

4. Conmy, *California's Community Property Law*, 11–12; Grace Ganz Blumburg, *Community Property in California* (Gaithersburg, MD, 1999), 83–98.

5. Elizabeth Eddy Fisk Diaries, Fisk Family Papers, Heritage Room, A. K. Smiley Public Library.

6. An extensive body of literature, generally regarded as the "organizational synthesis," argues that between 1870 and 1920 American society underwent a transformation from entrepreneurial capitalism to corporate capitalism. In the process, Americans organized themselves into bureaucratic hierarchies and replaced an apprentice system of training with professional, academic training. Professionalization and organization represented an attempt to bring order out of chaos. See Louis Galambos, "The Emerging Organizational Synthesis in Modern American History," *Business History Review* 44 (1970): 279–90; Galambos, "Technology, Political Economy, and Professionalization: Central Themes of the Organizational Synthesis," *Business History Review* 57 (1983): 471–93; Robert Wiebe, *The Search for Order: 1877–1920* (New York, 1967); Alfred D. Chandler, *The Visible Hand: The Managerial Revolution in American Business* (Cambridge, MA, 1977).

7. Helen G. Fisk correspondence, Fisk Family Papers.

8. Elizabeth Eddy, October 5, 1887, Elizabeth [Eddy] Fisk Diaries, Fisk Family Papers.

9. Ibid., November 18, 1887, February 23, 1888. In earlier entries, Elizabeth carefully recorded the prices and locations of property that she and Will had looked at. See entries for January 13, February 2, March 4, and October 5, 1887.

10. Elizabeth Eddy, February 24, 1887, Elizabeth [Eddy] Fisk Diaries, Fisk Family Papers. The early relationship that Elizabeth developed with Jane Hale and Marion Park extended into the Contemporary Club. All three women were long-term members of the club.

11. Elizabeth Eddy, March 4, 1887, Elizabeth [Eddy] Fisk Diaries, Fisk Family Papers.

12. For interpretations that emphasize speculation as the motivator behind Southern California and western development, see Kevin Starr, *Americans and the California Dream, 1850–1915* (New York, 1973); Starr, *Inventing the Dream: California Through the Progressive Era* (New York, 1985); Starr, *Material Dreams: Southern California Through the 1920s* (New York, 1990); Donald Worster, *Rivers of Empire: Water, Aridity, and the Growth of the American West* (New York, 1985); Mike Davis, *City of Quartz: Excavating the Future in Los Angeles* (New York, 1990). These works argue that Southern California today is the result of greedy, manipulative, and dishonest real estate speculators who sought personal gain at the expense of the nonwhite population and of the environment.

13. Carey McWilliams, *Southern California: An Island on the Land* (1946; reprint, Salt Lake City, 1973), 113, 118–28.

14. *Redlands Citrograph,* December 24, 1887.

15. Ronald Tobey and Charles Wetherell, "The Citrus Industry and the Revolution of Corporate Capitalism in Southern California, 1887–1944," *California History* 74 (Spring 1995): 6–21.

16. *Oakland Enquirer,* January 16, 1904.

17. *A Pictorial History of Redlands and Prospect Park* (Redlands, CA, 1968), 61–62.

18. Elizabeth [Eddy] Fisk, February 27, April 9, August 5, 1891; May 12, 1892; January 12, 1894; February 23, 1895; February 29, April 21 and 22, 1896, Elizabeth [Eddy] Fisk Diaries, Fisk Family Papers.

19. *Redlands Citrograph,* November 7, 1891.
20. *Golden Jubilee Redlands California: 1888–1938* (Redlands, CA, 1938), 7; and *A Pictorial History of Redlands and Prospect Park,* 49–50.
21. *Redlands Citrograph,* August 13, 1887.
22. *Redlands Citrograph,* September 3, 1887.
23. Elizabeth Eddy, June 2, 1888, Elizabeth [Eddy] Fisk Diaries, Fisk Family Papers.
24. Ibid., May 7, 1887.
25. Ibid., April 12, 1887.
26. Ibid., February 27, April 9, August 5, 1891; May 12, 1892; January 12, 1894; February 29, April 21–22, 1896; October 7, 1904; February 26, 1908. Elizabeth [Eddy] Fisk Financial Records, Fisk Family Papers. Scale is an insect infestation of citrus trees that can have a devastating economic impact on a grove. Heavy infestations of scale can cause premature drop of leaves, dieback of twigs and branches, stunting and distortion of fruit, and fruit drop before it is mature. Some types of scale attach directly to the fruit and form a virtually unremovable scale cover on the fruit causing rejection in most fresh fruit markets. Other types of scale can kill the tree.
27. Elizabeth Fisk, March 5, 1900, Elizabeth [Eddy] Fisk Diaries, Fisk Family Papers.
28. Ibid., February 3, 1898.
29. Ibid., May 22, 1900; 19 March 1901.
30. Ibid., June 20, 21, 29, 1904.
31. Ibid., May 14, 1917.
32. *Redlands Citrograph,* August 17, 1891.
33. "Clara Foltz, San Francisco, California," *Law Student's Helper* 1 (October 1893).
34. Ibid.
35. "Mary Lynde Craig," *Law Student's Helper* 1 (October 1893).
36. *Oakland Enquirer,* January 1, 1906.
37. *Oakland Enquirer,* April 9, 1909; *Oakland Achievement,* November 1915, p. 7; December 1915, p. 2; and Oakland Business and Professional Women's Club, "History of the Business and Professional Women's Club of Oakland," [n.p.], 1.
38. *Oakland Enquirer,* September 3, 1910.
39. *Oakland Enquirer,* March 6, 1906.
40. *Oakland Enquirer,* April 27, 1906.
41. *Oakland Enquirer,* May 30, 1906, and June 9, 1906.
42. *Oakland Enquirer,* May 18, 1907.
43. Joseph E. Baker, "Oakland and Roundabout," *Sunset Magazine,* October 1907.
44. *Oakland Enquirer,* June 3, 1909.
45. "Women's Clubhouses," *Club Woman* 5 (January 1900): 153. See also *Club Woman* 10 (October 1902): 40–41.
46. "Opportunity Knocks at our Door," *Business Women's Herald,* July 16, 1923.

47. Ibid.

48. *Oakland Enquirer,* June 25, 1907, January 16 and July 14, 1908, and August 12, 1909.

49. *Oakland Enquirer,* August 14, 1909.

50. *Oakland Enquirer,* September 2, 1909.

51. *Oakland Enquirer,* November 26, 1909.

52. *Oakland Enquirer,* September 3, 1910.

53. Ibid.

54. Redlands Chamber of Commerce to Miss E. B. Wilmarth, February 8, 1906, Public Relations Files, Redlands Chamber of Commerce Papers, Heritage Room, A. K. Smiley Public Library.

55. Redlands Chamber of Commerce to Mrs. Martha Mather, December 11, 1908, Public Relations Files, Redlands Chamber of Commerce Papers.

56. Redlands Chamber of Commerce to Mrs. Emma Blair Gray, May 28, 1909, Public Relations Files, Redlands Chamber of Commerce Papers.

57. Mrs. Della E. Boyer to the Redlands Chamber of Commerce, February 12, 1906; Mrs. F. W. Davis to the Redlands Chamber of Commerce, April 25, 1907; Mrs. E. Hosfield to the Redlands Chamber of Commerce, August 1, 1907; Mrs. W. E. Gaston to the Redlands Chamber of Commerce, September 3, 1907; Mrs. Allie Wicken to the Redlands Chamber of Commerce, March 9, 1908; and Mrs. Martha Mather to the Redlands Chamber of Commerce, December 3, 1908, Public Relations Files, Redlands Chamber of Commerce Papers.

58. Redlands Chamber of Commerce to Mrs. J. DuPlessis, January 25, 1917, Public Relations Files, Redlands Chamber of Commerce Papers.

59. Mrs. Mary Robinson to the Redlands Chamber of Commerce, May 16, 1907, Public Relations Files, Redlands Chamber of Commerce Papers.

60. Redlands Chamber of Commerce to Mrs. Mary Robinson, May 27, 1907, Public Relations Files, Redlands Chamber of Commerce Papers.

61. Redlands Chamber of Commerce to Mrs. Jodie Ansley, July 27, 1907, Public Relations Files, Redlands Chamber of Commerce Papers.

62. Miss Emma Bellinger to the Redlands Chamber of Commerce, February 10, 1909, Public Relations Files, Redlands Chamber of Commerce Papers.

63. Mrs. L. M. Ragin to the Redlands Chamber of Commerce, January 12, 1914, Public Relations Files, Redlands Chamber of Commerce Papers.

64. Mrs. C. E. Blunk to the Redlands Chamber of Commerce, February 1, 1918, Public Relations Files, Redlands Chamber of Commerce Papers.

Chapter 2

1. Karen J. Blair, *The Clubwoman as Feminist: True Womanhood Redefined, 1868–1914* (New York, 1980).

2. Ibid., xi–xii.

3. Sarah Deutsch, "Learning to Talk More Like a Man: Boston Women's Class-Bridging Organizations, 1870–1940," *American Historical Review* 97 (April 1992): 379–404; and Robyn Muncy, *Creating a Female Dominion in American Reform, 1890–1935* (New York, 1991); Darlene Roth, *Matronage: Patterns in Women's Organizations, Atlanta, Georgia, 1890–1940* (Brooklyn, NY, 1994).

4. Muncy, *Creating a Female Dominion,* xiii–xiv. See also Daniel Scott Smith, "Family Limitation, Sexual Control, and Domestic Feminism in Victorian America," in *Clio's Consciousness Raised,* edited by Mary Harman and Lois W. Banner (New York, 1976), 119–36; and Barbara Welter, "The Cult of True Womanhood, 1820–1860," *Journal of Urban History* 13 (August 1987): 394–425.

5. Roth, *Matronage,* 11, 56.

6. Neal Graffy, "The Santa Barbara Woman's Club: The First Forty Years," *Noticias* 38 (Autumn 1992): 41–42.

7. "The Woman's Parliament of Southern California," *Land of Sunshine* 8 (May 1898): 284.

8. Ibid., 287.

9. One of the best is Carl Abbott, *Boosters and Businessmen: Popular Economic Thought and Urban Growth in the Antebellum Middle West* (Westport, CT, 1981).

10. "The Woman's Parliament of Southern California," *Land of Sunshine* 8 (May 1898): 287.

11. Masthead, *California Independent.*

12. "The Woman's Parliament of Southern California," *Land of Sunshine* 8 (May 1898): 286.

13. Ibid.

14. Elizabeth L. Kenney et al., *Laws Relating to Women and Children* (Los Angeles, 1910). Minutes of club meetings of the Redlands Contemporary Club, 1910–1915, May 8, 1911, Minute Books, Redlands Contemporary Club Papers, Heritage Room, A. K. Smiley Public Library.

15. "The Woman's Parliament of Southern California," *Land of Sunshine* 8 (May 1898): 286.

16. "California," *Club Woman* 2 (April 1898): 18.

17. Howard P. Chudacoff and Judith E. Smith, *The Evolution of American Urban Society,* 3rd ed. (Englewood Cliffs, NJ, 1988), 174–207.

18. Elizabeth Eddy, November 19, 1888, Elizabeth [Eddy] Fisk Diaries, Fisk Family Papers, Heritage Room, A. K. Smiley Public Library.

19. Elizabeth Fisk, June 7–8, 1897, Elizabeth [Eddy] Fisk Diaries, Fisk Family Papers.

20. Ibid., January 17, 1898.

21. L. A. Ingersoll, *Century Annals of San Bernardino County, 1769–1904* (Los Angeles, 1904), 441.

22. *Redlands Citrograph,* August 13, 1887.

23. Starr, *Material Dreams,* 231.

24. McWilliams, *Southern California,* 144.

25. Ibid., 146.

26. Charles B. Hosmer Jr., *Presence of the Past: A History of the Preservation Movement in the United States Before Williamsburg* (New York, 1965), chap. 6. The importance of appropriating history and culture for the middle class is addressed by James Livingston in *Origins of the Federal Reserve System: Money, Class, and Corporate Capitalism, 1890–1913* (Ithaca, NY, 1986). Livingston argues that the corporate-industrial elite claimed to be the heirs to the civilizing culture

of Western Europe to create legitimacy for a new form of capitalism. They defined themselves and their communities as the source of cultural authority.

27. Charles A. Moody, "Santa Barbara," *Land of Sunshine* 15 (1901): 401–13.

28. Graffy, "Santa Barbara Woman's Club," 45.

29. Minutes of club meetings of the Redlands Contemporary Club, 1894–99, May 11, June 6, 1896, Minute Books, Redlands Contemporary Club Papers.

30. Ibid., May 9, 1898. Minutes of club meetings of the Redlands Contemporary Club, 1899–1904, March 5, 1900.

31. Minutes of club meetings of the Redlands Contemporary Club, 1899–1904, November 9, 1903.

32. Minutes of club meetings of the Redlands Contemporary Club, 1904–7, November 14, 1904.

33. Minutes of club meetings of the Redlands Contemporary Club, 1899–1904, annual report, April 1902.

34. Minutes of club meetings of the Redlands Contemporary Club, 1921–22, annual report.

35. Minutes of club meetings of the Redlands Contemporary Club, 1904–7, January 15, 1906.

36. Minutes of club meetings of the Redlands Contemporary Club, 1907–10, March 29, 1909.

37. Minutes of club meetings of the Redlands Contemporary Club, 1910–15, January 31, 1910.

38. Minutes of club meetings of the Redlands Contemporary Club, 1910–15, January 31, 1911.

39. Minutes of club meetings of the Redlands Contemporary Club, 1915–19, February 3, 1919.

40. Riverside Woman's Club, Scrapbook, 1912. Riverside Woman's Club Records. Special Collections, Riverside Public Library.

41. "The San Francisco District Convention," *Club Woman* (November 1913): 15.

42. Chudacoff and Smith, *Evolution of American Urban Society,* 176.

43. *Oakland Enquirer,* January 22, 1908.

44. "History of the Oakland Business and Professional Women's Club," 1–4. Oakland Business Women's Club Papers. Oakland History Room, Oakland Public Library.

45. "Club Ideals," *Business Women's Herald,* December 10, 1923.

46. *Business Women's Herald,* August 27, 1923.

47. *Business Women's Herald,* October 29, 1923.

48. "In Five Years—What Then?" *Business Women's Herald,* January 11, 1926.

49. "Boost," *Business Women's Herald,* September 3, 1923.

50. *Business Women's Herald,* October 29, 1923.

51. "Looking Forward," *Business Women's Herald,* December 10, 1923.

52. *Yearbook,* Redlands Contemporary Club, 1920–21, Redlands Contemporary Club Papers.

53. Minutes of the board of directors of the Redlands Contemporary Club,

1922–23, October 3, 1922; and Minutes of club meetings, 1922–23, December 4, 1922.

54. Minutes of the board of directors of the Redlands Contemporary Club, 1922–23, February 6, 1923.

55. Minutes of club meetings of the Redlands Contemporary Club, 1923–24, April 28, 1924.

56. Minutes of club meetings of the Redlands Contemporary Club, 1923–24, May 12, 1924.

57. Minutes of club meetings of the Redlands Contemporary Club, 1924–25, February 3 and 16, 1925.

58. Agreement for Sale of Real Estate, County of San Bernardino, California, January 1, 1917, Fisk Business Records, Fisk Family Papers.

59. Ruth Eddy Sargent, "Publicity Problems of a Small California Community (as Exemplified by Redlands)," 1925, Public Relations Records, Redlands Chamber of Commerce Papers, Heritage Room, A. K. Smiley Public Library.

60. Ibid.

61. Ibid.

62. Ibid.

63. Ibid.

64. Paula Baker, "The Domestication of Politics: Women and American Political Society, 1780–1920," *American Historical Review* (June 1984): 620–47.

Chapter 3

Substantial sections of this chapter have previously appeared in the *Journal of the West.* Lee M. A. Simpson, "Boosters in Petticoats: California Women and the Chamber of Commerce, 1880–1930," *Journal of the West* 42, no. 4 (Fall 2003). Reprinted with permission of *Journal of the West*, 1531 Yuma, Manhattan, KS 66502 USA.

1. An extensive body of literature in women's history documents the contributions of women to late-nineteenth- and early-twentieth-century municipal reform movements throughout the United States. A sampling of this work includes Lois W. Banner, *Women in Modern America: A Brief History,* 2nd ed. (New York, 1984); Robyn Muncy, *Creating a Female Dominion in American Reform, 1890–1935* (New York, 1991); Mary P. Ryan, *Womanhood in America: From Colonial Times to the Present* (New York, 1975); Kathryn Kish Sklar, "Hull House in the 1890s: A Community of Women Reformers," *Signs* 10 (1985): 657–77; Dorothy Schneider and Carl J. Schneider, *American Women in the Progressive Era, 1900–1920* (New York, 1994); and Glenna Matthews, *The Rise of Public Woman: Woman's Power and Woman's Place in the United States, 1630–1970* (New York, 1992).

2. Andrea Tuttle Kornbluh, "City Sex: Views of American Women and Urban Culture, 1869–1990," *Urban History Yearbook,* 1991, 60–83. See also Mary Ritter Beard, *Women's Work in Municipalities* (1915; reprint, New York, 1972).

3. *Redlands Chamber of Commerce Bulletin* 1, no. 2 (May 1912), Internal Affairs, Redlands Chamber of Commerce Papers, Heritage Room, A. K. Smiley Public Library.

4. For studies of Progressive era municipal politics and the backlash against Gilded Age corruption, see Eric Monkkonen, *America Becomes Urban: The Development of U.S. Cities and Towns, 1780–1980* (Berkeley, CA, 1988); Kevin Starr, *Inventing the Dream: California Through the Progressive Era* (New York, 1985); and Robert Wiebe, *The Search for Order, 1877–1920* (New York, 1968).

5. *Oakland Enquirer,* December 12, 1907.

6. Marc A. Weiss, *The Rise of the Community Builders: The American Real Estate Industry and Urban Land Planning* (New York, 1987).

7. See Greg Hise and William Deverell, *Eden by Design: The 1930 Olmsted-Bartholomew Plan for the Los Angeles Region* (Berkeley, CA, 2000).

8. For work that stresses speculation in western urbanization, see Gunther Barth, *Instant Cities: Urbanization and the Rise of San Francisco and Denver* (Albuquerque, NM, 1988); Mike Davis, *City of Quartz: Excavating the Future in Los Angeles* (New York, 1990); Starr, *Inventing the Dream; and* Starr, *Material Dreams: Southern California Through the 1920s* (New York, 1990). For studies that emphasize planned and controlled growth, see Weiss, *Rise of the Community Builders;* Monkkonen, *America Becomes Urban*; and Mansel Blackford, *The Lost Dream: Businessmen and City Planning on the Pacific Coast* (Columbus, OH, 1994).

9. Correspondence in the Redlands Chamber of Commerce papers indicates that the chamber was more concerned with attracting investors than people who sought only clerical or blue collar employment opportunities. Many women, for example, wrote to the chamber asking about opportunities for work as stenographers or clerks. The chamber responded that the city had an oversupply of competent clerks and suggested that the women look for work elsewhere. In contrast, when women indicated an interest in starting a business or buying citrus property, they received more encouragement from the chamber. Public Relations Files, Redlands Chamber of Commerce Papers, Heritage Room, A. K. Smiley Public Library.

10. *Redlands Citrograph,* March 17, 1888.

11. *Redlands Citrograph,* December 29, 1888, and January 5, 1889.

12. *Redlands Citrograph,* December 8, 1888.

13. Karen Blair, *The Clubwoman as Feminist* (New York, 1980). Blair argues that women joined social and civic clubs from "an emotional need to express one's identity and make a lasting contribution." Club membership afforded women the opportunity to engage in "self-expression" (xi–xii).

14. *Redlands Citrograph,* March 16, 1889.

15. *Redlands Citrograph,* May 18, 1889.

16. *Redlands Citrograph,* January 18 and April 26, 1890.

17. There are few references to the Ladies Annex in the minute books of the Los Angeles Chamber of Commerce. In general, those that do appear regard asking the ladies to serve as hostesses or to decorate the chamber offices with flowers and fruit. Minute Books of the Los Angeles Chamber of Commerce, August 19, September 18 and 25, and October 6 and 30, 1891. A request by the ladies to make money by selling ice cream at the chamber was denied on the grounds of being "impracticable." Minute Books of the Los Angeles Chamber

of Commerce, June 5, 1890. Los Angeles Chamber of Commerce Papers, Special Collections, University of Southern California.

18. *Los Angeles Times*, March 20, 1890.

19. *Los Angeles Times*, May 4, June 2, October 2, and December 16, 1890; May 26 and June 9, 1891.

20. *Los Angeles Times*, December 16, 1890.

21. *Los Angeles Times*, June 2, 1891.

22. Ibid.

23. *Los Angeles Times*, May 26 and June 2 and 9, 1891.

24. Cletus Daniel argues that between 1870 and 1910, Californians engaged in a struggle to determine the nature of the state's economic development. Would the state develop in the Jeffersonian tradition of the small family farmer, or would it instead encourage large-scale, industrialized agriculture that placed individual profit above social welfare? The debate took place in rural and urban communities, in chambers of commerce, men's clubs, and women's clubs. Daniel suggests that by 1905 the debate was over and individual profit pursued in large-scale, industrialized agriculture had triumphed. California cities would thus follow an economic development model in which the provision of social services would be subsumed to programs designed to enhance individual and city wealth. Daniel, *Bitter Harvest: A History of California Farmworkers, 1870–1941* (Berkeley, CA, 1981), 15–39.

25. *Los Angeles Times*, June 2, 9, and 20, 1891.

26. *Los Angeles Times*, September 15, 1891.

27. *Los Angeles Times*, June 30, 1891.

28. *Oakland Enquirer*, July 19, 1910.

29. Ibid.

30. *Oakland Enquirer*, July 19, August 2, 1910.

31. *Oakland Enquirer*, October 13, 1910.

32. *Oakland Enquirer*, October 25, 1910.

33. Mrs. George M. Lockwood to the Redlands Chamber of Commerce, [no date], Internal Concerns Files, Redlands Chamber of Commerce Papers.

34. Mrs. George M. Lockwood, "What They Do in a One Man's Town" (paper presented to the Redlands Contemporary Club [no date, ca. 1917], Internal Concerns Files, Redlands Chamber of Commerce Papers.

35. Janette Sturges to the Redlands Chamber of Commerce, September 17, 1923, Public Relations Files, Redlands Chamber of Commerce Papers.

36. Mrs. Milo Smith to the Redlands Chamber of Commerce, October 31, 1924, Public Relations Files, Redlands Chamber of Commerce Papers.

37. Jane Taltavall to the Redlands Chamber of Commerce, April 28, 1926; and A. E. Isham to Taltavall, April 30, 1926, Public Relations Files, Redlands Chamber of Commerce Papers.

38. *Oakland Enquirer*, October 31, 1910.

39. Myra Kingman Miller to the chamber of commerce, March 18, 1908, Events Files, Redlands Chamber of Commerce Papers.

40. Affidavit for Mrs. Mary Lynde Craig from the Redlands Chamber of

Commerce, September 26, 1908, Events Files, Redlands Chamber of Commerce Papers.

41. Secretary to Mrs. D. J. Carpenter, April 10, 1914, Events Files, Redlands Chamber of Commerce Papers.

42. "Promises City Planning Law," *Oakland Achievement* 1, no. 2 (March 1915): 4; Joseph E. Caine to Reinhardt, February 15, 1919, and Reinhardt to Caine, February 17, 1919, Office of the President Papers, 1916–19, Special Collections, Mills College Library.

43. Lavenson to Reinhardt, October 23, 1916, January 25 and February 8, 1918; and Reinhardt to Lavenson, February 7 and 11, 1918, Office of the President Papers, 1916–19.

44. Fitch to Reinhardt, December 21 and 29, 1916, and Reinhardt to Fitch, December 27, 1916, and January 2, 1917, Office of the President Papers, 1916–19.

45. K. L. Hamman to Reinhardt, February 18, 1919, Office of the President Papers, 1916–19.

46. S. Glen Andrus to Reinhardt, October 13 and November 6, 1916; J. T. Nickey to Reinhardt, n.d.; Mrs. L. M. Spiegl to Reinhardt, January 9, 1920; E. A. Walcott to Reinhardt, May 18, 1920; William Loewi to Reinhardt, November 27, 1920; J. T. Edwards to Reinhardt, January 10, 1921; Telegram, M. C. Raymond to Reinhardt, January 12, 1921; Fred Brandt to Reinhardt, May 24, 1921; Roscoe D. Wyatt to Reinhardt, September 2, 1921; Ben C. Dailey to Reinhardt, October 10, 1921, Office of the President Papers, 1916–19.

Chapter 4

1. The day-to-day operations of city government have not received adequate attention from urban historians, who have focused their efforts on the larger issues of economic growth or the more detailed topics of political machines and municipal government reform. Eric Monkkonen, *America Becomes Urban: The Development of U.S. Cities and Towns, 1780–1980* (Berkeley, CA, 1988), 132.

2. Winston W. Crouch and Dean E. Henry, *California Government: Politics and Administration* (Berkeley, CA, 1949), 185.

3. California became the second state in the union to permit home rule for cities. Missouri had done so in 1875 but allowed only larger cities a limited amount of home rule. Crouch and Henry, *California Government*, 208.

4. Crouch and Henry, *California Government*, 208.

5. For histories of Los Angeles and San Francisco, see Kevin Starr, *Material Dreams: Southern California Through the 1920s* (New York, 1990); and Starr, *Inventing the Dream: California Through the Progressive Era* (New York, 1985). On Orange County, see Stephanie Pincetl, "The Politics of Influence: Democracy and the Growth Machine in Orange County, U.S." in *The Urban Growth Machine: Critical Perspectives Two Decades Later*, edited by Andrew E. G. Jonas and David Wilson (Albany, NY, 1999), 195–212.

6. Larry Burgess, *Redlands: Remembrance and Reflection* (Redlands, CA, 1981).

7. *Redlands Citrograph*, January 18, 1890.

8. *Redlands Citrograph,* May 4, 1889, and August 8, 1890.
9. *Redlands Citrograph,* August 17, 1889.
10. See the petition of Mrs. R. W. Brown to the City Trustees for plowing out a gutter on Cypress Avenue. The city hired Robert Chestnut to complete the work. *Redlands Citrograph,* January 25, 1890, and February 8, 1890.
11. *Redlands Citrograph,* April 26, 1890.
12. *Riverside Daily Press,* April 5, 1901.
13. *Riverside Daily Press,* March 23 and 31 and April 6 and 13, 1905.
14. *Riverside Daily Press,* January 31 and February 9, 1900.
15. *Riverside Daily Press,* March 13, 1900.
16. *Riverside Daily Press,* May 22, 1900.
17. *Riverside Daily Press,* June 13, 1905.
18. Riverside *Daily Press,* June 14, 1905.
19. *Oakland Enquirer,* May 14, 1906.
20. *Oakland Enquirer,* May 8, 1906.
21. *Oakland Enquirer,* April 26, 1907.
22. Michael Doucet and James Weaver, *Housing the North American City* (Montreal, 1991), 17.
23. *Oakland Enquirer,* May 10, 1907.
24. *Oakland Enquirer,* May 30, 1907.
25. *Oakland Enquirer,* January 8, 1907.
26. Paula Baker, "The Domestication of Politics: Women and American Political Society, 1780–1920," *American Historical Review* 89 (June 1984): 620–47.
27. Mansel Blackford, *The Lost Dream: Businessmen and City Planning on the Pacific Coast* (Columbus, OH, 1993), 69.
28. *Oakland Enquirer,* March 1, 1906.
29. *Oakland Enquirer,* June 7, 1906.
30. *Oakland Enquirer,* April 5, 1906.
31. *Oakland Enquirer,* June 27, 1906.
32. *Oakland Enquirer,* May 22, 1906.
33. *Oakland Enquirer,* January 29, 1909.
34. *Oakland Enquirer,* October 18, 1907; *Oakland Enquirer,* November 22, 1907.
35. *Oakland Enquirer,* November 22, 1907.
36. *Oakland Enquirer,* December 4, 1907.
37. *Oakland Enquirer,* December 10, 1907.
38. *Oakland Enquirer,* December 17, 1907.
39. *Oakland Enquirer,* August 22, 1908.
40. *Oakland Enquirer,* February 7, 1911.
41. *Oakland Enquirer,* February 18, 1911.
42. *Oakland Enquirer,* February 21, 1911; *Oakland Enquirer,* February 24, 1911.
43. *Oakland Enquirer,* February 24, 1911.
44. *Oakland Enquirer,* February 25, 1911.
45. *Oakland Enquirer,* February 27, 1911.
46. *Oakland Enquirer,* March 2, 1911; *Oakland Enquirer,* March 3, 1911; *Oakland Enquirer,* March 4, 1911; *Oakland Enquirer,* March 6, 1911.

Chapter 5

1. Mel Scott, *American City Planning Since 1890* (Berkeley, 1971); Maureen Flanagan, "The City Profitable, the City Livable: Environmental Policy, Gender, and Power in Chicago in the 1910s," *Journal of Urban History* 22 (January 1996), 163–90; William H. Wilson, *The City Beautiful Movement* (Baltimore, 1989); Greg Hise and William Deverell, *Eden by Design: The 1930 Olmsted-Bartholomew Plan for the Los Angeles Region* (Berkeley, 2000); Marc A. Weiss, *The Rise of the Community Builders: The American Real Estate Industry and Urban Land Planning* (New York, 1987); Mansel Blackford, *The Lost Dream: Businessmen and City Planning on the Pacific Coast* (Columbus, OH, 1993); Marguerite Duncan-Abrams, "The History of the Riverside Planning Commission, 1914–1928" (master's thesis, University of California, Riverside, 1994); Gabriele G. Carey, "From Hinterland to Metropolis: The Origins of Land Use Planning in Orange County, California, 1925–1955" (Ph.D. diss., University of California, Riverside, 1997).

2. Robyn Muncy, *Creating a Female Dominion in American Reform, 1890–1935* (New York, 1991); Karen Blair, *The Clubwoman as Feminist: True Womanhood Redefined, 1868–1914* (New York, 1980).

3. Weiss, *Rise of the Community Builders.*

4. Blackford, *Lost Dream,* 4.

5. Ibid., 1.

6. Kevin Starr, *Inventing the Dream: California Through the Progressive Era* (Oxford, 1985); and Starr, *Material Dreams: Southern California Through the 1920s* (Oxford, 1990).

7. Blackford, *Lost Dream,* 13–30.

8. Joseph Baker, *Past and Present of Alameda County California* (Chicago, 1914), 1:356.

9. Ibid.

10. Quoted in Elizabeth Bagwell, *Oakland: The Story of a City* (Novato, CA, 1982), 119. This refrain would echo through Oakland's promotional literature through the 1930s as the Oakland elite came to recognize the commercial value of beautiful homes, safe neighborhoods, and good schools. See the *Oakland Tribune* yearbooks, 1909–40.

11. Blackford, *Lost Dream,* 64.

12. *Oakland Enquirer,* August 6, 1909.

13. *Oakland Enquirer,* January 1, 1906.

14. Blackford, *Lost Dream,* 16.

15. *Oakland Enquirer,* January 1, 1906.

16. Blackford, *Lost Dream,* 64.

17. *Oakland Enquirer,* June 6, 1906.

18. *Oakland Enquirer,* October 3, 1906.

19. *Oakland Enquirer,* October 6, 1906.

20. *Oakland Enquirer,* January 2, 1907.

21. *Oakland Enquirer,* January 8, 1907.

22. *Oakland Enquirer,* February 5, 1907.

23. *Oakland Enquirer,* January 9, 1907.

24. *Oakland Enquirer,* January 11, 1907.
25. *Oakland Enquirer,* February 5, 1907.
26. *Oakland Enquirer,* January 2, 1909.
27. *Oakland Enquirer,* January 1, 1906.
28. *Oakland Enquirer,* April 16, 1906.
29. *Oakland Enquirer,* August 6, 1909.
30. *Oakland Enquirer,* August 9, 1909.
31. "Promises City Planning Law," *Oakland Achievement* 1 (March 1915): 4.
32. Lavenson to Reinhardt, October 23, 1916, and January 25, 1918, Office of the President, Papers, 1916–19, Special Collections, Mills College Library.
33. Reid to Reinhardt, October 25, 1918, and Reinhardt to Reed, October 29, 1918, Office of the President Papers, 1916–19.
34. Charles E. Hewes to Reinhardt, February 28, 1919, Office of the President Papers, 1916–19.
35. E. C. Elliott to Reinhardt, November 21, 1919, Office of the President Papers, 1916–19.
36. Jesse J. Dunn to Reinhardt, February 11, 1920, Office of the President, Papers, 1916–19.
37. *Riverside Daily Press,* January 29, 1914.
38. *Riverside Daily Press,* November 30, 1915.
39. *Riverside Daily Press,* November 30, 1915.
40. *Riverside Enterprise,* March 14, 1916.
41. Riverside Planning Commission Minutes, 1919. Special Collections. Library. University of California Riverside.
42. Riverside Woman's Club membership notes and scrapbooks, 1896–1927. Riverside Woman's Club Handbook, 1896. Riverside Woman's Club Papers. Local History Room. Riverside Public Library.
43. Riverside Planning Commission Minutes, 1918–21.
44. Minutes of board of directors meetings of the Redlands Contemporary Club, 1906–13, October 10, 1910, Redlands Contemporary Club Papers, Heritage Room, A. K. Smiley Public Library.
45. Minutes of club meetings of the Redlands Contemporary Club, 1910–15, January 31, 1911.
46. Minutes of the board of directors of the Redlands Contemporary Club, 1906–13, May 4, 1912.
47. Minutes of club meetings of the Redlands Contemporary Club, 1922–23, April 9, 1923.
48. Ibid., October 29, 1923.
49. Ibid., March 17, 1924.
50. Minutes of the Redlands Chamber of Commerce, April 9, 1924, Chamber of Commerce Papers.
51. Minutes of club meetings of the Redlands Contemporary Club, 1925–26, April 26 and May 3, 1926.
52. Ibid., May 3, 1926.
53. Minutes of club meetings of the Redlands Contemporary Club, 1926–27, November 1, 1926.

54. Minutes of board of directors meetings of the Redlands Contemporary Club, 1926–27, November 15, 1926.

55. Minutes of the Redlands Chamber of Commerce, January 26, 1927, Chamber of Commerce Papers.

56. Alan Dawley, *Struggles for Justice: Social Responsibility and the Liberal State* (Cambridge, MA, 1991), 1.

Chapter 6

1. Quoted in Frank J. Taylor, "Blue Ribbon Citizen," *Survey Graphic* (March 1940), 180.

2. Carey McWilliams, *Southern California: An Island on the Land* (1946; reprint, Salt Lake City, 1990), 77. For more on the Anglo preservation movement in Southern California, see Kevin Starr, *Inventing the Dream: California Through the Progressive Era* (New York, 1986), 64–127; Starr, *Material Dream: Southern California Through the 1920s* (New York, 1990), 263–302.

3. Norman Tyler, *Historic Preservation: An Introduction to Its History, Principles, and Practice* (New York, 2000), 33–34.

4. William H. Wilson, "The Ideology, Aesthetics, and Politics of the City Beautiful Movement," in *The Rise of Modern Urban Planning, 1800–1914*, edited by Anthony Sutcliffe (New York, 1988), 166–98.

5. Starr, *Material Dreams*, 278.

6. Although Chase took the title of secretary, her work extended far beyond traditional clerical duties. She worked more as Hoffmann's partner, contributing to the organization of the committee, initiation of projects, and public education. According to her biographer, Roseanne Barker, Chase made a conscious decision as a college undergraduate never to do clerical work. "In college, typing was required and everybody wanted me to be secretary of their committees. I said I was never going to do that, I'd do something on my own." Quoted in Roseanne Marie Barker, "Small Town Progressivism: Pearl Chase and Female Activism in Santa Barbara, 1909–1929" (Ph.D. diss., University of California, Santa Barbara, 1994), 241.

7. Quoted in Ronald Nye, "The Influence of the Chase Family on Santa Barbara History" (paper presented at the West Coast Symposium on Family History, University of California, Santa Barbara, May 1, 1976), 4.

8. *Santa Barbara News-Press*, November 17, 1968.

9. Pearl Chase Diaries, 1905–9, Chase Family Papers, Community Development and Conservation Collection (CDCC), Special Collections, University of California, Santa Barbara, Library.

10. Nye, "Influence of the Chase Family."

11. Hezekiah G. Chase, Pearl's father, died intestate. His probate records indicate that he transferred ownership of the property at 2012 Anacapa St. to Pearl Chase in 1949. Probate Records, Santa Barbara County Superior Court.

12. Pearl Chase, "A Brief Report of H. G. Chase, Real Estate, 1903–1953," 1, Chase Family Papers, CDCC.

13. *Santa Barbara News-Press*, January 30, 1951.

14. Barker, "Small Town Progressivism," 235.

15. [Pearl Chase] to S. S. Cook, July 11, 1924, Better Homes Papers, CDCC.

16. Clarke A. Chambers, *Seedtime of Reform: American Social Service and Social Action, 1918–1933* (Minneapolis, 1965), 135–38.

17. Mrs. W. L. Lawton to Bernhard Hoffmann, February 22, 1924, Letterhead, Better Homes Papers, CDCC.

18. Michael Doucet and James Weaver, *Housing the North American City* (Montreal, 1991), 119.

19. Pearl Chase, interview by Gibbs Smith, "Oral History," 1972, tape 1, side 1, p. 10, and tape 3, side 1, p. 11. Oral History Collection, Special Collections Library, University of California, Santa Barbara.

20. Ibid.

21. Barker, "Small Town Progressivism," 257–58.

22. Pearl Chase, "History of the H. G. Chase Real Estate Co."

23. *Santa Barbara Morning Press,* September 19, 1922.

24. S. J. McKinnon to Pearl Chase, April 22, 1931, Better Homes Papers, CDCC.

25. W. C. Paulton to Pearl Chase, May 20, 1931, Better Homes Papers, CDCC.

26. Pearl Chase to Building and Loan Associations, May 20, 1931, Better Homes Papers, CDCC.

27. Duncan McDuffie to Pearl Chase, December 9, 1924, Better Homes Papers, CDCC.

28. Duncan McDuffie to Pearl Chase, June 17, 1929, Better Homes Papers, CDCC.

29. Report, Pearl Chase, December 30, 1924, Better Homes Papers, CDCC.

30. Memorandum for Mr. F. A. Hoefer, President, County National Bank and Trust Company to Pearl Chase, January 26, 1925, Better Homes Papers, CDCC.

31. Letterhead, Earle Ovington to Pearl Chase, April 18, 1925, Better Homes Papers, CDCC.

32. Pearl Chase to Lloyed Tilton, May 11, 1925, Better Homes Papers, CDCC.

33. Pearl Chase to Norman McFadden, May 21, 1925, Better Homes Papers, CDCC.

34. Pearl Chase to Lloyd Tilton, May 25, 1925, Better Homes Papers, CDCC.

35. Better Homes Committee, "How to Own Your Own Home," 1925, Better Homes Papers, CDCC.

36. James Ford to Pearl Chase, September 1, 1925, Better Homes Papers, CDCC.

37. Herbert U. Nelson to Pearl Chase, November 20, 1931, Better Homes Papers, CDCC. See enclosed lesson plans.

38. Ibid., Lesson XI, 3.

39. Ibid., 2.

40. Ibid., Lesson XII.

41. Ronald Tobey, Charles Wetherell, and Jay Brigham, "Moving Out and Settling In: Residential Mobility, Home Owning, and the Public Enframing of

Citizenship, 1921–1950," *American Historical Review* 95 (December 1990), 1395–422; and Doucet and Weaver, *Housing the North American City,* chap. 6.

42. Howard C. Gates, Typescript "Better Homes Week," April 27, 1938, Better Homes Papers, CDCC.

43. [Better Homes in America], "Better Homes in America Is Engaged in Active Promotion of Home Ownership Because," [n.d.], Better Homes Papers, CDCC.

44. Doucet and Weaver challenge the interpretations of Manuel Castells, David Harvey, and Mathew Edel, Elliott Sklar, and Daniel Luria. Doucet and Weaver, *Housing the North American City,* 166–73.

45. Quoted in Frank J. Taylor, "Blue Ribbon Citizen," 180.

46. Barker, "Small Town Progressivism," vii.

47. [Pearl Chase], Memorandum, April 3, 1925, Better Homes Papers, CDCC.

48. Architectural Advisory Committee, Minutes, July 7, 1925, Plans and Planting Papers, CDCC.

49. "Santa Barbara's Opportunity," [n.d.]. This unsigned typescript was probably written by Hoffmann but was included in Chase's personal papers, indicating her approval of its content. Chase Family Papers, CDCC.

50. Ibid.

51. Elma C. Levy to Bernhard Hoffmann, July 21, 1925, Plans and Planting Papers, CDCC.

52. *Santa Barbara Daily News,* October 1, [1925?]

53. [Pearl Chase] typescript, [n.d.], Chase Family Papers, CDCC.

54. Edwin Bergstrom to Bernard [*sic.*] Hofmann, July 11, 1925, Plans and Planting Papers, CDCC.

55. Bernhard Hoffmann to Paul Plunkett, July 22, 1925, Plans and Planting Papers, CDCC.

56. Bernhard Hoffmann to editor, *Santa Barbara Morning Press,* August 4, 1925, Plans and Planting Papers, CDCC.

57. "Meeting of the State Street Property Owners," typescript, [n.d.], Chase Family Papers, CDCC.

58. Michael A. Levy to Mrs. John Kahn, August 20, 1925, Plans and Planting Papers, CDCC.

59. Helen Dean Bogsa to Bernhard Hoffmann, [n.d.], Chase Family Papers, CDCC.

60. [Pearl Chase] to Theodora Kimball Hubbard, February 9, 1927, Better Homes Papers, CDCC.

61. Ibid.

62. Mark A. Weiss, *The Rise of the Community Builders: the American Real Estate Industry and Urban Land Planning* (New York, 1987), 12.

63. LeRoy E. Bowman to Pearl Chase, March 14, 1929, Better Homes Papers, CDCC.

64. Marie B. Maulsby to Pearl Chase, June 14, 1929, Better Homes Papers, CDCC.

65. *Santa Barbara News-Press,* January 30, 1951.

66. Harry B. Brainerd to William A. Boring, June 10, 1927, and Isabel Norton Fish to Pearl Chase, February 12, 1928, Better Homes Papers, CDCC.

67. L. Deming Tilton to Pearl Chase, July 26, 1928, and June 12, 1929, Better Homes Papers, CDCC.

68. E. E. East to Pearl Chase, April 23, 1929, Better Homes Papers, CDCC.

69. Tilton to Chase July 1, 1929, and August 5, 1929, Better Homes Papers, CDCC.

70. O. Bartlett to Community Arts Association, July 8, 1927, Better Homes Papers, CDCC.

71. Mrs. James M. Smith to [Pearl Chase], March 9, 1928, Better Homes Papers, CDCC.

72. Hazel G. McCabe to Pearl Chase, January 30, 1928, Better Homes Papers, CDCC.

73. Herb Andree and Noel Young, *Santa Barbara Architecture from Spanish Colonial to Modern* (Santa Barbara, CA, 1975), 8.

Conclusion

1. Gerald D. Nash, *The American West in the Twentieth Century: A Short History of an Urban Oasis* (Albuquerque, NM, 1977), 191.

2. Carl Abbott, *The Metropolitan Frontier: Cities in the Modern American West* (Tucson, AZ, 1993), 111.

Bibliography

I. Primary Sources

A. MANUSCRIPT COLLECTIONS

Department of Special Collections, Library, University of California, Santa Barbara

Community Development and Conservation Collection

Allied and Protective and Improvement Association Papers
Architectural Advisory Committee Papers
Architectural Board of Review Papers
Awards and Honors Scrapbooks
Better Homes Papers
California Roadside Council Papers
Chase Family Papers
City of Santa Barbara Papers
Clubs and Associations Papers
Community Arts Association Papers
County of Santa Barbara Papers
Ephemera Collection
Local History Essay File
Newspaper Clippings File
Pamphlets Collection
Plans and Planting Papers
Photograph Collection
Santa Barbara Beautiful Papers
Santa Barbara Chamber of Commerce Papers
Small House Design Competition Papers

Oral History Collection

Bancroft Library, University of California, Berkeley

Berkeley Club Papers
Charles Henry Cheney Papers

Gledhill Library, Santa Barbara Historical Society
Oral History Collection
Scrapbook Collection
Department of Special Collections, Library, Mills College
Aurelia Henry Reinhardt Papers
Personal and Family Papers, 1824–1948
Office of the President Files, 1916–43
Rosalind Keep Files, 1916–48
American Association of University Women, 1919–32
Writings of Aurelia Henry Reinhardt, 1905–47
Newspaper Clippings, 1914–48
Department of Special Collections, Library, University of Southern California
Los Angeles Chamber of Commerce Papers
Heritage Room, A. K. Smiley Public Library, Redlands, California
John and Elizabeth Fisk Family Papers
Correspondence from Friends
Elizabeth H. Fisk Diaries
Elizabeth H. Fisk Personal Correspondence
Helen Graves Fisk Business Correspondence
Helen Graves Fisk Business Papers
Helen Graves Fisk Personal Correspondence
John P. Fisk Correspondence
Ruth Eddy Sargent Personal correspondence
Redlands Contemporary Club Papers
Club Minutes, 1896–1944
Board of Directors Minutes, 1896–1944
Club Yearbooks, 1896–1944
Redlands Chamber of Commerce Records
Board of Directors Minutes
Correspondence Files
History Room, Oakland Public Library
Business and Professional Women's Club Papers
Local History Room, Riverside Public Library
Riverside Woman's Club Papers
Mary Darling Scrapbooks
San Bernardino County Archives
Office of the Recorder, Index to Deeds, 1854–1926
Office of the County Clerk, Index to Superior Court Cases

B. PRINTED PRIMARY SOURCES

Baker, Joseph E. "Deep Water in the Harbor Means Commercial Greatness for Oakland." *Oakland Tribune,* December 31, 1900, waterfront edition,December p. 1.

Better Homes in America. *Better Homes in America: Do You Want Better Homes in Your Community?* Washington, D.C.: Better Homes in America, 1925.

Blake, Evarts, I. *Greater Oakland*. Oakland: Pacific Publishing Co., 1911.

Brown, Rexwald. "A New Santa Barbara." *American Review of Reviews* 72 (August 1925): 159–62.

Chase, Pearl. "Better Homes in Santa Barbara." *New Santa Barbara*. Santa Barbara: Plans and Planting Committee, c. 1926: 48–56.

———. "Santa Barbara Resurgent." *Survey* 54 (August 1925): 469–72.

Crane, Hattie Elliot. "Woman's Place in the Government and Conduct of Society." *Overland Monthly and Out West Magazine* 59 (April 1912): 359–66.

Crawford, Evelyn. "The Woman and the Club in California." *Overland Monthly and Out West Magazine* 53 (February 1909): 120–25.

Gibson, Mary S. *A Record of Twenty-five Years of the California Federation of Women's Clubs, 1900–1925*. Vol. 1. N.p., 1927.

Greater San Francisco and Its Environs. San Francisco: Pacific Novelty Co., 1921.

Greater San Francisco Association. *Greater San Francisco: The Clearing House of California for Her Commerce with the World*. San Francisco: International Printing Co., 1912.

Greater San Francisco Committee. *Greater San Francisco Primer*. San Francisco: n.p., 1907.

Home Builder's Plan Book: A Collection of Architectural Designs for Small Houses Submitted in Competition by Architects and Architectural Draftsmen in Connection with the 1921 'Own Your Home' Exhibitions, New York and Chicago. New York: Building Plan Holding Corporation, 1921.

Kenney, Elizabeth L., William Chambers, and Willoughby Rodman. *Laws of California Relating to Women and Children*. Los Angeles: Baumgardt Publishing Co., 1910.

MacFadden, Hamilton. "The Community Arts Association of Santa Barbara, California." *Playground* (December 1924): 530–34.

Mitchell, Edward H. *Greater San Francisco as Seen Today*. San Francisco: Edw. H. Mitchell, 1908.

Nob Hill Apartment Co., *Greater San Francisco*. San Francisco: n.p., 1909.

Oakland Chamber of Commerce. *Oakland: The City of Opportunity*. Oakland: Chamber of Commerce, 1909.

Plans and Planting. *Small House Designs*. Santa Barbara: Plans and Planting, 1924.

Purdy, Helen Throop. *Greater San Francisco and Its Environs*. San Francisco: Pacific Novelty Co., 1921.

Winter, Alice Ames. *The Business of Being a Club Woman*. New York: n.p., 1925.

C. NEWSPAPERS AND JOURNALS

Business Woman's Herald (Oakland, California)

The Citrograph (Redlands, California)

The Club Woman (General Federation of Women's Clubs, Boston)

Land of Sunshine

Los Angeles Times

Oakland Enquirer

Oakland Tribune

Oakland Tribune Yearbook

Riverside Daily Press
Riverside Enterprise
Santa Barbara Daily Independent
Santa Barbara Independent
Santa Barbara Morning Press
Santa Barbara News-Press

II. Secondary Sources

A. BOOKS

Abbott, Carl. *Boosters and Businessmen: Popular Economic Thought and Urban Growth in the Antebellum Middle West*. Westport, CT: Greenwood Press, 1981.

———. *The Metropolitan Frontier: Cities in the Modern American West*. Tucson: University of Arizona Press, 1993.

Andree, Herb, and Young, Noel. *Santa Barbara Architecture from Spanish Colonial to Modern*. Santa Barbara: Capra Press, 1975.

Baker, Joseph E., ed. *Past and Present of Alameda County, California*. Vol. 1. Chicago: S. J. Clarke Publishing Co., 1914.

Barth, Gunther. *Instant Cities: Urbanization and the Rise of San Francisco and Denver*. Albuquerque: University of New Mexico Press, 1988.

Bauer, John E. *The Health Seekers of Southern California, 1870–1900*. San Marino, CA: Huntington Library, 1959.

Beard, Charles A. *An Economic Interpretation of the Constitution*. 1913. Reprint, New York: McMillan, 1956.

Beard, Mary Ritter. *Women's Work in Municipalities*. 1915. Reprint, New York: Arno Press, 1972.

Berg, Barbara. *The Remembered Gate: Origins of American Feminism, the Woman, and the City, 1800–1860*. New York: Oxford University Press, 1978.

Binheim, Max, ed. *Women of the West: A Series of Biographical Sketches of Living Eminent Women in the Eleven Western States of the United States of America*. 1929 ed. Los Angeles: Publishers Press, 1928.

Black, Naomi. *Social Feminism*. Ithaca, NY: Cornell University Press, 1989.

Blackford, Mansel G. *The Lost Dream: Businessmen and Planning on the Pacific Coast*. Columbus: Ohio State University Press, 1993.

———. *The Politics of Business in California, 1890–1920*. Columbus: Ohio State University Press, 1977.

Blair, Karen J. *The Clubwoman as Feminist: True Womanhood Redefined, 1868–1914*. New York: Holmes and Meier, 1980.

———. *The Torchbearers: Women and Their Amateur Arts Associations in America, 1890–1930*. Bloomington: Indiana University Press, 1994.

Boyer, Christine. *Dreaming the Rational City: The Myth of American City Planning*. Cambridge, MA: Harvard University Press, 1983.

Brown, Dorothy M. *Setting a Course: American Women in the 1920s*. American Women in the Twentieth Century Series. Boston: Twayne Publishers, 1987.

Cavallo, Dominick. *Muscles and Morals: Organized Playgrounds and Urban Reform, 1880–1920*. Philadelphia: University of Pennsylvania Press, 1981.

Chafe, William H. *The American Woman: Her Changing Social, Economic, and Political Roles, 1920–1970*. New York: Oxford University Press, 1972.

———. *The Paradox of Change: American Women in the 20th Century*. New York: Oxford Press, 1991.

Chambers, Clarke A. *Seedtime of Reform: American Social Service and Social Action, 1918–1933*. Minneapolis: University of Minnesota Press, 1965.

Chambers, John Whiteclay, III. *The Tyranny of Change: America in the Progressive Era, 1900–1917*. New York: St. Martin's Press, 1980.

Chandler, Alfred D. *The Visible Hand: The Managerial Revolution in American Business*. Cambridge, MA: Harvard University Press, 1977.

Charles, Jeffrey A. *Service Clubs in American Society: Rotary, Kiwanis, and Lions*. Urbana: University of Illinois Press, 1993.

Chudacoff, Howard P., and Smith, Judith E. *The Evolution of American Urban Society*. 5th ed. Englewood Cliffs, NJ: Prentice Hall, 2000.

Conmy, Peter Thomas. *The Historic Spanish Origin of California's Community Property Law and Its Development and Adaptation to Meet the Needs of an American State*. San Francisco: n.p., 1957.

Cott, Nancy F. *The Bonds of Womanhood: Woman's Sphere in New England, 1790–1835*. New Haven, CT: Yale University Press, 1975.

———. *The Grounding of Modern Feminism*. New Haven, CT: Yale University Press, 1988.

Cott, Nancy F., ed. *A Heritage of Her Own: Toward a New Social History of American Women*. New York: Simon and Schuster, 1979.

Cronon, William. *Nature's Metropolis: Chicago and the Great West*. New York: W. W. Norton, 1992.

Daniel, Cletus. *Bitter Harvest: A History of California Farmworkers, 1870–1941*. Berkeley: University of California Press, 1981.

Davies, Pearl Janet. *Women in Real Estate: A History of the Women's Council, National Association of Real Estate Boards*. Chicago: Women's Council of NAREB Committee on History, 1963.

Davis, Mike. *City of Quartz: Excavating the Future in Los Angeles*. New York: Vintage Books, 1990.

Davis, Reda. *California Women: A Guide to Their Politics, 1885–1911*. San Francisco: California Scene, 1968.

Dawley, Alan. *Struggles for Justice: Social Responsibility and the Liberal State*. Cambridge, MA: Harvard University Press, Belknap Press, 1991.

Degler, Carl. *At Odds: Women and the Family in America from the Revolution to the Present*. New York: Oxford University Press, 1980.

Dinkin, Robert J. *Before Equal Suffrage: Women in Partisan Politics, from Colonial Times to 1920*. Westport, CT: Greenwood Press, 1995.

Doucet, Michael, and James Weaver. *Housing the North American City*. Montreal: McGill-Queen's University Press, 1991.

Ebner, Michael H., and Eugene M. Tobin, eds. *The Age of Urban Reform: New Perspectives on the Progressive Era*, National University Publications Interdisciplinary Urban Series. Port Washington, NY: Kennikat Press, 1977.

Epstein, Barbara Leslie. *The Politics of Domesticity: Women, Evangelism, and Temperance in Nineteenth-Century America*. Middletown, CT: Wesleyan University Press, 1981.

Farley, Marco. *The Legacy of Pearl Chase*. Santa Barbara: Santa Barbara Trust for Historic Preservation, 1988.

Fisher, Irving D. *Frederick Law Olmsted and the City Planning Movement in the United States*. Architecture and Urban Design Series, No. 15. Ann Arbor, MI: UMI Research Press, 1986.

Fitzpatrick, Ellen. *Endless Crusade: Women Social Scientists and Progressive Reform*. New York: Oxford University Press, 1990.

Frankfort, Roberta. *Collegiate Women: Domesticity and Career in Turn-of-the-Century America*. New York: New York University Press, 1977.

Ginzberg, Lori D. *Women and the Work of Benevolence: Morality, Politics, and Class in the Nineteenth-Century United States*. New Haven, CT: Yale University Press, 1990.

Golden Jubilee Redlands California: 1888–1938. Redlands, CA: Citrograph Printing Co., 1938.

Goldin, Claudia. *Understanding the Gender Gap: An Economic History of American Women*. New York: Columbia University Press, 1990.

Harris, Barbara J. *Beyond Her Sphere: Women and the Professions in American History*. Westport, CT: Greenwood Press, 1978.

Harrison, Cynthia. *On Account of Sex: The Politics of Women's Issues, 1945–1968*. Berkeley: University of California Press, 1988.

Hayden, Dolores. *The Grand Domestic Revolution: A History of Feminist Designs for American Homes, Neighborhoods, and Cities*. Cambridge: Massachusetts Institute of Technology Press, 1981.

Hewitt, Nancy A. *Women's Activism and Social Change: Rochester, New York 1822–1872*. Ithaca, NY: Cornell University Press, 1984.

Hinckley, Edith Parker. *On the Banks of the Zanja: The Story of Redlands*. Claremont, CA: n.p., 1951.

Hirschman, Albert. *The Strategy of Economic Development*. New Haven, CT: Yale University Press, 1958.

Hise, Greg, and William Deverell. *Eden by Design: The 1930 Olmsted-Bartholomew Plan for the Los Angeles Region*. Berkeley: University of California Press, 2000.

Horowitz, Helen Lefkowitz. *Alma Mater: Design and Experience in the Women's Colleges from Their Nineteenth-Century Beginnings to the 1930s*. New York: Alfred A. Knopf, 1984.

Hummer, Patricia M. *The Decade of Elusive Promise: Professional Women in the United States, 1920–1930*. Studies in American History and Culture, No. 5. Ann Arbor, MI: UMI Research Press, 1979

Ingersoll, L. A. *Century Annals of San Bernardino County, 1769–1904*. Los Angeles: n.p., 1904.

Issel, William, and Robert W. Cherny. *San Francisco, 1865–1932: Politics, Power, and Urban Development*. Berkeley: University of California Press, 1986.

Jensen, Joan M., and Gloria Ricci Lothrop. *California Women: A History*. Golden State Series. San Francisco: Boyd and Fraser, 1988.

Jonas, Andrew E. G., and David Wilson. *The Urban Growth Machine: Critical Perspectives Two Decades Later*. Albany: State University of New York Press, 1999.

Jones, Billy M. *Health-Seekers in the Southwest, 1817–1900*. Norman: University of Oklahoma Press, 1967.

Jurmain, Claudia K., and James J. Rawls, eds. *California: A Place, a People, a Dream: A Journey Through California History*. San Francisco: Chronicle Books, 1986.

Kelley, Mary, ed. *Woman's Being, Woman's Place: Female Identity and Vocation in American History*. Boston: G. D. Hall, 1979.

Kincaid, Laurence. *History of the Greater San Francisco Bay Region*. New York: Lewis Historical Publishing Co., 1966.

Lebsock, Suzanne. *The Free Women of Petersburg: Status and Culture in a Southern Town, 1784–1860*. New York: W. W. Norton, 1984.

Limerick, Patricia Nelson. *The Legacy of Conquest: The Unbroken Past of the American West*. New York: Norton, 1988.

Livingston, James. *Origins of the Federal Reserve System: Money, Class, and Corporate Capitalism, 1890–1913*. Ithaca, NY: Cornell University Press, 1986.

Lubove, Roy. *The Urban Community: Housing and Planning in the Progressive Era*. Englewood Cliffs, NJ: Prentice-Hall, 1967.

Mathews, Glenna. *The Rise of Public Woman: Woman's Power and Woman's Place in the United States, 1630–1970*. New York: Oxford University Press, 1992.

McWilliams, Carey. *Southern California: An Island on the Land*. 1946. Reprint, Salt Lake City: Peregrine Smith, 1990.

Monkkonen, Eric. *America Becomes Urban: The Development of U.S. Cities and Towns, 1780–1980*. Berkeley: University of California Press, 1988.

Mowry, George E. *The California Progressives*. Berkeley: University of California Press, 1968.

Muncy, Robyn. *Creating a Female Dominion in American Reform, 1890–1935*. New York: Oxford University Press, 1991.

Nash, Gerald D. *The American West Transformed: The Impact of the Second World War*. Lincoln: University of Nebraska Press, 1985.

North, Douglass. *The Economic Growth of the United States*. Englewood Cliffs, NJ: Prentice-Hall, 1961.

Olin, Spencer C. *California's Prodigal Sons: Hiram Johnson and the Progressives, 1911–1917*. Berkeley: University of California Press, 1968.

O'Neal, Owen H., ed. *History of Santa Barbara County, State of California: Its People and Its Resources, pt. II*. Santa Barbara: Harold McLean Meier, 1939.

A Pictorial History of Redlands and Prospect Park. Redlands, CA: Prospect Park Fund, 1968.

Pomeroy, Earl. *The Pacific Slope: A History of California, Oregon, Washington, Idaho, Utah, and Nevada*. Seattle: University of Washington Press, 1965.

Reps, John. *The Making of Urban America: A History of City Planning in the United States*. Princeton, NJ: Princeton University Press, 1965.

Rosenberg, Rosalind. *Beyond Separate Spheres: Intellectual Roots of Modern Feminism*. New Haven, CT: Yale University Press, 1982.

Roth, Darlene Rebecca. *Matronage: Patterns in Women's Organizations, Atlanta, Georgia, 1890–1940*. Brooklyn, NY: Carlson Publishing, 1994.

Rothman, Sheila M. *Woman's Proper Place: A History of Changing Ideals and Practices, 1870 to the Present*. New York: Basic Books, 1978.

Ryan, Mary P. *Cradle of the Middle Class: The Family in Oneida County, New York, 1790–1865*. Cambridge, MA: Harvard University Press, 1981.

Schackel, Sandra. *Social Housekeepers: Women Shaping Public Policy in New Mexico, 1920–1940*. Albuquerque: University of New Mexico Press, 1992.

Scharf, Lois, and Joan Jensen, eds. *Decades of Discontent*. Westport, CT: Greenwood Press, 1983.

Schultz, Stanley. *Constructing Urban Culture: American Cities and City Planning, 1800–1920*. Philadelphia: Temple University Press, 1989.

Schwarz, Judith. *Radical Feminists of Heterodoxy: Greenwich Village, 1912–1940*. Lebanon, NH: New Victoria Press, 1986

Scott, Anne Firor. *The Southern Lady: From Pedestal to Politics, 1830–1930*. Chicago: University of Chicago Press, 1970.

Scott, Mellior. *American City Planning Since 1890*. Berkeley: University of California Press, 1969.

Smith-Rosenberg, Carroll. *Disorderly Conduct: Visions of Gender in Victorian America*. New York: Oxford University Press, 1985.

Sochen, June. *The New Woman: Feminism in Greenwich Village, 1910–1920*. New York: Quadrangle Press, 1972.

Solomon, Barbara Miller. *In the Company of Educated Women: A History of Women and Higher Education in America*. New Haven, CT: Yale University Press, 1985.

Stansell, Christine. *City of Women: Sex and Class in New York, 1789–1860*. Urbana: University of Illinois Press, 1986.

Starr, Kevin. *Inventing the Dream: California Through the Progressive Era*. New York: Oxford University Press, 1985.

———. *Material Dreams: Southern California Through the 1920s*. New York: Oxford University Press, 1990.

Stewart, Elinore Pruitt. *Letters of a Woman Homesteader*. 1914. Reprint, Boston: Houghton Mifflin, 1988.

Stratton, Joanna L. *Pioneer Women: Voices from the Kansas Frontier*. New York: Simon and Schuster, 1981.

Sutcliffe, Anthony, ed. *The Rise of Modern Urban Planning, 1800–1914*. New York: St. Martins Press, 1980.

Tobin, Eugene M. *Organize or Perish: America's Independent Progressives, 1913–1933*. New York: Greenwood Press, 1986.

Tompkins, Walker A., and Russell A. Ruiz. *Historical High Lights of Santa Barbara*. Santa Barbara: Santa Barbara National Bank, 1970.

Tompkins, Walker A. *Santa Barbara History Makers*. Ed. Barbara Hathaway Tompkins. Santa Barbara: McNally and Loftin, 1983.

Umbeck, John R. *A Theory of Property Rights with Application to the California Gold Rush*. Ames: University of Iowa Press, 1981.

Vicinus, Martha. *Independent Women: Work and Community for Single Women, 1850–1920*. Chicago: University of Chicago Press, 1985.

Wandersee, Winifred D. *Women's Work and Family Values, 1920–1940*. Cambridge, MA: Harvard University Press, 1981.

Weiss, Marc A. *The Rise of the Community Builders: The American Real Estate Industry and Urban Land Planning*. New York: Columbia University Press, 1987.

Wiebe, Robert. *The Search for Order: 1877–1920*. New York: Hill and Wang, 1967.

Wilson, Chris. *The Myth of Santa Fe: Creating a Modern Regional Tradition*. Albuquerque: University of New Mexico Press, 1997.

Wilson, William H. *The City Beautiful Movement*. Baltimore: Johns Hopkins University Press, 1989.

Woloch, Nancy. *Women and the American Experience*. New York: McGraw-Hill, 1984.

Worster, Donald. *Rivers of Empire: Water, Aridity, and the Growth of the American West*. New York: Oxford University Press, 1985.

Wright, Gwendolyn. *Building the Dream: A Social History of Housing in America*. New York: Pantheon Books, 1981.

B. ARTICLES

Abbot, Carl. "The Metropolitan Region: Western Cities in the New Urban Era." In *The Twentieth-Century West: Historical Interpretations*, edited by Gerald D. Nash and Richard W. Etulain, 71–98. Albuquerque: University of New Mexico Press, 1989.

———. "Frontiers and Sections: Cities and Regions in American Growth." *American Quarterly* 37 (1985): 395–410.

Altman, Karen E. "Consuming Ideology: The Better Homes in America Campaign." *Critical Studies in Mass Communication* 7 (September 1990): 286–308.

Anderson, Karen. "Western Women: The Twentieth-Century Experience." In *The Twentieth-Century West: Historical Interpretations*, edited by Gerald D. Nash and Richard W. Etulain, 99–122. Albuquerque: University of New Mexico Press, 1989.

Anderson, Kristi. "Women and Citizenship in the 1920s." In *Women, Politics, and Change*, edited by Louise A. Tilly and Patricia Gurin, 177–98. New York: Russell Sage Foundation, 1990.

Antler, Joyce. "'After College, What?': New Graduates and the Family Claim." *American Quarterly* 32 (Fall 1980): 409–34.

Armitage, Susan. "Women and Men in Western History: A Stereopticon Vision." *Western Historical Quarterly* 16 (October 1985): 381–391.

Baker, Paula. "The Domestication of Politics: Women and American Political Society, 1780–1920." *American Historical Review* 89 (June 1984): 620–47.

Brown, Victoria. "Fear of Feminization: Los Angeles High Schools in the Progressive Era." *Feminist Studies* 16 (Fall 1990): 493–519.

Chase, Pearl. "Bernhard Hoffmann—Community Builder." *Noticias* (Summer 1959).

Cohen, Miriam, and Michael Hanagan. "The Politics of Gender and the Making of the Welfare State, 1900–1940: A Comparative Perspective." *Journal of Social History* 24 (Spring 1991): 469–84.

Conway, Jill. "Women Reformers and American Culture, 1870–1930." In *Our*

American Sisters: Women in American Life and Thought, 3rd ed., edited by Jean E. Friedman and William Shade, 432–43. Lexington: D. C. Heath, 1982.

Cook, Blanche Weisen. "Female Support Networks and Political Activism: Lillian Wald, Chrystal Eastman, Emma Goldman." *Chrysalis* 3 (1977): 43–61.

DuBois, Ellen, et al. "Politics and Culture in Women's History: A Symposium." *Feminist Studies* 6 (Spring 1980): 26–64.

Fairbanks, Robert B. "From Better Dwellings to Better Community: Changing Approaches to the Low-Cost Housing Problem, 1890–1925." *Journal of Urban History* 11 (May 1985): 314–34.

Flanagan, Maureen A. "Gender and Urban Political Reform: The City Club and the Woman's City Club of Chicago in the Progressive Era." *The American Historical Review* 95 (October 1990): 1032–50.

Freedman, Estelle. "Separatism as Strategy: Female Institution Building and American Feminism, 1870–1930." *Feminist Studies* 5 (Fall 1979): 512–29.

Galambos, Louis. "The Emerging Organizational Synthesis in Modern American History." *Business History Review* 44 (1972): 279–90.

———. "Technology, Political Economy, and Professionalization: Central Themes of the Organizational Synthesis." *Business History Review* 57 (1983): 471–79.

Gittell, Marilyn, and Teresa Shtob. "Changing Women's Roles in Political Volunteerism and Reform of the City." *Signs* 5 (Spring 1980 Supplement): S66–S78.

Glassberg, David. "History and the Public: Legacies of the Progressive Era." *Journal of American History* 73 (March 1987): 957–980.

Glover, Katherine. "Blue Ribbon Citizen: The Stateswoman." *Survey Graphic* 29 (March 1940): 180–181.

Graffy, Neal. "The Santa Barbara Woman's Club: The First Forty Years." *Noticias* 38 (Autumn 1992): 41–52.

Hartig, Anthea M. "'In a World He Has Created': Class Collectivity and the Growers' Landscape of the Southern California Citrus Industry, 1890–1940." *California History* 74 (Spring 1995): 100–111.

Harris, Katherine. "Homesteading in Northeastern Colorado, 1873–1920: Sex Roles and Women's Experience." In *The Woman's West*, edited by Susan Armitage and Elizabeth Jameson, 165–78. Norman: University of Oklahoma Press, 1987.

Hewitt, Nancy A. "Beyond the Search for Sisterhood: American Women's History in the 1980s." In *Unequal Sisters: A Multi-cultural Reader in U.S. Women's History*, edited by Ellen Carol DuBois and Vicki L. Ruiz, 1–14. New York: Routledge, 1990.

Hutchinson, Janet. "The Cure for Domestic Neglect: Better Homes in America, 1922–1935." In *Perspectives in Vernacular Architecture II*, edited by Camille Wells, 168–78. Columbia: University of Missouri, 1986.

Issel, William. "'Citizens Outside of Government': Business and Public Policy in San Francisco and Los Angeles, 1890–1930." *Pacific Historical Review* 58 (May 1988): 117–46.

Jameson, Elizabeth. "Women as Workers, Women as Civilizers: True Womanhood in the American West." In *The Women's West*, edited by Susan Armitage and Elizabeth Jameson, 145–64. Norman: University of Oklahoma Press, 1987.

Jenkins, William D. "Housewifery and Motherhood: The Question of Role Change in the Progressive Era." In *Woman's Being, Woman's Place: Female Identity and Vocation in American History*, edited by Mary Kelley, 142–53. Boston: G. K. Hall, 1979.

Jensen, Joan M., and Darlis A. Miller. "The Gentle Tamers Revisited." *Pacific Historical Quarterly* 49 (May 1980): 173–213.

Kerber, Linda K. "Separate Spheres, Female Worlds, Woman's Place: The Rhetoric of Women's History." *Journal of American History* 75 (June 1988): 9–39.

Kornbluh, Andrea. "City Sex: Views of American Women and Urban Culture, 1869–1990." *Urban History Yearbook* (1991): 60–83.

Lebsock, Suzanne. "Women and American Politics, 1880–1920." In *Women, Politics, and Change*, edited by Louise A. Tilly and Patricia Gurin, 35–62. New York: Russell Sage Foundation, 1990.

Lesser, Susan Tank. "Paradigms Gained: Further Readings in the History of Women in the Progressive Era." In *Gender, Class, Race, and Reform in the Progressive Era*, edited by Noralee Frankel and Nancy S. Dye, 180–93. Lexington: University of Kentucky Press, 1991.

Lotchin, Roger. "City and Sword in Metropolitan California, 1919–1941." *Urbanism Past and Present* 7 (Summer–Fall 1982): 1–16.

———. "The City and the Sword: San Francisco and the Rise of the Metropolitan-Military Complex, 1919–1941." *Journal of American History* 65 (March 1979): 996–1020.

———. "The Darwinian City: The Politics of Urbanization in San Francisco Between the Wars." *Pacific Historical Review* 48 (August 1979): 357–81.

Luckingham, Bradford. "The American Southwest: An Urban View." *Western Historical Quarterly* 15 (July 1984): 261–80.

———. "The Urban Dimension of Western History." In *Historians and the American West*, edited by Michael Malone, 323–43. Lincoln: University of Nebraska Press, 1983.

McCormick, Richard L. "The Discovery That Business Corrupts Politics: A Reappraisal of the Origins of Progressivism." *American Historical Review* 86 (February-June): 247–74.

Molotch, Harvey. "The City as a Growth Machine: Toward a Political Economy of Place." *American Journal of Sociology* 82 (September 1976): 309–32.

Moses, H. Vincent. "'The Orange Grower Is Not a Farmer': G. Harold Powell, Riverside Orchardists, and the Coming of the Industrial Agriculture, 1893–1930." *California History* 74 (Spring 1995): 22–37.

Mowry, George. "The California Progressive and His Rationale: A Study in Middle Class Politics." *Mississippi Valley Historical Review* 36 (September 1949): 239–50.

Peterson, Jon. "The City Beautiful Movement: Forgotten Origins and Lost Meanings." *Journal of Urban History* 2 (August 1976): 415–34.

Pincetl, Stephanie. "The Politics of Influence: Democracy and the Growth Machine in Orange County, U.S." In *The Urban Growth Machine: Critical Perspectives Two Decades Later*, edited by Andrew E. G. Jonas and David Wilson, 195–212. Albany: State University of New York Press, 1999.

Pomeroy, Earl. "The Urban Frontier of the Far West." In *The Frontier Challenge*, edited by John G. Clark, 7–29. Lawrence: University of Nebraska Press, 1971.

Putnam, Jackson K. "The Persistence of Progressivism in the 1920s: The Case of California." *Pacific Historical Review* 35 (November 1966): 395–411.

Rodgers, Daniel T. "In Search of Progressivism." *Reviews in American History* 10 (December 1982): 113–32.

Scott, Anne Firor. "On Seeing and Not Seeing: A Case of Historical Invisibility." *Journal of American History* (June 1984): 7–21.

Shammas, Carole. "Re-assessing the Married Women's Property Acts." *Journal of Women's History* 6 (Spring 1994): 9–31.

Smith, Daniel Scott. "Family Limitation, Sexual Control, and Domestic Feminism in Victorian America." In *Clio's Consciousness Raised*, edited by Mary Hartman and Lois W. Banner, 119–36. New York: Octagon Books, 1976.

Smith-Rosenberg, Carroll. "The Female World of Love and Ritual: Relations Between Women in Nineteenth-Century America." *Signs* 1 (Autumn 1975): 1–29.

Splitter, Henry Winfred. "Health in Southern California, 1850–1900." *Journal of the West* 8 (October 1969): 526–58.

Taylor, Frank J. "Blue Ribbon Citizen: The Townswoman." *Survey Graphic* 29 (March 1940): 178–80.

Tobey, Ronald, Charles Wetherell, and Jay Brigham. "Moving Out and Settling In: Residential Mobility, Homes Owning, and the Public Enframing of Citizenship, 1921–1950." *American Historical Review* 95 (December 1990): 1395–1422.

Tobey, Ronald, and Charles Wetherell. "The Citrus Industry and the Revolution of Corporate Capitalism in Southern California, 1887–1944." *California History* 74 (Spring 1995): 6–21.

Underwood, June O. "Civilizing Kansas: Women's Organizations, 1880–1920." *Kansas History* 7 (Winter 1984–85): 291–306.

———. "Western Women and True Womanhood." *Great Plains Quarterly* 5 (Spring 1985): 93–107.

Welter, Barbara. "The Cult of True Womanhood: 1820–1860." *American Quarterly* (Summer 1966): 151–74.

Wilson, William H. "The Billboard: Bane of the City Beautiful." *Journal of Urban History* 13 (August 1987): 394–425.

C. THESES AND PAPERS

Antler, Joyce. "The Educated Woman and Professionalization: The Struggle for a New Feminine Identity, 1890–1920." Ph.D. diss., State University of New York at Stony Brook, 1977.

Barker, Roseanne. "Small Town Progressivism: Pearl Chase and Female Activism in Santa Barbara, 1909–1929." Ph.D. diss., University of California, Santa Barbara, 1994.

Carey, Gabriele G. "From Hinterland to Metropolis: Land Use Planning in Orange County, California, 1925–1955." Ph.D. diss., University of California, Riverside, 1997.
Conway, Jill Kathryn. "The First Generation of American Women Graduates." Ph.D. diss., Harvard University, 1968.
Duncan-Abrams, Marguerite. "The History of the Riverside Planning Commission, 1914–1928." Master's thesis, University of California, Riverside, 1994.
Gallaway, Sara Essa. "Pioneering the Woman's Club Movement: The Story of Caroline Maria Severance in Los Angeles." Ph.D. diss., Carnegie-Melon University, 1985.
Gullett, Gayle Ann. "Feminism, Politics, and Voluntary Groups: Organized Womanhood in California, 1886–1986." Ph.D. diss., University of California, Riverside, 1983.
Hutchinson, Janet Anne. "American Housing, Gender, and the Better Homes Movement, 1922–1935." Ph.D. diss., University of Delaware, 1989.
Miller, Dorothy Grace. "Within the Bounds of Propriety: Clara Burdette and the Women's Movement." Ph.D. diss., University of California, Riverside, 1984.
Nye, Ronald. "The Influence of the Chase Family on Santa Barbara History." Paper presented at the West Coast Symposium on Family History, University of California, Santa Barbara, May 1, 1976.

Index

In this index an "f" after a number indicates a separate reference on the next page, and an "ff" indicates separate references on the next two pages. A continuous discussion over two or more pages is indicated by a span of page numbers, e.g., "57–59."